PERMISSION TO TEACH

from His Grace
for His Glory

Jeanne
Nordstrom

PERMISSION TO TEACH

A PERSONAL ODYSSEY IN THE CLASSROOM

JEANNE NORDSTROM

TATE PUBLISHING
AND ENTERPRISES, LLC

Published by Tate Publishing & Enterprises, LLC
127 E. Trade Center Terrace | Mustang, Oklahoma 73064 USA
1.888.361.9473 | www.tatepublishing.com

Tate Publishing is committed to excellence in the publishing industry. The company reflects the philosophy established by the founders, based on Psalm 68:11,
"The Lord gave the word and great was the company of those who published it."

Book design copyright © 2015 by Tate Publishing, LLC. All rights reserved.
Cover design by Samson Lim
Interior design by Angelo Moralde

Published in the United States of America
ISBN: 978-1-68028-285-6
Biography & Autobiography / Educators
15.05.05

To the many students I have taught—and especially those students who gave me permission to teach another year.

Acknowledgments

God provided many supports, long before I even knew I needed them. Let me share some of the valuable gifts He prepared for me:

The talented team at Tate Publishing, especially Michelle Ybãnez and Eric Michael DelaTorre.

The late Tom Mullen, my first editor who helped me envision and shape this book.

My many colleagues—teachers, staff, custodians, and administrators—who offered support, insight, and perspective, but most importantly, friendship and laughter.

My friends through the years who have been like family.

My unofficial tech support, Becky and Pam, for their help and friendship.

My twin sister, Judy, whose friendship and invaluable editing skills met needs I never knew I had.

My best friend, Pat, who was always ready, no matter what I needed.

Contents

A Personal Genesis 17

Out of Touch 27

Making Lemonade 33

By the Numbers 39

Ready or Not 41

Holding Your Ground 51

Author, Author 57

Kids Will Say Most Anything 65

The Rewards of Persistence 75

Sweet Memories 81

You Only Cheat Yourself 87

Many Happy Returns 99

Teacher's Pet 109

Irrepressible 119

Help! I Need a Geek 133

Construction Daze 143

Movin' In, Movin' On 159

Time Travel 167

Tutoring the Teacher 179

Shhh! She's Got Her Hands on Our Book! 193

Gotta Laugh 205

Redemption 221

Monkey See, Monkey Do 229

Low Tide 239

You Reap What You Sow 263

Pass It On 283

Tried and True (For Me, Anyway) 291

View from the Custodial Cart 309

Time to Go 321

Permission to Retire 333
Epilogue 341
Notes 347

Preface

Unless otherwise noted, names of characters in this book are aliases. Some characters are compilations of more than one student, teacher, staff member, or administrator because these behaviors were not limited to one individual, one classroom, or even one school. Aliases are also used to protect identities, and in some cases, circumstances have been altered to more carefully obscure identities. It is not my intention to highlight specific individuals. Although the events and the student writings are authentic, these examples come from four different states, six different grade levels, and also college-level students.

Prologue

I will lift up mine eyes unto the hills,
from whence cometh my help.

—*Psalms 121:1*, KJV

My first "permission to teach" came through God's grace. College had been a struggle for me, and I often lost sight of my future during that challenging time. Yet I persevered throughout all of it and earned my teaching degree, eager to begin my career. Notice I didn't say I was prepared to teach—that was a much slower process. My college degree opened the door to a classroom of my own, but preparing a young adult to teach is a daunting task as well as an ongoing process. Through my years of schooling, I had accumulated plenty of facts and pieces of knowledge, but I wondered if I had the talent to spark the imagination of children and keep their attention.

Being on the other side of the desk certainly altered my whole perception of the classroom. And as it turned out, teaching was nearly a perfect fit for me.

Like most every other adult, I had experienced a variety of teaching styles throughout my years as a student. The excellent teachers stood out in sharp relief against the background of others who were just putting in their time. More than anything else, I wanted to be a member of the first group. But how would I know? I needed a measuring stick.

My first year in the classroom I decided that I could evaluate my effectiveness through more than students' academic successes. Although a school's primary goals are to increase student knowledge and hone thinking skills, test scores and projects are not the only measure of achievement and effectiveness. The teachers who had stretched me intellectually also had inspired me to turn in my best performance. They had encouraged me to believe I could succeed even when I didn't believe it myself. Reflecting on the impact these inspired mentors had on my learning, I realized how my ability to spark young minds would be integral to my ultimate success. I would have gladly welcomed the opportunity to work with any of the inspiring teachers from my past.

I wanted my classroom to be a special place, a place where children wanted to be. I also wanted my students to feel encouraged, excited, and challenged to reach their potential. Not an easy goal—igniting that internal spark as special teachers had for me—but a worthy one.

As a student, I had performed to my best ability, especially under the tutelage of gifted, enthusiastic teachers who saw learning as an adventure, but I had not set lofty goals for myself; achievable goals, yes, but never lofty ones. Perhaps I could consider myself a successful teacher for a given year if I were able to inspire just one student to reach for a deeper understanding and a level of comprehension beyond the expectation.

Because I myself had struggled with learning, I could use my experience to help others. Chances were good that during my school years, I had experienced many of their same struggles. To achieve success, I also often had to rely on a healthy dose of elbow grease. I was prepared to help my students to want to apply their own elbow grease as well. Sure I had times as a student when it would have been easier for me just to give up, but I hadn't. And I knew this same determination could be useful when motivating students.

After much thought and reflection, I finally decided on my personal litmus test to judge my effectiveness in the classroom. It was a simple but closely guarded secret: one of my students had to ask that I be promoted to the next grade with them. During most of my years in teaching, I did not change grade levels, but I always wanted to hear the question, "Will you be my teacher again next year?"

In some years, this request came from many students, while in others it came as quite a surprise from a student I least expected. Occasionally, even parents called to ask if I would please teach their child one more year. After one particular group of seventh-grade math students heard that they would have a different teacher for their eighth-grade year, they wrote a letter to the principal requesting that I be allowed to again teach them math. The principal shared the letter with me, and he noted that all fifteen students had signed it, even though he was not able to grant their request. No matter who asked or how they asked, this question always lifted my spirits and gave me permission to teach another year. And I was blessed to hear this request every single year of my career, and each time the invitation warmed my heart.

Keep your lives free from the love of money and be content with what you have, because God has said, "Never will I leave you; never will I forsake you." So we say with confidence, "The Lord is my helper; I will not be afraid. What can mere mortals do to me?"

—Hebrews 13:5–6, NIV

A Personal Genesis

Do not be afraid or discouraged, for the Lord God, my God,
is with you. He will not fail you or forsake you until all the
work for the service of the temple of the Lord is finished.

—*1 Chronicles 28:20b*, NIV

A young married couple, still in their teens, had a daughter. A second daughter was born the following year. And a third pregnancy two years later surprised even the doctor when twins arrived. The father, who wanted sons, used to joke, "When God sends me girls two at a time, I quit." By age twenty-two, these parents were raising four daughters on a gas station attendant's income. This story is familiar to me: I am one of the twins.

Having twins can be exciting, but it placed an extra burden on our struggling family. Times were difficult for most families in those postwar years, and ours was no exception.

Adding to the financial strain, our mother contracted polio when she was twenty-four years old, which left her restricted to a wheelchair. This disability was a huge obstacle. Life in a wheelchair certainly was challenging to overcome in those times since society had not yet made accommodations for the disabled. For example, many were the times when we girls would carry a measuring tape into a public restroom to see if our mother's wheelchair would fit though the doorway. Even when the entrance was wide enough, there was still the issue of stall doors inside. At that time, stall doors in public restrooms were usually about eighteen to twenty inches wide, not nearly wide enough to accommodate the twenty-four-inch width of her wheelchair. Some days we had to check many locations to find a restroom that would accommodate our mother's wheelchair.

This was just one of many challenges my family had to deal with in my childhood. We also had to overcome the trials of low income, too many children, and too little job training. At that time, we were unaware how those humbling, uncertain circumstances would eventually make us stronger.

Life, for me, was challenging from the moment I was born. I have often teased my fraternal twin sister that not only did I have to experience her labor pains and then mine, but also I was slower reaching the oxygen. I have even halfheartedly blamed some of my life situations on being born second.

One of the blessings of twins is that you don't have to adjust all your shopping habits. At least my family didn't. To save money in a budget already stretched to its limit, my parents would buy a piece of clothing, a trinket, or a treat for Michele, another one for Bonnie, and one for Judy and me to share.

It became second nature for me to share. I had half of a crib, followed by half of a twin bed until I was five, and either a quarter or a half of a room until I was twenty. Judy and I went halves on clothes, toys, time, and even baths. You name it, we shared it. Many of the photos in my baby scrapbook were cut in half so Judy could have her part. But best of all, my twin never considered me an intruder. The opposite was true. We were best friends and clung to each other as a matched set. Often we even simultaneously spoke the same entire sentence together, word for word, with exactly matched cadence.

Shortly before we started kindergarten, our parents asked if we had made new friends in our Sunday school class. We answered in unison, "We have each other. We don't need friends." They fixed that situation when we entered school that September and endured our first separation. Judy attended the morning kindergarten class while I was placed in the afternoon one.

For me, being a twin was the best gift. We shared everything—everything they'd let us from chickenpox to choosing a college. Many times we felt like one inseparable unit. Imagine my surprise when I discovered Judy was stronger academically, and it showed on tests and grade cards. It was only a slight difference but noticeable to me. She, for her part, gave me credit for reading people much better.

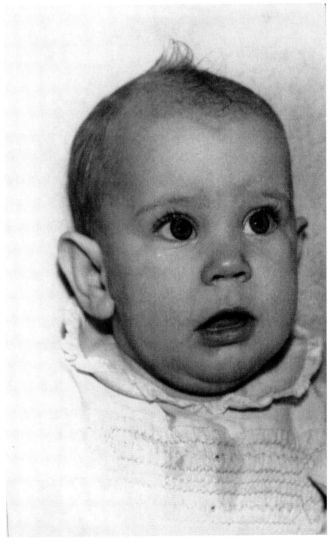

My half of a baby photo from my scrapbook.

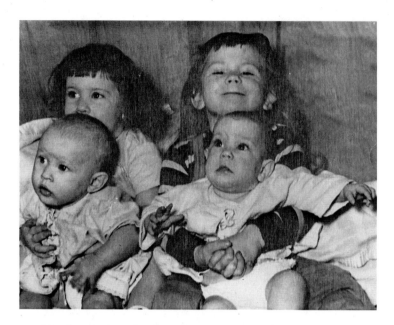

The four little girls when the twins were a few months old.

The four sisters in their Easter dresses.

My twin, Judy, carrying the Olympic torch
while I held her Olympic flag.

Education played a significant role in my family. Our parents
stressed the importance of academic success in securing a good
future, realizing a more successful career, and creating a more fulfilling life. And sacrifice from every family member was a large
part of that vision. During my childhood, our mother enrolled
in college and then graduated when I was fourteen, just one year
before my oldest sister completed high school. Our mother's time
in college demanded commitment and extra effort from everyone, further straining the family's finances and shifting almost
all household tasks to the daughters. However, her college degree
not only enabled her to develop and use her God-given talents,
but also provided more financial stability for the family.

I knew that my mother was smart, but just how smart became
evident when she graduated Phi Beta Kappa from college, the
top woman in her class. The impetus to further our education was
drilled into us while we were surrounded with daily reminders as

our mother studied and prepared for her degree. Later, she also joined Mensa, a group open to people who scored in the top 2 percent on intelligence tests worldwide.

During our childhood, our father had directed a local teen canteen where he mentored high school students and helped provide a fun, safe place for teens to gather and socialize at the local YWCA. I looked up to these older high school kids. Many of them went on to college, and when they came home for visits, we heard exciting tales of collegiate life. It sounded wonderful to me, and I looked forward to the freedom and opportunities they described.

The year after Mother graduated from college, my oldest sister enrolled at the same college where she was awarded their highest scholarship. In recognition of her academic achievements, Michele received full tuition and books for four years. This local liberal arts college was known for its exceptional standards, making her scholarship quite an honor. I know Michele deserved this scholarship. I had watched her maintain excellent grades throughout her school years and receive statewide recognition in math. I especially remember a day when she came home from junior high school sporting all As on her grade card, but one was an A-. This grade upset our mother who demanded an explanation. I secretly began to grow more concerned about the Bs I was earning.

While Michele was majoring in chemistry at college, I was struggling through chemistry as a junior in high school. Seeing my struggle, my teacher approached me during class one day to discuss my grade. He knew I needed help in order to complete the class successfully, so he offered to tutor me under one condition. "Name it," I responded. His condition was that I never take another chemistry class, and I have kept my word to this day.

I don't want to paint an unrealistic picture of my academic skill, but I have found intelligence is relative to those around you. I was surrounded by intelligent siblings, a smart dad, and an astonishingly brilliant mother—a mixed blessing. Academic expectations were high in my family, and my IQ looked inadequate, at least to me. I have learned over time that I have what it takes; but for much of my formative life, I doubted my ability.

My next sister, Bonnie, entered the same college easily enough the following year. And two years later, it was time for Judy and me to enroll.

Growing up, my sisters and I were a tightly knit group. Since we were all born in a space of three years and four months, we looked more like a roving dormitory than a family. For one year, all four of us were in college at the same time. Tuition assistance at this private institution was one of the first clear gifts that let me feel God's presence. Many more would follow.

Tuition was costly, but the college had a program to help employees' children who wanted to enroll there. After her graduation, our mother took a job at the college. Midway through our sophomore year, my twin sister and I qualified for tuition assistance. But we still needed student loans and summer jobs to cover the tuition until we met the requirements. We also needed to finance four years of textbooks and living expenses. Tuition assistance was a "God send" that put college within my reach and eased the financial burden for my family.

Once we hammered out the college financial plan, I could then focus on the academic challenges. Since I was the only daughter not inducted into the National Honor Society during high school, how did I expect to keep my head above water academically? My grades, although above average, were not on par with my college peers. Even more, I feared I didn't possess the intellectual qualities required to succeed at this academically rigorous college. To make matters worse, test taking was not my strength, and my SAT scores reflected this. Since this college was known for its exceptional education and for its practice of basing course grades mostly on a midterm and a final exam, was it any wonder the admissions committee was skeptical about accepting me.

Like most liberal arts colleges, this one had a foreign language requirement for the bachelor of arts degree. Both my twin and I had studied French in high school, so we were hoping the placement exam would eliminate some of the foreign language requirement.

As mentioned, I generally didn't perform well on standardized tests, and the French placement exam was no exception. My disappointing score meant that I would have to take two of the three terms without receiving any credits toward graduation. Judy, in contrast, got credit for two terms of French and needed only one more term to complete her foreign language requirement.

I felt defeated. I was already two classes behind, and the school year hadn't yet started. But I was not going to go down without a fight. Through persistent efforts, I found an alternative. I could study another language, take all three terms, and then earn the three required foreign language credits. Someone suggested that Spanish would be my best choice, and I said, "Sign me up!" To this day, I still confuse French and Spanish vocabulary, but at least I fulfilled the language requirement.

For some, this bumpy introduction to college might spell impending calamity, but not for me. Not even the dean of admissions could thwart me when he told me to my face that my SAT scores were low compared with other freshmen, my sunny nature indicated I was not serious enough for college, and he would see me flunk out before my freshman year ended. This was far from the confidence builder I was looking for. But I knew I had to succeed because I didn't see any other financially workable path to a baccalaureate degree. What I couldn't see at the time was how God's plan for me required all of these humbling experiences.

College life did not turn out to be the joy I had anticipated it would be; instead, it was a series of struggles. But these struggles weren't wasted; I used them as building blocks for my teaching career.

When it came time for me to declare a major in my sophomore year, the admonition from the admissions dean still resonated in my head. Worried that I might not survive in a variety of academic disciplines, I spent a lot of time pondering my course of study. I opted for a practical approach to my education and was seeking a major where I could successfully complete my degree and then support myself. I hadn't been able to visualize how some fields of study, such as philosophy, would lead to immediate professional employment.

It seemed many doors had already closed for me—low test scores and a disappointing B grade average in high school, followed by self-doubt and the questions voiced by administrators. So before declaring my major field, I met with the academic dean, an affable fellow who seemed truly interested in helping students make wise personal choices. As we discussed my abilities, interests, and challenges, he listened intently. After some consideration, he suggested, "Why don't you become a teacher, Jeanne? You could write your ticket anywhere." So I made a practical choice—education. Whether my choices were limited or I just felt they were, it turned out that elementary education, grades K through eighth in those days, was a sensible decision for me. The teaching market was nearly saturated when I graduated, but I continued to feel God's presence throughout my career, because I was blessed with a teaching job every year for the next four decades.

However, I do remember clearly a very special day—the day it became obvious to me that I had chosen the right field of study. My whole world brightened that first day of student teaching in my senior year of college when I met the students in Mrs. Custard's third-grade class. This was no ordinary class—this was my first group of students; and because of that, they were special. They enjoyed my teaching and returned the affection I felt for them. What a blessing, after all of these years preparing to teach; I was just where I needed to be! Even in later years as retirement grew closer, I still felt great affection and admiration for my mentor, Eleanor Custard (not an alias). She was a veteran teacher who cared for all of her students no matter what age.

After successfully completing student teaching, the last two terms of college requirements, and the mandatory departmental comprehensive written and oral exams, I was finally ready to graduate. I had been holding my breath for four long years. I walked across that outdoor stage and shook the president's hand on that sunny June day when he handed me my diploma. Back at my seat, I clutched the lovely folder that held my diploma. After the difficulties I had experienced earning my bachelor's degree, I almost thought I heard someone whisper, "Don't tell anyone where you got this diploma." But I double checked the diploma. My name was written on it, and the president had signed it. Now the idea of teaching didn't seem so scary or far away.

Some say when God closes a door, He opens a window. For me, God opened a side door; teaching was the ideal career for me. When I viewed my college experience from the security of graduation day, I gained a sense of perspective on my life and began to see His greater power at work.

Some people can recall exactly when they first knew what they wanted to do when they grew up. Not me. My process was gradual. I needed closed doors to keep me from making wrong choices. I found plenty of blocked entries—but I walked through the one that was open, and it would lead me to my future.

And God is faithful; he will not let you be tempted beyond what you can bear. But when you are tempted, he will also provide a way out so that you can endure it.

—1 Corinthians 10:13b, NIV

Out of Touch

Have mercy on me, my God, have mercy on me, for in you I
take refuge. I will take refuge in the shadow of your wings
until the disaster has passed.

—Psalm 57:1, NIV

Under normal conditions, history and geometry share little common ground. But for me, these two college classes provided as much training in teaching methods as any of my education classes, and the lessons I learned from the professors who taught these two courses had a lasting impact on my teaching style.

The history professor regularly ran overtime with his lecture. Students stopped listening long before the bell sounded, so his continuing to lecture past the bell was futile. Yet he persisted in presenting lengthy lectures. The particular class session I recall best has become legendary among students and staff at this college.

The summer before this particularly memorable day, I was stocking shelves at the college bookstore with my friend John, who was two years ahead of me. John, both brilliant and witty, was helping me unpack a shipment of history texts. With a sly grin, he turned to me and asked, "Have you taken Western Civilization yet?"

"No, I'm taking it this next year. Why?"

"I wondered if you wanted a preview of a lecture by one of the professors I am sure you will have," John said.

"Sure," I answered.

John slid his glasses down his nose, opened a history book from the box he was unpacking, and broke into a classic Ted Smith lecture. John's mannerisms instantly transformed him into the persona of Dr. Smith, known for his monotone style. Staring down his nose at the text, John broke into a dry lecture on some long-forgotten emperor from ancient times. Without looking up, John continued to motion toward a make-believe chalkboard pretending there was an ancient Roman timeline of historical events relating to antiquity. I was in stitches before Professor John completed his discourse.

The following January, I had a chance to compare the real thing with John's perfectly pitched rendition. If my classmates had seen the bookstore routine, we would have all been suppressing laughter. I was the only one who was amused and smiling inwardly. No one else saw the humor in that dry lecture.

Ted Smith was completely oblivious to time and student interest. Once he started his lecture, little could derail his monologue. He talked to the podium, rarely glancing up, while he lapsed into Latin mutterings and pointed to illegible columns of names he had scrawled on the chalkboard. The sound of the bell signaling the end of class had no recognizable impact on his delivery. He ignored students who sat glued to their seats, agonizing over how to flee at the end of class, even five minutes after the dismissal bell had rung. But Dr. Smith droned on, sometimes calling down errant students trying to escape. "Sit down," he admonished. "I am not finished. Class is not dismissed." Students sat back down with a groan, waiting for him to stop talking so they could hurry on to their next assigned classes.

This required history class was held in a new state-of-the-art performance theater. The whole history department taught this class; lecture topics were assigned according to each professor's specialty. Even we students learned of the friendly rivalry among the professors to see who could detain us longest in the lecture hall. Students grumbled about this situation because we were always late to our next classes, but we felt powerless to change it.

The theater's comfortable seats and soft lighting made it even more challenging for the students to focus on the dry, tedious history lectures. This environment was not conducive to learning.

Whenever Dr. Smith lectured, the chalkboard was wheeled in—already covered in scrawls and unreadable past the second row. In the center of the contemporary, elliptical stage stood a podium with a microphone. However, the microphone was useless since the professor muttered his lecture, often lapsing into Latin and really confusing the class.

One day in early March, word passed among the students that class would feature a surprise, student-generated dimension that day. Throughout the entire lecture, I wondered what the surprise was. Fellow classmates who were involved in theater productions were eyeing each other with mischievous glances and looking mighty smug as the lecture dragged on.

Meanwhile, Dr. Smith was gathering momentum on some long-forgotten point of history. Time moved slowly while we waited in anticipation for the end of class. A friend and fellow classmate had worked with the theater productions and had knowledge of the inner workings of the auditorium, especially the elliptical hydraulic orchestra pit where the lecture podium now stood. This student also had the requisite key to the sound and lights booth.

As the end of class approached, Dr. Smith droned on as usual. Only this time when the dismissal bell sounded, suddenly the stage lights began blinking, a warning alarm sounded, and the podium, microphone, chalkboard, history text, and professor all began a slow descent before our very eyes. Even as the orchestra pit descended, Dr. Smith continued his lecture undeterred. For once, class ended on time. In unison, all of us stood, cheered, clapped, and then walked out. Ted Smith took it like a seasoned veteran. He tipped his head toward the student in the control booth and continued delivering his lecture as he dropped into the depths of the abyss. After this episode, many of us feared that sections of this particular lecture would appear on the final exam.

Word spread quickly about the drama in history class that day. And from that lecture forward, our history professors made sure they wrapped it up on time.

When I entered the teaching profession, I wondered if I would ever require such a dramatic wake-up call to know that I was out of touch with the very students I was assigned to teach.

While Dr. Smith's example reinforced the importance of respecting class schedules, Dr. Julius Jones presented another teaching method I knew I did not want to emulate. Dr. Jones taught my college geometry class, and I had taken high school geometry from a gifted teacher. As a result, I arrived as prepared as anyone. Geometry proofs may not have been high on my list of fun, but I had more than a passing knowledge of them.

In class, Dr. Jones began working a complicated geometry proof starting on the left side of an old-fashioned slate chalkboard. After a few minutes of thinking and writing, he stopped, stepped back, and stared at his proof. He didn't turn to us with an explanation of his progress, but rather moved back to the board, which ran the full length of the room. He resumed filling the chalkboard with his mathematical scribbles.

I checked my watch—wanting to know how much class time remained—while we all watched quietly as our professor continued writing and thinking. Fifteen minutes elapsed before he filled the board and turned to us. Surprised to find all of his students still in their seats, watching, he muttered, "Oh, you're still here."

I'm not sure how the others in Dr. Jones's room reacted, but I felt insignificant. My reaction today would have been much different. Now I would be irritated since I was paying for an education I wasn't receiving.

Would I eventually become a teacher who forgot she was teaching students? How does a teacher stay in touch with those she is educating? These were important points, and I didn't want to lightly pass over them in my training.

My history and geometry classes left lasting impressions on me. The teachers were preoccupied. I did not sense malice on their part, just a lack of engagement. Their interest in the subject matter far outweighed their attention to their students.

Over the years, I have worked with and been taught by excellent teachers. I have seen their influence alter the lives of their students. The talented ones reach down into the well of discouragement and lift students up. Somehow these instructors detect a hidden energy behind the students' anger, apathy, or lack of interest and channel that to engage students and enrich their lives.

I also have experienced the other end of this spectrum—ineptitude, arrogance, and even disdain on the part of educators. Some teachers have dished out the curdled milk of soured human kindness. In short, I've learned as much from the bad examples as from the good ones.

No matter what age, no matter what subject, I always taught the same thing throughout my career—students. Content ranks second in importance when it comes to the learner. The best lesson plans fail if the student isn't engaged in the learning process. Education was not a spectator sport in my room. For me, a lesson was classified as a success only when students were actively involved in gaining knowledge.

Let us not become weary in doing good, for at the proper time we will reap a harvest if we do not give up.

—Galatians 6:9, NIV

Making Lemonade

God is our refuge and strength, an ever-present
help in trouble.

—*Psalm 46:1*, NIV

The challenge of arranging my class schedule during junior year of college tested my faith in college professors, the registration process, and whether I'd have the stamina to withstand the trial. When I tried to sign up for foundations of education—a prerequisite course for student teaching—I felt as if I had received a whole shipment of sour lemons. This class was taught only once a year, and there was a cap on enrollment. Each student needed the professor's signature on the enrollment card to complete registration in the foundations course. If I missed this chance, I would have to pay extra tuition and delay graduation for a year.

My academic adviser, a professor from the religion department, did not appear to understand the stringent and sequential course schedule required of education majors. These students had to complete all of their education requirements by the end of their junior year in order to student teach in the fall of their senior year. And that is just what I was trying to accomplish through the registration process during my junior year.

Course registration, outdated by today's standards, was fraught with confusion, tension, and anxiety. Sometimes getting the classes you wanted or needed to graduate required the luck of a successful gambler. In short, registration was a full day of headaches for students and professors.

At the beginning of my junior year, the registrar was converting the course registration process to a computerized system using FORTRAN computer cards. Each course had an enrollment limit with a corresponding number of enrollment FORTRAN cards. Students who entered the gymnasium that morning to register saw tables lining the perimeter with names of departments taped to the tables. Professors representing individual departments sat at the tables with a box of FORTRAN cards for each course offered by that department. Students formed long lines in front of the tables, eager to snap up one of the coveted computer cards that reserved a space in the class. Registration involved a strategy to jockey for a position that would ensure that students were in the right line to get a course card for required courses that had limited enrollment. When all the FORTRAN cards for a given class were distributed, the course was deemed to be "closed" to further registration, and the unfortunate students who failed to secure computer cards for their preferred courses would have to wait for another semester or another year, depending on the department schedule.

I ran into a roadblock when trying to register for foundations of education that day. The foundations professor would not give me an enrollment card but had allowed a few sophomores to enroll in this upper-level course, apparently without question. But I needed this course now, because it was only offered once a year. If I couldn't take this class during my junior year, my student teaching, and hence my graduation, would be delayed a full year. Frustrated that my academic adviser from the religion department had no suggestions to help me solve this dilemma, I sought advice from Dr. Jerome Storm (not an alias), one of my professors in the education department.

As I anxiously explained my predicament, Jerry Storm listened intently to my concern.

When I had finished describing the problem, Dr. Storm sent me back to registration with clear instructions to return to his office as soon as the registrar officially closed enrollment in the foundations class. I looked on as my hopes for graduating on time begin to fade; I was starting to panic.

I watched in despair as the required class closed, and then I rushed back to Dr. Storm's office. Discouraged and feeling helpless, I nearly shouted, "The class is closed and now I have no idea how I will graduate on time!"

Dr. Storm confidently announced, "Registration for Foundations 11 Independent Study taught by Dr. Jerome Storm is now open. Would you like to enroll?"

"Yes!"

In retrospect, this was one of the brightest moments of my four years in college. In addition to graduating on time, I would benefit from what would become one of the most valuable and influential courses in my education taught by a dynamic, talented, and knowledgeable professor. I did not understand at that moment, however, the vital impact this one course, and this one professor, an ex-marine, would have on my career.

Each Tuesday and Thursday morning, Dr. Storm delivered a lecture to me, his only student. His compact office—crowded with his desk, his overflowing bookshelves, and one visitor's chair—was an inspiring learning environment. As the lone student, I always had to be prepared.

The unqualified vote of confidence I received from this gifted teacher and quintessential mentor proved to be one of the best lessons ever for me. What began as one of my most exasperating challenges ended up being one of my greatest gifts. Jerry Storm demonstrated his faith in my ability by taking on this extra teaching responsibility. He also provided a wonderful example of creative problem solving. His genuine interest in resolving my registration dilemma became a personal role model of generosity and devotion to help students throughout my career despite resistance from higher ups or arcane administrative procedures.

I learned many lessons in that foundations class, and in general, from Dr. Storm, an exacting professor who demanded the best from his students. I have used numerous techniques that I learned through his wisdom and style. I can still quote some of his sayings that influenced my educational philosophy. For example, "You can have thirty years of experience or one year repeated thirty times," he would say.

He shared that gem with me when I commented on a problem I had encountered in my children's literature class. Before literature class began one day, I noticed the professor arranging his notes on the podium, carefully unfolding them. I was seated near the front, close enough to notice the yellowed edges of the paper and glimpse the date—eleven years earlier! Had so little changed in children's literature since I had been in the fourth grade?

I wanted every year in my classroom to be fresh and different, so at the close of each year, my lesson plan book was carefully packed away for future reference only. I started each school year with new lesson plans building on the knowledge I had acquired in previous years. No warmed-over lesson plans for me or for my students, regardless of how many times I had taught the material. For example, while teaching junior high, I regularly taught the same math concept three times in a given day. And with my long history as a math instructor, I could have taught any given concept more than fifty times. So if I had let myself, I could have become bored with any number of math theories I was teaching.

One afternoon, during my last math class of the day, a student asked, "Haven't you taught this math two other times already today?"

"Yes," I replied.

"Doesn't it get boring!"

"Why, yes," I answered honestly, "it certainly can."

"How can you stand it?" he asked.

"Some people say I teach math, but I don't," I said.

This confused him, but nearby students listening in joined the conversation, and before I could answer, another classmate said, "She doesn't teach math. She teaches students."

Very perceptive and so right. Each year my students were new and so was my approach.

The college I attended had less than one thousand students so most of us knew each other. We were a family of sorts, and a rather small one at that in comparison to a large university. When one of our professors made a career move, as Jerry Storm did at the end of my junior year, it had an impact on students. I had been looking forward to my student teaching experience with both eagerness and apprehension. Dr. Storm, the college's student teacher supervisor, was a taskmaster. I had heard about his stringent requirements from previous student teachers, but I still looked forward to having his guidance. I knew I could build my classroom skills with his wise mentoring.

As my junior year drew to a close, Dr. Storm pulled me aside before my science methods class one day to tell me he would be leaving at the end of the year and taking a teaching position in another state. Distracted and disappointed by this news, I got very little from class that day. I felt sure whoever filled his position would not fill his shoes.

When I talked to the student teachers from the class ahead of me, they were disgruntled by their student-teaching experience. Some had been placed with cooperating teachers who had not helped them develop their classroom skills. Some seniors told me they felt their mentor teachers had walked out when they walked in, leaving them to fend for themselves. I wanted a cooperating teacher who would guide me, helping cultivate my skills.

One of Dr. Storm's last responsibilities before leaving for a new position was to coordinate student teaching assignments for the upcoming fall semester. I asked him if I could choose my mentor teacher. "That is certainly unorthodox," he said. "But let's see what you find."

So I asked another professor's wife, a highly respected biology teacher in a nearby district, for a recommendation. "Is there an elementary teacher in your district who is exceptional?" She talked with her network, and one name rose above all others, Eleanor Custard.

I gave Mrs. Custard's name, grade level, and credentials to Dr. Storm for consideration. Mrs. Custard didn't have her master's degree, which made it more difficult. But she had a wonderful reputation in the classroom and also had twenty-two years of experience. It required some doing, but before he left, Dr. Storm managed to have Mrs. Custard assigned as my mentor. It was more than a stroke of good fortune. Once again, Dr. Storm taught by example. His tenacity and commitment to students set a high standard for me to follow in my own teaching career. If I couldn't have Jerry Storm to guide me through my student teaching, at least I would now have Eleanor Custard's wisdom and experience, which proved to be a solid foundation for building a teaching career.

> *Now to him who is able to do immeasurably more than all we ask or imagine, according to his power that is at work within us.*
>
> —*Ephesians 3:20*, NIV

By the Numbers

Does he not see my ways and count my every step?

—*Job 31:4*, NIV

American culture doesn't stand still, and neither does the teaching profession. Take the following statistics listed on the US Census Bureau website; they offer a glimpse of the broad sweeping changes and cultural shifts that occurred across this nation during my four-plus decades of teaching. The numbers and percentages in the left column below provide a snapshot of the United States from 1970 when I was student teaching. Those in the right column come from the 2010 US Census statistics compiled two years before I retired. The numbers speak for themselves.

Some General Comparisons in US Population, 1970–2010

	1970	2010
US population	203.0 million	308.7 million
Life expectancy	70.8 years	77.8 years
High school graduates	55%	85%
College graduates	11%	28%
Households with cable TV	4%	83% [cable/satellite]

Some Numbers of My Own

4	Number of states I taught in
12	Number of different homes I lived in
6	Number of dogs I had

9	Superintendents I worked for
15	Principals I reported to
12	Secretaries who assisted everyone
10	Custodians who kept classrooms clean and floors gleaming
12	Classrooms I taught in
7	Different school buildings I worked in
3500	Approximate number of students I taught
122	Students I taught whose parents were my colleagues
20	Percentage of teachers at my school when I retired who had once been my students
7	Specific grade levels I taught
3rd–9th; college	Range of grade levels I taught
45	Years of educational service (equivalency with college instruction)
7500	Approximate days in the classroom
1	Private school instruction
7	Teaching licenses (different types from various states)
1	Administrative license
4	Years spent in post-bachelor training
6	Number of teacher's desks I used
10	Number of cars I wore out
966	Number of paychecks I cashed
$31,087	Average yearly income

As you know, we count as blessed those who have persevered.

—James 5:11a, NIV

Ready or Not

*He tends his flock like a shepherd: He gathers the lambs in his
arms and carries them close to his heart; he gently leads those
that have young.*

—*Isaiah 40:11,* NIV

My first teaching position was most unusual. I was hired to
teach in a private junior high boarding school in an isolated rural setting surrounded by the natural beauty of mountain peaks, clear streams, and old-growth forest. I went from the
role of student to one of teacher and houseparent in short order.
Ready or not, I was now swimming in the deep end of the educational pool with no auxiliary floatation devices. Twenty-five
seventh, eighth, and ninth graders traveled from several regions
of the country to this remote location to attend this small school.
Each family paid $2,000 for tuition—a huge sum in those days
when beginning teachers' annual salaries averaged $7,828.[1]

The cumulative tuition of $50,000 powered the school, cover-
ing the housing, meals, supplies, maintenance and utilities, faculty salaries, and vehicles for transportation. Saying the budget
was stretched tight was an understatement, which did not give
full credit to the talent and innovation of the headmaster, who
ably managed the school's limited financial resources.

In addition to teaching English and math, I handled office
chores, filled in for the cook occasionally on her day off, drove the
school van when needed, performed an assortment of odd jobs,
and was a twenty-four-hour-a-day houseparent to five inquisi-
tive, rambunctious teenage boys. My pay for this position was
$250 each month, roughly twenty-five percent of the average US
teacher's salary at that time.[2] However, $50 was then deducted
from each paycheck to cover my room and board since I lived in

school housing as a houseparent. (In effect, I had to pay rent for the privilege of being a houseparent.) On top of that, $32.57 was deducted for state and federal taxes. After these deductions, I was left with a mere $167.43 each month.

For this princely sum, I worked every day of the week. I taught classes Monday, Wednesday, Thursday, and Friday. Tuesday was my official day off when my workload was lighter. For that day, I was only expected to get the boys up, prepare their breakfast, send them off to class by 8:00 a.m., be ready for them to return about 4:00 p.m., prepare dinner for them, and then monitor their evening activities until bedtime. But while they were at school between eight and four on Tuesday, I was not responsible for anyone but me.

I also worked weekends when the staff monitored students' Saturday chores, supervised activities and games, and chaperoned occasional outings. However, every fifth weekend, I was free of responsibility. I couldn't afford to get away, but I did relish the two days with no school-related duties.

I was just a twenty-one-year-old college graduate when I accepted this position, but I looked more like I was fifteen. Sure, I had a college degree—I was a genuine, licensed classroom teacher. Despite the requisite college diploma and a valid teaching license, the responsibility of this residential position looked overwhelming to me. I was well-prepared for teaching the English and math classes. Although the school didn't have the conventional classrooms I was used to, I still enjoyed teaching junior high subjects in a classroom that was not just a teaching space but also served many other functions, one of which was the library. My youth and eagerness helped compensate for the absence of supplies and limited choices of textbooks.

I was more anxious about the constant demands of being a houseparent and a Jill of all trades. This challenge would most certainly test me, and although I was already more responsible and mature than many of my former college classmates, this assignment was sure to help me become even more mature, and quickly. The auxiliary responsibilities of this position presented the biggest challenges, especially the role of houseparent. This school was experimental, and I was a part of that experiment. Taking on the role of the authority figure in these students' home lives instantly made me a natural adversary for some of them. Worse, I soon discovered that my role of houseparent came without any real power, other than the power of persuasion. Four of the five students in my house were generally agreeable and willing to respect the few established rules of the house, but Dave, the fifth student, was a trial.

Dave had already been expelled by three different public schools before his parents enrolled him in this private one. He took pride in his rebellious, defiant attitude, and through his posture, facial expressions, body language, and general demeanor, he telegraphed to everyone around that he was not about to cooperate or change his ways. He was exceedingly difficult to motivate in the morning and refused to change his clothes or shower. He failed to show up for most classes and treated those around him with disdain. Dave was not in any classes that I taught, but being his houseparent created conflict between us.

I did not know the conditions underlying his acceptance at this school, but it was only a matter of time before he had angered or alienated most of the staff and his fellow students. I figured his belligerent behavior had been well-honed long before he arrived on our doorstep. The staff tried to redirect Dave's energy through the variety of classroom and outdoor activities offered at our school. But it was an incessant battle of breaking school rules, refusing to be a part of the community, and running away. When Dave ran away the third time, he burned his last bridge with the headmaster. Dave had received two warnings after his earlier disappearances, but with this latest incident, the consensus among the entire staff was that it was too risky to let Dave remain in residence when he could not be trusted. It was with a heavy heart that the headmaster called Dave's parents in March and sent him home.

I sensed that Dave knew if he broke enough rules that he would eventually be expelled from our school. This may have been his goal; I can't know for sure. But he didn't seem surprised or angry when he was expelled. Dave's dad told the staff that he appreciated all that we had done to help his son and accepted our decision because we had been in close communication with him throughout the school year. No one, not even Dave, was caught off guard with this resolution to the problem. After Dave left, life at home with the remaining four boys calmed down considerably.

At the other end of the behavior scale was Tyler, who also lived in my house. Tyler was a very motivated, respectful student. He enjoyed having "brothers" since he was an only child. Basketball was his favorite sport with outdoor activities taking a close second. As one of the older students, Tyler provided an inspiring role model for the younger ones, particularly in the maturity he showed in his daily choices. He often talked of following in his father's footsteps and becoming a surgeon, after his projected successful high school basketball career, of course.

Since this was a boarding school, our students came from many faraway places and a variety of family situations. I left after a year of teaching there and sadly lost track of the students. I regret that I didn't get to know if Tyler and the others achieved their dreams.

One advantage of being a small school was that staff could quickly respond to the academic needs of individual students, adjusting the curriculum to accommodate various learning levels and learning styles. Each Friday, for example, we held staff meetings where the teachers evaluated student progress and prepared for the upcoming week's activities and classes. As a staff, we had some lively discussions assessing where we felt our students needed more help or what we could offer that would most effectively meet their academic and social needs. The individual instructors, however, mostly determined the scope and sequence of their courses. Occasionally, one class would involve the entire school as an unexpected science lesson did one day in late winter outside the classroom building.

This classroom facility, built with the smooth, large rocks harvested from the nearby river, was located at the edge of a dense forest. Six large wood-framed windows on three sides of the building offered spectacular views of the natural landscape. This particular day, the sun was shining brightly causing the windows to mirror the blue skies and the evergreen trees from the nearby forest. A pileated woodpecker had found one of these windows and mistook his reflection for a competing pileated. In his attempts to scare off this challenger, the woodpecker was chipping out huge chunks of the wood that held the window in place. If he wasn't stopped soon, his enthusiastic drilling would damage the window beyond repair.

This bird was a dead ringer for the cartoon character Woody the Woodpecker, except that he was very large: he was about eighteen inches long, weighed three-quarters of a pound, and had a thirty-inch wingspan. His drumming rattled the whole building, all six rooms, and the sound carried for a great distance.

Upon locating the source of all this noise, the head teacher sent out word for all the students to hurry quickly to the classroom building. As the science teacher also, he wanted the students to see this fine animal up close while they could and before the woodpecker ruined the window frame. After the science lesson was over, the window was covered with a large, heavy tarp that kept "Woody" from intimidating the phantom contender who challenged his territory. The tarp was taken down after a few weeks, and the window was repaired. In the meantime, though, our students and staff got to observe and enjoy an impromptu science lesson.

The school was situated in a rural setting, and students relished outings to "civilization." Small groups of students with a staff chaperone traveled to neighboring towns for library visits and the occasional opportunity to eat out. The science teacher also offered regular field trips where students explored the woodlands, played in the cascading mountain river and the spring-fed pond, and hiked nearby mountains. The rural location, however, didn't mean a lack of cultural experiences. Daily, our head teacher enriched us all—students and staff alike—by reading excerpts of classic books as well as E. B. White's recently published *The Trumpet of the Swan* during lunchtime. The staff also planned fun Friday night activities for the students—movies, games, and intramural sports—changing the activities from week to week. A few teachers even taught the students traditional folk dances and invited local families to join us.

All students lived in houses on the school property with houseparents who also doubled as staff. Three of the school's student-residence houses were located about a half mile from the school on a gravel lane. Calling this lane the Cove Road gave it more credibility than it actually deserved. The ruts on this mountainous path were deep enough to shake important parts off of a vehicle. Three times a year, the school's maintenance crew used the tractor to drag an old scraper blade across the lane's surface in a gesture to smooth out as many lumps and potholes as possible.

The year before I arrived, the maintenance crew had rerouted the dirt road to make way for construction of a new home for the school's founder. The mound of dirt and gravel left over from building the new section of road was used to redirect the traffic. Students who rode bikes liked this embankment, and used it as an obstacle to jump as they traveled the half-mile mountain path between their homes in the cove and the school buildings.

Mostly this obstacle provided harmless fun until one weekend when Benjamin made the jump. Ben loved this pastime and jumped the embankment on a daily basis. However, over time, the hard landings had loosened the nut and bolt that secured his front tire. One Saturday afternoon as he was flying over the embankment, Ben's front tire came loose and fell off, leaving just the two wheel prongs on the front of his bike in its place. Ben realized in midair that he had a problem when he saw his front wheel take independent flight. But propelled by speed in midair, he was powerless to do anything more than hang on and brace for the impending impact. Ben and his bike landed hard on the other side of the embankment. The prongs, now free of the front wheel, dug into the dirt, stopping the bike short. In the next moment, Ben sailed over the handlebars and landed face first in the dirt.

The first staff member to arrive at the scene saw the damage to Ben's face, and especially his nose, and quickly realized the injuries were more serious than the local clinic was equipped to handle. Besides, the clinic was only open weekdays. In the meantime, two other staff members had arrived on the scene, and they ran to get the van to transport Ben to the nearest emergency room, a ninety-minute ride by car. The bike accident had happened about one that afternoon, but it was after midnight before the two staff members and Ben arrived back at school. The ER took x-rays, stitched up Ben's face, and gave him pain medication before releasing him. Banged up and bandaged, somewhat wiser, and definitely a bit more cautious, Ben jumped back into school life and bike riding, sporting his bumps and bruises as a mark of honor.

This school had only been in operation a few years when I joined the staff, and not long after my arrival, a former alumna returned, high school diploma in hand, seeking a job. Wanting to accommodate this graduate and also with an eye toward helping the school's finances, the headmaster offered Darlene the cook's job. Funding for the school was tight and the kitchen, like every other department, had to do its part to conserve precious financial resources. To that end, the kitchen's storeroom contained a lot of government surplus, including cheese, one of the cheapest items available through a federal program. Darlene had no choice but to plan many meals around those yellow blocks of protein.

While finances limited the choices of what Darlene could cook, the larger problem was that Darlene was not a cook. She had no experience in a commercial kitchen, and barely any practice cooking even on a small scale. It didn't appear that Darlene saw that as a barrier to success, even though her new job required preparing large quantities of food two times a day for hungry teens and the school's staff.

Junior high students can be most unforgiving in many areas when it comes to assessing the adults around them. But what they ate was a particularly sensitive topic. Discussing meals that Darlene had prepared required great diplomacy on the part of the adults, who often had to stifle their own reactions to the bland, the over-seasoned, or the sometimes downright distasteful food served in our dining hall. One day, I was seated across from the headmaster as he plunged headlong into the chili, eating spoonful after spoonful without complaint. However, I couldn't help but notice the sweat that was beading on his forehead and above his upper lip. Whether it was cayenne, red pepper flakes, or black pepper, I couldn't tell because I had avoided the chili that day, but the headmaster bravely soldiered through the entire bowlful. Among the least favorite meals were the casseroles Darlene concocted, especially when we couldn't recognize the ingredients. These casseroles grew increasingly unrecognizable as the year progressed and as Darlene grew tired of trying to be creative. Frustrated students began calling these dishes "compost casserole." The staff tried to discourage negative, blatant student reaction, but silently we agreed with their assessment. The evenings I cooked meals at home were a welcome relief from the usual casserole fare.

Scott, a kind, gentle seventh grader who lived in my house, approached me one day after a particularly bad meal at the dining hall and quietly said, "Miriam, Donna, and you have all cooked for us on Darlene's day off and we enjoyed your meals. Why is it that the only one who can't cook is hired as our cook?" I guess this was just one of the life lessons these junior high kids were getting—the mysteries of adults' decisions that defy explanation, such as not correcting errors when making hiring mistakes.

One thing I particularly noticed that year was the absence of parent complaints, and I wondered why. Considering all the time on task the staff spent with students, I figured the staff must have been doing something right. Dave was the only student who didn't complete the entire school year, and even his father accepted the way his son was cared for at our school and also understood the decision that required his son to leave.

One thing's for sure—I certainly grew a lot that year. I had plenty of opportunities to practice decision-making and setting appropriate boundaries, as well as handling frustration and physical and mental exhaustion. Not surprisingly, the staff burnout rate under these challenging circumstances was extremely high. Most of the teaching staff lasted only one, two, or at most three years. One year of a boarding school position satisfied me. I found a job the following year where I did not live in a 980-square-foot house with five teenage students; where the school day ended long before 10:00 pm; where weekends were mine; and most notably where the salary was commensurate with the customary rate for a teacher, allowing me greater economic freedom and more financial options. I moved three states away and sadly never saw any of my first-year students again; I have no idea if my efforts brought forth fruit in these students' lives, but God knows, and He allowed me to have a teaching position each year for the next four decades.

> *For I am convinced that neither death nor life, neither angels nor demons, neither the present nor the future, nor any powers, neither height nor depth, nor anything else in all creation, will be able to separate us from the love of God that is in Christ Jesus our Lord.*
>
> *—Romans 8:38–39,* NIV

Holding Your Ground

The Lord bless you and keep you; the Lord make his face shine on you and be gracious to you; the Lord turn his face toward you and give you peace.

—Numbers 6:24–26, NIV

If you need instant gratification, don't become a teacher. Daily, teachers till the ground, plant the seeds, fertilize the soil, water the plants, and cultivate the crop—but most of the harvesting is done far into the future, out of their view. The rare opportunity to experience closure is both a blessing and a strong motivator.

The classroom is a colossal experiment in human interaction. No owner's guide for upkeep and maintenance accompanies those students that we teach. Trial and error sum up my classroom experience best, and I had plenty of both. Throughout my career, I experienced many special moments that have demonstrated God's blessings for my students and me.

Take Scott, a former third grader, for example. He didn't appear at first to be one of those blessings. I met him when he walked into my classroom as a new student on the first day of school when I was teaching in the rural Midwest. Scott was a cute kid, and for an eight-year-old, he was also assertive and confident.

Everything was different for Scott that year—new town, new school, new classmates, and a new teacher. I wanted his transition to be as smooth as possible. His mind, however, was not set on the same goal as mine. He bossed other students around in class as well as during recess and at lunch. In general, Scott behaved badly much of that first day.

Scott also tried to push me around, but that met with little success. First, he made a point of ignoring my instructions. And when that didn't work, he openly defied my directions. All day long, his attitude bordered on belligerent. The activities of that opening day seemed to turn into challenges of autonomy for Scott. Most students used their best manners at least for the first few days, but it appeared that Scott was showing the worst he had to offer from the outset.

The other third graders in the class knew each other pretty well from previous grades together, but Scott was meeting these new classmates for the first time. I, too, was meeting these students for the first time and wanted to learn as many names as possible that day. This was one way I could welcome my students and show them that I was looking forward to having them in my room.

At the end of the afternoon, we played a name game as a fun way to finish our first day together. The object of the game was to practice each other's names aloud by starting with one person and one name, and then one at a time adding the other students—and their names—to the group at the front of the room. As each person was added, all of the names were repeated in order. I offered to let Scott, our newest class member, go first so he could avoid having to name a long line of children. But no, that was not for him. He announced loudly, "I want to be last." How challenging it is for a student who chooses to pursue his own folly headlong.

That first day Scott was in my classroom had been arduous for all of us, at least from my perspective. He had demanded attention, had been uncooperative, and in general had made a nuisance of himself. In hopes that he would settle down soon and start using good manners, I had gone easy on him with gentle reminders, trying to guide him while avoiding a standoff. Now he wanted his turn at naming all twenty-three fellow students after just a few hours in our class. Sometimes as the teacher, you just have to step back and let human nature run its course.

Scott totally flopped when it came time to name his classmates. He'd been so wrapped up in himself and what he wanted all day that he had failed to learn many names during recess or class time. Now here it was at the end of the day, and he was in front of the whole class stumbling over the few names he could recall. What could have been a wonderful first day making new friends and settling into his new school ended up being anything but enjoyable. As the entire class filed down the hall to board the school buses, one petulant, embarrassed third grader headed home from my classroom.

It wasn't a complete surprise on that second morning when the principal approached me in the hall. Before the students arrived, he wanted to discuss a problem. Very early that morning, before most of the teachers had arrived, the principal had received a call from Scott's mother complaining about her son's first day at his new school. The principal said Scott's mother had been shrill and unpleasant, demanding that her son be immediately removed from my class and placed in another room. She delivered her ultimatum as nonnegotiable.

I asked the principal to share her specific objections to my classroom. He summed it up by saying, "She accused you of being a witch and said that you were mean to her son." Well, here was a new perspective on that previous day. I agreed that Scott could have thought I looked stern when he tried to usurp my authority in the classroom. But her son was one of the most out-of-control students I'd experienced on the first day of any school year. And when I tried to save him from an embarrassing situation, he thwarted my attempts.

Here was a headstrong eight-year-old who had convinced his mother, without any other facts from any other sources, that he had been ill-treated by his teacher. His mother rose quickly to his aid demanding that the school transfer her child to another room by the second day of the year. From what the principal said, as well as what I had witnessed the previous day, this youngster had control of many things at home. And being in my classroom when he was new and unaccustomed to the procedures and people, he must have been frightened as well as frustrated that he couldn't wrestle from me the power he appeared to have at home.

In our conversation, the principal indicated that he was inclined to grant the mother's (son's) request and quietly transfer Scott to another room to be done with the matter. And this may have been the easiest solution for me, but I didn't see it as the best solution for Scott. I didn't feel it was the right choice that day and explained to the principal why I thought the transfer would lead to more problems.

I asked the principal, "Are you ready to field the variety of requests you'll be receiving once parents realize the power of a loudly registered complaint, especially one based on emotions rather than facts?" Schools don't function in a vacuum. People in the community talk, and granting this simple transfer had the potential to open the floodgates for other parents' requests to modify their children's placement for whatever reason.

My other students and I would be willing to acknowledge how trying that first day had been. Scott and I had been caught in a clash of wills that I didn't particularly care to repeat. Yet I couldn't voice a valid reason to transfer Scott out of my room, and I had no intention of relinquishing my authority to a spoiled eight-year-old. Somewhere deep inside of me, I felt confident that Scott and I would be fine, and he would receive a good education in my room. I assured the principal that Scott and I could work out our differences.

I noticed a minor shift in Scott's attitude during our second day together. He wasn't exactly well-behaved, but the bravado from the first day was gone. I calmly went about the business at hand and treated him like any other student—calling on him when he participated and gently correcting him when he misbehaved.

We got off to a slow start that first week, but as time progressed, I could perceive an improvement.

My students and I enjoyed wonderful learning activities on those early fall days, including a field trip to the Mississippi River where we learned how the locks and dam worked. We were permitted to walk across the metal grids of the locks and get an up close look at the river and the process of lifting and lowering the boats.

I also read aloud to my class every day, and these books seemed to spark Scott's curiosity. He was an attentive listener who appeared to enjoy the literary adventures our class shared. This one specific activity helped smooth out many wrinkles among all the students—not just with Scott.

By December, Scott was one of the students most excited by the Christmas puppet show we performed for other classes. He enjoyed art class when we painted the scenery, and he eagerly participated in the required practices we needed to prepare our presentation. By then the classroom was humming like a well-oiled machine needing only occasional tune-ups.

Considering our difficult first day, my year with Scott leveled out to a satisfying and workable teacher-student relationship. The classroom can turn into a scary place for students when the authority figure fails to exert her power. When that leader abdicates her authority, it can be usurped by the strongest, but not necessarily the nicest, student. Then all the other students are subject to this tyrant's whim. I held firmly to my position—refusing to abdicate to Scott as it appeared other adults in his world had. Eventually he settled down and learned to trust me and his classmates.

Early that spring, we saved milk cartons from lunch for a science project. We rinsed out the cartons thoroughly and then filled them with soil. Next, we planted tiny marigold seeds in each carton. Once the tender seedlings sprouted, we cared for them by keeping them warm and moist. We hoped they would grow into recognizable marigold plants in time for Mother's Day. On the second Friday in May, the students took their delicate plants home to present as gifts to their mothers. During the coming days, students reported how they had planted their flowers in their gardens with their mothers' help.

That next fall, Scott and his classmates entered the fourth grade with new room assignments and the promise of new experiences and responsibilities. Anticipation always runs high on the first day of a fresh school year. We teachers enjoyed watching former students return and locate their new rooms. But Scott's entry that August was different from the other students' return.

He came bursting into the school clutching a large, bright yellow marigold. He hurried past his new room, rounded the corner, and headed straight for his former classroom. When he found me there, he thrust his flower in my face and proclaimed with a happy grin, "Look what *we* grew!"

Scott had managed to coax his plant into a beautiful flower over the summer. Then he had shared the credit with me. There are times when we have to hold our ground and know, with patience and God's help, difficult situations can turn around and become blessings. In that moment, Scott and I shared the same feeling: Look what we grew, indeed.

Bear with each other and forgive one another if any of you has a grievance against someone. Forgive as the Lord forgave you.

—*Colossians 3:13*, NIV

Author, Author

Train up a child in the way he should go: and when he is old,
he will not depart from it.

—*Proverbs 22:6,* KJV

Can you name your favorite author? My third graders certainly could. They chose this one particular author above all others. His children's books were classics: timeless topics, real-life applications, inspired creativity, lessons in loyalty and honor, and a joy to share out loud because of their rhythm and cadence.

My third graders were not alone in their selection of E. B. White. He was described as "one of the most influential modern American essayists, largely through his work for *The New Yorker* magazine."[1] But even a writer of his talent understood the frustration of putting pen to paper when he said that he found writing difficult and bad for one's disposition, but he kept at it.[2] "I admire anybody who has the guts to write anything at all," he told George Plimpton and Frank H. Crowther in a 1969 interview published in *The Paris Review.*[3]

Yet, here he was in his early fifties creating his second book for children. He described how he got started in the world of children's literature in an interview with Bill Caldwell for one of Caldwell's books.

> But I got into writing for children by a complete accident. Little children visiting always wanted me to tell them stories, and I wasn't able to tell them a good story, so I decided to arm myself with materials. And I wrote a couple of chapters of *Stuart Little*. Stuart Little was a bit of a fluke, but it was a successful book financially and spiritually. Then *Charlotte's Web* was a deliberate attempt

to write something for children. And "Charlotte" has kept me alive, been my bread and butter.[4]

Despite his success, White said he often found himself at a loss for words. With more than ten prestigious literary awards for writing aimed at adults, he could also pen a child's story that people of all ages could enjoy.[5]

Charlotte's Web, the bestselling children's paperback of all time,[6] was a perennial favorite in my classroom. E. B. White's enduring story focuses on friendship and commitment. Spiders across the country are granted immunity from harm, at least temporarily, after children meet Charlotte and her friends, Wilbur the pig and Templeton the rat, in this classic tale.

Some of E. B. White's inspiration for children's stories came from his Maine farm, as he told Bill Caldwell:

> I love lambs. I had triplets once. Don't like triplets, I'd rather have a good pair of twins....My lambs are out in the pasture now, not here in the sheep pen....(Opening a door to a two holer [outhouse])....And this is a very lucky room for me. This is where I first saw Charlotte. Watched a spider spinning her web in here one day....Let's walk on down to the water now. I'll show you the dock and the boathouse—fishhouse (sic)—I've got for writing in. I keep my typewriter down here, by the water....My normal routine is to come down here in the morning so I can get away from all the mess up at the house. Right now I am finishing a book. [*The Trumpet of the Swan*]....I'll unlock the fish house, so we can take a look inside...I've just had its face lifted, got the place fixed up a bit. I used to lug my typewriter all the way down from the house, now I just leave it here and lock the door...but I don't need a lot of stuff around when I am writing here. I just bring down what I need that day. All I need really is typewriter and paper. I write by the window, at this table. I sit on the bench with my back to the wall.[7]

White's inspiration for Charlotte came from his farm, while his inspiration for *Stuart Little* came from a dream. "In a letter White wrote…how he came to conceive of Stuart Little: many years ago I went to bed one night in a railway sleeping car, and during the night I dreamed about a tiny boy who acted rather like a mouse."[8] Stuart and Charlotte are wonderful stories, but my own personal favorite is *The Trumpet of the Swan*. White had written about a mouse-boy and a literate spider—was it a far stretch to tell the story of a mute trumpeter swan that needed a real trumpet to live his life?

Louis, a trumpeter swan born without a voice, and his friend, Sam Beaver, shared adventures from Montana to Massachusetts. Louis's father, realizing his son would never live a full life without a voice, stole a trumpet. With this trumpet, Louis could court and woo a female—a lifelong companion in the swan world. Louis considered it his responsibility to restore his father's honor by repaying the debt of the pilfered trumpet. Louis and Sam shared many escapades while Louis sought gainful employment.

White was a master at creating word pictures. One of my classes was so excited they wanted to share the story with others. Since *The Trumpet of the Swan* has twenty-two chapters and I had twenty-two students, each one studied a chapter and created a picture to illustrate what they visualized in their own minds.

After they created their rough drafts on Manila paper, they produced finished drawings on eighteen-by-twenty-four-inch construction paper. The students were pleased with their illustrations and wanted to display them in the hall.

Each picture had an endearing quality, but one in particular captured my imagination. Joey had a clear vision of camp life when he depicted the following scene for our story.

Louis's friend Sam helped him get his first job as a camp bugler. But when summer came to an end, Louis still needed to earn more money. The bugle calls he had learned did not require the use of the trumpet keys. To get a better paying job, Louis knew he'd have to be able to play more like the famous trumpeter Louis Armstrong rather than a camp bugler. The swan asked Sam to separate the toes on his right foot so he could press the keys of his trumpet.

Joey brought this scene to life by filling his paper with a large camp tent, canvas flaps tied back. Inside were two camp cots. Louis sat on one with his left foot dangling and his right held straight out for Sam, who sat on the opposite cot. With a razor, Sam carefully separated the webbed toes for Louis.

When the pictures from every student were exhibited in order, we liked the way they told the story. So did other students and teachers in our building. We wondered aloud what E. B. White would think of them.

My students were eager to share with their favorite author and suggested writing him letters. Reading-circle discussions about *The Trumpet of the Swan* had already produced a lively exchange of ideas, an increased vocabulary, and an art activity. Now it also was going to foster an English lesson on how to write a letter.

Once the letters were finalized, the students and I gathered their letters and pictures illustrating the chapters only to discover I didn't have any envelopes large enough to mail them in. Checking the supply cabinet, I found a large piece of tagboard, which is a stiff yet flexible cardboard. So I fashioned an envelope to accommodate our materials.

The post office in our rural town was three blocks from school, close enough for a social studies walking field trip. The postmaster was happy to show my students around and explain how our letter would travel to Maine. We learned about postmarks and routing techniques. Mail destined for the same state or regional zip code area was bundled and a sticker with a letter from the alphabet was fixed to the top envelope.

Our trip near the end of March turned out to be a lucky day for some local taxpayers. With the April 15 federal tax deadline looming, people had begun mailing in their tax forms. As the postmaster was explaining to us the various parts of the post-mark, my students noticed that the date on the meter was accidentally set for April, not March—an error the postmaster was glad to correct before any of the forms left his office.

Once we arrived back at school, I prepared the students for disappointment in case E. B. White was unable to respond to their letters and drawings. They were satisfied to know that they had thanked him for his exciting adventures, but maintained hope they'd hear from him.

Four weeks later, an envelope arrived with E. B. White's return address. It was addressed to Ms. Favreau's Third Grade (my name was Jeanne Favreau at the time), and it had a yellow circle with an S routing symbol on it. We knew our letter had been on the top of the bundle of mail headed to our rural community from Maine. Everyone crowded around as I read our letter out loud.

The envelope with the routing symbol from the top of the postal bundle.

North Brooklin, Maine
April 13, 1976

Dear Third Graders and Ms. Favreau:

Your fine letters and
beautiful pictures have arrived, and I want to thank you
all for the work you put in. I love the drawings of the
scenes from THE TRUMPET OF THE SWAN, and I gather from the
letters that you enjoyed the story. I have received many
thousands of letters over the past few years, but the
envelope that came from you was the biggest one I ever got.
I don't know how you managed to find such a big envelope.

I want to thank Jeanne
Favreau for reading the stories and for her kindness in
telling me about her experience in the classroom. It does
me a lot of good, at my age, to know that some of the things
I have written in the past have meant something to the
reader. I am quite old now and have almost forgotten that
I ever wrote them.

Spring has finally come to
Maine, after a snowstorm that we had here only day before
yesterday. My goose, Felicity, is laying and has a nest of
straw in the barn. She started laying around St. Patrick's
Day and will probably continue to lay until the Fourth of
July. She lays one very big white egg every other day, and
she buries them up in the straw so they won't freeze. I have
another goose named Apathy, and she isn't much at laying eggs
but she gets broody and likes to sit, so I take Felicity's
eggs and put them under Apathy and she hatches them out, after
twenty-eight or twenty-nine days.

Tomorrow I am expecting 75
day-old chicks in the mail, shipped from Connecticut where
there is a big hatchery. I have my brooder stove all ready
and tomorrow I will drive to Bangor and go to the post office
and call for the baby chicks. Then I will drive them home---
fifty miles---and place them under the brooder, at a temperature
of 90 degress, which will be like a mother to them. Baby chicks
need warmth more than they need anything else.

I have been asked to read
the story of THE TRUMPET OF THE SWAN for a recording, and I
have agreed to do it. But I don't think I will be able to get
around to it until next fall, as I have too many other things
on my mind. Thank you again for your letters and your drawings.

Sincerely,

EBWhite

Our letter from E. B. White.

Geese in the barn cellar on E. B. White's farm.

Barn cellar

·This is Felicity, two years ago, when she was hatching her goslings in the barn cellar.

The caption Mr. White penned
on the back of the picture.

We were awestruck that he would write to us at all, let alone send such an engaging, personal letter. Their favorite author's stories about his life on his farm struck a chord with them, but his warmth and caring demeanor were the best gift.

Mr. White shared his views on corresponding with his readers in Bill Caldwell's interview:

> I like to write children's books. It's very rewarding. The letters I get are fabulous. Thousands from children, and every once in a while I hear from teachers and librarians about the impact of the book.[9]

The true essence of E. B. White came through in his correspondence. Not only was he a man of character and fame, but he also possessed generous amounts of humility that was well-grounded in an appreciation of everyday life. I doubt my students understood the significance of receiving correspondence from an author of his stature. However, they did resonate to the thoughtful kindness E. B. White showed an unknown, but still important, class of eight- and nine-year-olds.

> *You, my brothers and sisters, were called to be free. But do not use your freedom to indulge the flesh; rather, serve one another humbly in love. For the entire law is fulfilled in keeping this one command: "Love your neighbor as yourself."*
>
> *—Galatians 5:13–14,* NIV

Kids Will Say Most Anything

The Lord gives strength to his people; the Lord blesses his people with peace.

—Psalm 29:11, NIV

Arriving at school forty-five minutes ahead of my students on a cold, dreary February morning, I noticed workers on ladders attaching cables along the outside of the school building. Climbing the stairs to my classroom on the second floor, I mentally prepared for the day's activities. Soon my fifth graders arrived, and we settled into our lessons. Near the end of reading that morning, I saw a baseball cap shuffling its way across the bottom edge of our classroom windows. This didn't surprise me since I had seen the ladders propped against the building earlier. The fifth graders, however, had entered the building through another door and were unaware of the work being done outside our room.

Jack, a gifted student with a great sense of humor, glanced up and eyed the baseball cap creeping along the bottom edge of our second-story windows. Without hesitation, he elbowed his neighbor, pointed to the cap, and whispered, "I told that encyclopedia salesman to stop bothering me." Neither his friend nor I could stifle our laughter. The whole class wanted to be a part of the fun so Jack shared his comment with everyone. His cleverness made him more a class comedian than a class clown. He had the gift of sizing up a situation and putting a comical spin on it. This noteworthy comment stood out because of its sophistication, a rare occurrence in my work with ten-year-olds.

I became more aware of laughter's good effect on this particular class that summer when I bumped into Jack and his mother at our local county fair. This fair, with a history of more than one hundred years in our rural farming community, was the highlight of the year for our students, and it offered a great place to reconnect with old friends. After I greeted Jack and his mom, I inquired about how their summer was going. After Jack's mother shared a few activities they had enjoyed, she asked, "Do you have a few minutes to wait with me while Jack goes to find his father?"

"Sure," I answered as Jack disappeared into the crowd.

While Jack was gone, his mom continued the conversation. "My husband has always wanted to meet you. He can't believe the stories Jack brought home from school this past year because he never had a teacher who enjoyed laughter the way you do. Jack persuaded his father that you really found his humor funny, but part of his dad still doubts Jack's perception. I know my husband would be disappointed if he didn't get to meet you."

Shortly, Jack returned with his father. I convinced his dad that not only did I find Jack funny, but his classmates did also. After spending just a few minutes talking and laughing with his family, I could see why Jack had been so much fun in my class. Conversation with the whole family came easily, even though I had just met Jack's dad. I also saw a similarly enjoyable sense of humor in his father's witty comebacks. For me, the nine-month school year was much too short when it came to students like Jack.

I have lost track of Jack over the years, but I never forgot his quick, humorous comment on that February day. Laughter was considered an indispensable ingredient of learning in my classroom. I still believe students gain knowledge better and retain more of it when their environment fosters laughter.

But along with laughter, sadness also intruded into my students' lives.

As a teacher, I never knew what burdens children would tote with them when they entered my classroom. For instance, Emily, a normally happy child, showed up one Monday morning rather subdued. I approached her at recess when we were free to talk. "Emily, you've been out of sorts today. Is anything wrong?" I asked.

"I'm sad," she answered. "My grandmother died over the weekend."

"I'm so sorry to hear that," I replied. "Tell me about your grandmother."

I spent much of that recess with Emily, who shared many special memories about her grandmother. She finished our conversation with, "Our favorite hobby was baking cookies together. It just won't be the same without her."

On the way home that afternoon, I related Emily's story to fellow teachers in my carpool. All three third-grade teachers, plus one teacher from second grade, shared the thirty-minute ride. As we traveled, we discussed student needs from our rooms so that we could develop greater insight and be more sensitive to important issues such as Emily's. After hearing about Emily's grandmother's passing, the other teachers agreed to watch over Emily as she adjusted to her loss.

The second-grade teacher then added, "I had an interesting situation in my room today which relates to yours. One of my little girls became quite upset and began crying while sitting at her desk during silent reading time. Her crying had turned to wailing by the time I knelt next to her chair. 'What is wrong?' I asked.

"She choked out, '*M-m*-my *g-g*-grand*m-m*-mother *d-d*-died!' As I tried to comfort her, great sobs racked her small body. 'I'm so sorry to hear this,' I told her. 'When did this happen?' She continued to cry and answered, '*T-t*-two *y-y*-years *a-a*-ago.'"

The sense of time is a whole different matter for children than for adults. Perhaps the delayed response increased the girl's intensity of her feelings. Or maybe something reminded her of her grandmother that day, perhaps a happy memory that dredged up fresh feelings of sadness and loss. None of us knew; we could only speculate. However, that afternoon, we each got an important lesson in how children process feelings differently than adults.

Another example of how children view the world came from a teacher and friend who would start the new school year in a brand new building. In mid-August, she was working in her new room arranging the classroom supplies when she heard youngsters talking outside the building. She could hear their voices grow louder as they went from room to room, peering in the windows. Their excitement grew as they got closer to her room.

"Look at *this* room."

"Yeah, it's almost ready! Look at all that new stuff."

"Come over here and look. This room even has books in it."

Their anticipation seemed to increase when the leader of the group peered into the windows of my friend's room and exclaimed, "Look at *this* room. It already has the teacher!" Adults know that teachers aren't ordered and shipped in the way furniture is, but this child did not seem so sure.

Another friend discovered that students could say important things, but as teachers, we might not be able to understand them, especially first graders.

On one particular January day, many first graders were suffering from winter colds, and one little boy who approached his teacher had a stuffy nose. His speech pattern was difficult to understand under normal circumstances, but this day, it was nearly impossible to decipher.

"N've gaught creyuns ah minos."

"What?" the teacher asked.

He repeated, "N've gaught creyuns ah minos."

"I can't understand you. Say it again," she directed him.

"N've gaught creyuns ah minos!" he said with exasperation.

Still unable to understand what he needed, she turned to his classmates. "What does Sammy need?"

Translating for him, a couple of students blurted out, "He's got crayons up his nose!"

These were not small crayons. No, they were the primary, monster-sized ones, and they were firmly lodged in his small nostrils. Looking at the child, the teacher said, "Well, get them out."

"Un kant," Sammy muttered, "dare schtuk."

"Well, blow," she said. And that's just what he did, with gusto.

Like scud missiles with mucous afterburners, the crayons shot across the room. The collective response of his fellow first graders revealed their feelings. "EEEWWW."

Later that year, this teacher experienced another unforgettable incident in her room. The superintendent had recently warned the staff that they needed to keep their rooms cleaner. This one-size-fits-all announcement often causes unexpected outcomes. Teachers who need the directive often ignore it thinking they aren't the problem. While conscientious teachers, already diligent, work even harder to meet the request. This teacher, one of the meticulous ones, wanted to be sure it was not her first graders at the root of the cleaning trouble. So she became even more vigilant in her pursuit of tidiness, not an easy task with a room filled with six-year-olds.

A few days later, following an art lesson using clay, the teacher spotted something on the floor near the door. Aware that each room was being monitored for cleanliness, she announced, "All right. Who dropped the clay?" Students turned to observe the offending item on the floor.

A soft-spoken girl nearby offered, "I don't think it's clay."

She was right. As the teacher drew closer, she found it did indeed resemble clay. One of her students hadn't made it to the bathroom in time and also had neglected to wear underwear to school that day.

Sometimes students will put unusual things in writing. One afternoon while teaching third grade, I was scheduled to attend a district meeting during the last two hours of school. Instead of hiring a substitute, the principal decided he would cover my class and teach the last lessons of the day.

I had a wonderful bunch of students that year and discipline issues rarely crossed my mind. I enjoyed reporting to work each day, so it came as a complete surprise when I returned the next morning to find my students had acted out during class time with the principal. My surprise turned to shock when the principal related the details of the trouble my students had caused. They had been noisy and disrespectful, and they had spoken out of turn during the science discussion—behaviors I was not used to experiencing from them.

My first order of business that morning was to discuss what had happened while I was gone. I didn't even try to hide my disappointment over their bad behavior. As we discussed the incident, it became apparent they needed, and wanted, to apologize to the principal. Real-life situations often provided some of the best opportunities for effective writing lessons in my room.

I was amazed at the behaviors they admitted to in their letters. I had to give my students credit for honesty. They owned up to their rudeness and asked the principal to forgive them. The confessions they wrote in their letters showed their sincerity. Here is one example.

Dear Mr. Turner,

I'm sorry about my talking. I don't know what was wrong. I didn't mean to be so noisy, but the words just kept coming out of my mouth. You're not as good a teacher as Mrs. Nordstrom, but she's not as good a principal as you are.

Sincerely,

Ken

Children's bodies sometimes did the talking for them. An example comes from a fifth grader who had kept a lie to himself since third grade. Two years may not seem like a long time to an adult, but it amounted to one-fifth of this child's lifetime.

Mrs. Pat Nelson (not an alias) and I both taught the fifth-grade classes, and we regularly worked together when discipline problems arose. That particular day, we were discussing a recess situation that involved Billy. A scuffle had broken out during the noontime football game, and it was unclear who started the problem. After we found out that Billy was only a witness to the incident and not the instigator, he then quietly admitted that he had another problem he wanted to confess to us. He told us he had been holding on to this problem for some time and said he just had to share it with someone. Billy took a deep breath and blurted out that he had stolen a stopwatch from his third-grade teacher's desk. Having confessed his burden and cleansed his conscience, he crumpled. As Billy collapsed right there in the hall, Mrs. Nelson hollered, "What's wrong?"

"He's fainted," I said. Startled by his reaction, we somehow managed to catch Billy before he hit the floor. Within seconds Billy sat up but found himself very embarrassed. Admitting his crime along with his fainting left him dumbfounded. When he was ready to talk again, we discussed the serious consequences of dishonest behavior.

With what we had just observed, we felt Billy had already paid a hefty price for stealing, and his face also showed true remorse. Neither Mrs. Nelson nor I felt the need to add more punishment to what he had already heaped on himself.

We explained to him that we felt he had paid enough for his misconduct and this matter would be a closed subject as far as we were concerned. However, we cautioned him that if either of us heard of any more stealing in his future, we would bring up his past transgression.

Billy finished his fifth-grade year and the rest of his school days without a hint of scandal. Mrs. Nelson and I were relieved we never had to mention the stealing episode again. Billy had indeed learned from that incident and grew into a fine young man.

Sometimes my encounters with students were not only unpredictable, but also embarrassing for me. Katelyn's story from my second year of teaching was one of these.

Open House was a September ritual in all of the districts where I taught. Teachers had the opportunity to meet students' parents and siblings, and students got to show their classrooms and projects to their families. The following morning, students often shared stories about things parents had learned from their visit the evening before. My third graders' comments were typical until it was Katelyn's turn. "My parents liked our class," she said. "But my dad said he never had a teacher with legs as pretty as yours." With a red face, I quickly closed sharing time and moved on to the first subject of the day.

Occasionally the embarrassment extended to parents as well. Take Sarah and her mother, for example. During sixth-grade recess, Sarah wanted to join the game of football in progress. When the boys refused to let her play, Sarah got mad. That was when the trouble started. After I found out about how Sarah had dealt with the boys, I knew I would need to become involved. After recess, Sarah and I discussed her behavior. I thought the best course of action to correct her mistake was to have her explain to her mom what had transpired during recess. We had phones in the office that allowed two people to talk with a third party. I placed the call to Sarah's mother and explained that her daughter had something to tell her and that Sarah and I were both on the phone.

"Mom? This is Sarah, and I got in trouble at recess. Yes, I made a mistake and that's why I have to call you. My punishment is telling you what I did. You see, I was trying to play football with the boys, and they weren't playing fair. I finally got so frustrated that I mooned them."

Her mom's voice resonated through both phones. "You what? Oh, Sarah, how could you?"

I coaxed Sarah to tell her mother the rest of the details from recess. In a small voice, Sarah added, "Twice."

Her mother's reaction was similar to mine. "You did it twice, Sarah? Once wasn't bad enough?"

My disciplining was often more effective when I let students ponder their behavior and worry about the consequences while I cleared my head. As Sarah finished her conversation with her mom, I decided that I would add only one comment. The call to her mom and the comment from me would close the incident.

"You know, Sarah, a problem like this one will haunt you if you continue to make choices like the one from today. This event could even define your future unless you alter your behavior. You wouldn't want your classmates writing about this event in your high school yearbook. I trust you'll pause and think before you react next time."

Sarah took this experience to heart and improved her recess behavior. I enjoyed teaching her; she was smart, capable, and motivated. And after that incident, she also developed a cooler head.

I saw Sarah many years later at her high school graduation. When I met her in the hall, she gave me a big smile, pulled me aside, and said, "I have been good, really good. You would be proud of me." She was so right.

Now and then, even high school kids could surprise me. During a working lunch at my desk, I noticed some former students crowded around my classroom door. Setting aside my slice of watermelon, I motioned for them to come in. These four sophomore girls had been in my math class during seventh and eighth grades. But that day, they needed some help on their high school algebra. Their math instructor had been out sick a few days and the substitute didn't possess the algebra skills to explain the assignment.

They spread their books and papers on my desk and we looked over their problems. High school algebra troubles often required a review of the identity and distributive properties that my students had studied with me in junior high math. Once I reviewed these rules with them, I saw other algebra properties we had studied pop into their heads as they solved the problems. I often joked with my students that the air molecules in my math classroom enhanced problem solving and many of my students agreed with me that there was something special about the air in my room.

After finishing the algebra assignment, the girls gathered their supplies and began buzzing about the activities going on in their lives. That happy laughter and a chance to help former students made a special lunch break for me. As they were leaving, the first student headed for the door but then turned and said, "I miss you!" The next one joined in, "I miss the way you explained everything so I could understand it."

"Thank you," I responded. "Being able to teach you is the gift I was given for the struggles I experienced in school."

Lunch was extra tasty for me that day. I hadn't packed anything out of the ordinary. It was the joy these students had left in their wake. The last one out the door looked over her shoulder and said, "I miss the wonderful smell of your room."

I am never sure of the impression I have left on my students, but you can be sure one of the best parts of my job is the surprise factor. Yes, God's blessings can come in unusual and unexpected ways.

Do not let any unwholesome talk come out of your mouths,
but only what is helpful for building others up according to
their needs, that it may benefit those who listen.

—Ephesians 4:29, NIV

The Rewards of Persistence

I will say of the Lord, "He is my refuge and my fortress, my
God, in whom I trust."

—*Psalm 91:2*, NIV

Some students inherently know when they have been a challenge to their teacher. Brian knew.

A fifth grader with chutzpa, Brian had been flexing his independence muscles throughout the school year. Struggles with him were daily fare—problems in the restroom, shoving in lunch line, or crashing in on others' games at recess. Brian needed constant intervention from the teaching staff. With 180 student days in a school year, the variety and number of times I witnessed or heard tales of Brian's escapades were countless. As his homeroom teacher, I was summoned each time his behavior went too far and he needed correction or punishment. I got plenty of practice in steering him toward acceptable behavior.

For Brian, the restroom was a hotbed of trouble. I usually stationed myself outside of the boys' bathroom, a preemptive move for the disturbances that often started there. One day, the racket coming from the restroom was so loud that I was compelled to step to the door. "Calm down in there," I called out, "or I will be forced to come in and monitor this restroom break."

I heard a boy from another class ask, "Would she really come in here?"

I heard Brian answer, "You have to see her in action. If she says she's coming in, then she will."

His comment let me know that my persistence in correcting his behavior was having the desired effect. My presence in the hall that day helped calm down the commotion in the restroom.

Brian taught me many lessons during his year in my classroom. Persistence was one of his best lessons. I sensed Brian had hidden potential, most of it hidden behind his bad behavior. I wanted to help him recognize and start to develop his abilities before he completed fifth grade. Brian was a bright boy, and I was hoping to help him direct his energy into making good use of his many talents. I had many days when I questioned my effectiveness, wondering if I had missed the target.

As I taught my classes, I looked for any opportunity to encourage Brian. Helping students who want, and need, to make different choices is most always a slow process. Two steps forward, one step back on a daily basis, and always on the lookout for a chance to recognize positive changes: homework turned in on time, good behavior playing at recess, restroom breaks without being rowdy, no pushing in the drinking fountain line. Dedicated consistency, that's the key.

By the end of the school year, I noticed that the restroom episodes were fewer and much farther apart. Most of the time, I was no longer needed to run interference solving recess problems or complaints from fellow teachers, unlike the previous September. Disruptions in lunch line rarely involved Brian anymore. His behavior, although not perfect, was greatly improved. I was about to complete the nine-month school year still standing. Brian had not worn me down; instead, my persistence paid off for Brian.

In spite of the unrelenting tug of war with Brian, my year with this class had been quite satisfying. As a celebration on the last day, I brought Hershey's Kisses to school as a treat. I asked the students to form two lines—a hug line and a hug-and-kiss line. (The Hershey Company had not created chocolate hugs yet, or I might have used them also.)

You can guess where my fifth-grade boys headed—straight to the hug line—while my girls went for the hug-and-kiss line. Students had no idea that I was carrying chocolate kisses in my paper bag, or my boys might have joined that line.

Was I ever surprised when I looked down the hug-and-kiss line and saw one lone boy, Brian, standing at the end. Starting with the hug line, I gave each boy a hug and told him something special I remembered from his year in my class. Then I moved to the other side of the room and gave each student there a hug and a chocolate kiss, as well as a significant memory.

When I reached Brian at the very end of the line, I gave him a hug and then a kiss wrapped in foil. He looked up at me and shook his head. "That won't do it for me," he said. "I want a kiss, a real kiss. I have been such a problem this year that you should have given up on me in November, but here we are in May, and you never quit trying to help me. I want a kiss."

I had not anticipated this situation, and it left me speechless. Through my experience with Brian, I knew what his earnest expression meant. Brian was a role model for persistence.

Kissing a student was not in my realm of experience or choice. Aware of propriety, I was in a quandary as to how I should proceed. So I paused and looked at him. I offered him a second Hershey's Kiss, but he was adamant about the real thing. Bending over, I placed a kiss on his forehead. Pleased, he beamed at me and then went about his business of gathering his things to go home.

Before my class headed for the buses that final day of fifth grade, all of my students had gotten chocolate kisses. It was a unanimous decision that each of the upcoming sixth graders needed, deserved, a chocolate kiss.

It seemed that before Brian moved on to the sixth grade, he needed reassurance from me that the strain of his daily trials had not made me an enemy.

Since the middle school was in a different town, I did not get to see Brian the following year, but I heard occasional updates about his progress, especially from his sister who was now in my fifth-grade class. She occasionally brought news about Brian, and twice that year, I saw Brian's mom. During conferences about her daughter, she also provided news about her son's progress, always accompanied with a smile. She wasn't sure what all had happened for Brian while he was in my room, but she was quite relieved that he had made so many improvements.

By the time Brian and I met again, he was finishing his junior year in high school. While shopping at the local Walmart store one evening, I noticed a lady standing in my aisle studying me. "Are you Mrs. Nordstrom?" she asked. I smiled and nodded yes. "Well, I am Mrs. Sawyer, Brian's mom. You were his fifth-grade teacher. Do you remember me?"

"Yes," I said. "And how is Brian doing in high school?"

"He's doing really well. He has been since he left fifth grade. Something special happened to him that year. He changed his ways and didn't get into as much trouble, and he applied himself in school after that. His father and I credit you with the trans-formation. As a matter of fact, Brian is here in the store with me tonight. I know he would be disappointed if he didn't get to see you. Do you have a few minutes to talk with him? I could find him if you would wait."

I assured her it would be my pleasure to see Brian again.

A few minutes later, Mrs. Sawyer reappeared with a 6'2" young man. After we hugged—no kisses this time—he stood back and looked me over. When I hugged him good-bye six years earlier, he was no taller than I was. Now, I just barely reached his shoulders.

With a big smile, Brian announced, "You have no idea how you changed my life. I had never had a teacher who was so per-sistent. You hung in there long enough for me to see the potential I had. School became much easier for me when I went to sixth grade, and I applied myself."

"I heard that you did well in junior high," I said. We then recalled some of the episodes we had shared together in fifth grade, and we got to laugh together over some of his escapades.

"Now, since you are a junior in high school, what are your plans for the future?" I asked.

"I'm planning to become a police officer. And you won't have to worry if I find you speeding. I could never give you a ticket after all the changes you made in my life."

"Thank you, Brian," I said. "But I'm not much of one to speed and most likely would not need such a gift. However, you will meet people along life's path who will need your understanding and patience. All I ask is that you pass on the spirit of generosity when it is appropriate."

We finished our conversation, shared another hug, and headed back to the errands we needed to finish.

I doubt my feet touched terra firma the rest of the evening. Knowing my efforts paid dividends like these increased my "pay."

Somewhere tucked in the back of my mind is the picture of Brian on the last day of fifth grade, and then at the end of his junior year. What an inspiration Brian was. It was up to me, with God's help, to assist the next student who needed guidance, and all the others who would follow.

[Love] keeps no record of wrongs.

—1 Corinthians 13:5b, NIV

Sweet Memories

A generous person will prosper; whoever refreshes others will be refreshed.

—Proverbs 11:25, NIV

Student questions often sparked memorable events. On a typical day, my students would ask hundreds of questions, literally. Most were academic in nature, directly related to the concepts we were studying, but on occasion, the inquiries were personal.

If we had a few free minutes and my students were respectful in their queries, I would answer their questions, most of which were simple. But occasionally, a student was bold and direct. When I attended junior high, my classmates and I rarely asked our teachers questions about their lives. However, I can remember wanting to know more about my teachers, especially my favorite ones who were also my role models when I became a teacher.

One wintry February morning, I showed up wearing a pale yellow sweater. Both the junior high math lesson and the gloomy overcast day needed all the help they could get to lift our spirits. I liked to brighten my class with a sunny attitude and a cheerful outfit, if possible.

As we began class, one student commented, "Nice sweater. I like that color." These students had been in my class less than ten days, and we were still getting to know each other. "Haven't I worn this sweater before?" I asked.

"No," one student piped up. "I don't remember your repeating an outfit yet." Other students agreed they had not seen this sweater and couldn't remember a repeat on any outfit I'd worn so far. I didn't realize that my students were so observant.

This sweater had been to school twice already—once when I was still knitting it, and once after it was finished. Its first visit was right before Christmas vacation; my first semester math classes needed a break, so we took a day to share hobbies that required math. Many students brought in their favorite games, and we all enjoyed seeing how many different ways students used math skills outside the classroom. I broke the ice that day by sharing how I used math in knitting. To illustrate, I brought the supplies and directions for a half-finished, yellow sweater I had been working on. By mid-January, before that class completed its semester in my room, I wore the finished sweater.

"Hey, look what she's wearing," one of the students announced. "It's the sweater we saw in pieces before Christmas."

A few weeks later, in a new semester with new students, I wore the yellow sweater for the second time, and that's why the sweater was new to these students. After teaching the math lesson on identity and commutative properties that morning, I made my way around the classroom helping individual students with their homework. When I finished helping Jenny, she said, "Your sweater looks so soft. Could I touch it?"

"If you'd like," I answered.

Then Dana said, "Mrs. Nordstrom, you look like sunshine today."

"Funny thing," I said. "Sunshine was my nickname when I was a child."

"Could we call you Miss Sunshine?" Nathan asked.

That would be one of the better nicknames I've been called in my career, I thought. And I answered, "That wouldn't bother me." So from then on, my first-block students sometimes called me Miss Sunshine.

A couple of days later, off the point and out of the blue, Tommy asked, "Is there a Mr. Sunshine?" Even though I had taught many years, I'm not sure it was ever possible to prepare for such sudden changes in topics when students blurt out what's on their minds.

Tommy had asked sincerely, so I answered, "There was, but not now. And I am certain that no one ever called him that. He left a few years ago and went his separate way." This short conversation, exposing divorce in my life, opened the door for students who had difficult situations in their families. Following this revelation, some students began to approach me quietly after class or in the hall to discuss problems they were struggling with in their lives. This one question encouraged students to relate their lives to mine and perhaps some of their pain, too.

One day, during a literature discussion with my sixth graders, Richie asked, "So what is it you got as a kid that we won't get?" No student had ever asked me that, and the depth of his question caught me by surprise. Many differences divided my childhood from theirs, but the one that stood out for me was innocence. The world had changed considerably since I was a youngster. In my childhood, my friends and I had been allowed freedom these students hadn't experienced. We could play in the woods, have a game of kick the can after dark, and ride our bicycles in the neighborhood, all without adult supervision.

I told the class of a time when I was walking home from kindergarten on a windy day. I lived only three blocks from school, and it was common to see children my age walking home alone. That day, the wind was blowing really hard, and a particularly strong gust caught me while I waited on the curb. I was a little kindergartener, and the gust blew me right into the street. I had been taught not to cross the street if a car was in sight. So I quickly backed up onto the curb and was blown into the street twice more, each time climbing back up on the curb waiting for traffic to clear.

A passing driver noticed my dilemma. He parked his car, came and stood beside me, and held me in place until it was safe. I then crossed the street and headed home. Because of the frightening news reports aired these days, a story like this would make many people gasp to hear it. But it was a more innocent era when this happened, a time when children played outside for hours with their friends without adults on the spot to physically watch over them. We even played a game now banned from many playgrounds, dodge ball—and suffered no psychological damage—and at twilight we enjoyed a game of hide and seek.

Luckily for me, a kind stranger happened by that windy day, and to this day I continue to believe that people who will help far exceed the number of those who want to do harm. But it is difficult to distinguish one from the other by looks, and we need to instruct our youngsters how to be safe.

During my childhood, I elaborated to the class we got to enjoy innocent fun with the neighborhood kids without adults fretting about every little thing we did. We felt like we had some freedom to play and just be kids.

"That sounds like fun to me," Richie added. "And it's fun picturing you as a little kindergartener trying to cross the street."

Sometimes I was the one who got to ask the questions. For instance, I was able to ask a special question while attending a high school graduation party for a former student from my junior high English and math classes. Kimberly not only scored really well in both of these subjects, but she also was one of the kindest students I've had the pleasure of teaching. When she was in my class, Kimberly managed to be the top scorer, often earning an A+ because she put forth the extra effort to earn any bonus points offered.

During her party, the usual graduation topics came up. "Where are you going to school in the fall?" I asked. Kimberly said she had been accepted by a nationally ranked state university. "What major are you leaning toward?"

"I'd like to major in education and become a junior high math teacher like you," she said.

"How did you decide on this major?" I asked.

"I watched you work with Allan in junior high math. He required lots of patience, and you never became impatient with him. You continued to explain the concepts, calmly trying to help him understand a subject that was very difficult for him."

I was humbled by Kimberly's unexpected response. I guess I had been teaching more than math when I was working with Allan, and I had not realized that my students were listening so carefully. God sometimes sends important messages in special packages.

The one question from my career that surprised me most came up during a talk one day in the hall while my students took their afternoon restroom and water fountain break. I had found that this unscripted interaction provided an opportunity to know my students in a broader context, both their afterschool and weekend activities.

Tammy, a shy sixth grader in my room, told me she had been attacked by her neighbor's dog when she was four and a half years old, and she still carried scars on her face seven years later. In the past, she had talked with me about the attack and the fear it created in her. She said that she had not allowed that event to poison her attitude toward all dogs, but she admitted that she still had problems trusting some dogs, especially large breeds like the one that had attacked her. I admired Tammy's upbeat approach to life. Since I had taught her older sister, I knew times were not easy at her house for a variety of reasons. In spite of her many challenges, Tammy managed to rise above her fears and worries and maintain a positive outlook.

But that day during the restroom break, she caught me off guard when she asked, "Did your mother love you?" I hadn't shared much about my family with my students, so they wouldn't know that the two words *love* and *mother* rarely found their way into the same sentence in my own experience. My students had learned to count on honest, straightforward answers from me. This particular question, however, jolted me, and I needed a moment to compose myself: I wanted my answer to be honest, but not too revealing or too painful.

Partly because I needed a moment to think, but mostly because I was curious what motivated Tammy to ask this question, I returned with, "Why do you ask?"

Her answer astonished me. "I heard that in order for you to love others, someone needs to love you first. And you love us so much I just wondered if your mother loved you." It was apparent to me at that moment how God had called me to this career and then blessed me in this calling.

I wanted to be tactful as well as truthful; and since I rarely discussed this, I did not have a ready answer. I was nervous and hesitant. "No," I slowly answered. "From my view, my mother didn't love me, but my father and my grandmother did. So I guess I am ahead if you only need one and I had two." Satisfied with my answer, Tammy never asked again. Our exchange served as a concrete reminder of why I answered my students honestly whenever they asked sincere questions.

During restroom breaks, I continued to hang out near the drinking fountain line. The water was cold, and the conversations with my students brought unbelievable opportunities to learn from them and gain sparkling insights. And they also refreshed my soul.

> *The Lord is not slow in keeping his promise, as some*
> *understand slowness. Instead he is patient with you, not*
> *wanting anyone to perish, but everyone to come to repentance.*
>
> —*2 Peter 3:9*, NIV

You Only Cheat Yourself

Create in me a pure heart, O God, and renew a steadfast spirit within me.

—*Psalm 51:10*, NIV

Cheating in school, and in life, has been with us since the beginning of civilization. It was a problem when I was in school, and it appears only to have grown more widespread in recent years. An article in *Teen Newsweek* from April 24, 2006 provided the following material for discussion in my classroom.

> The prevalence of cheating has skyrocketed during the past decade. In a study of 50,000 college and 18,000 high school students in the United States, more than 70 percent admitted that they have cheated. That's up from about 56 percent in 1993 and just 26 percent in 1963. Internet plagiarism has quadrupled in the past six years, according to the same study, which was conducted by Duke University's Center for Academic Integrity.
>
> McCabe [founder of Duke University's Center for Academic Integrity] says cheating increases when students move from elementary school to junior high. Instead of having just one teacher, students in junior high school have a different teacher for each subject. That makes some students feel there's less risk of being caught, McCabe says.
>
> In past surveys conducted by McCabe, two-thirds of junior high and middle school students report having cheated on tests, and nine of 10 say they've copied another student's homework.
>
> "We've passed the tipping point, where cheating is so common that it's an accepted social norm," says David Callahan, author of *The Cheating Culture*.[1]

During my years as an educator, I witnessed more deceitful behavior than I can even begin to recall. Each time I became aware of an incident, I met with the student, or students, and dealt with it promptly.

My personal experiences with cheating were limited, mostly because I knew it was wrong, and I knew my conscience would bother me. I also feared being caught in the embarrassing, humiliating loss of integrity, not to mention the castigation that would follow. In my youth, expectations from family, friends, and teachers were high and punishment was harsh, and hence they were all good deterrents for me. However, I can remember one time in high school when I risked it.

Reading *Wuthering Heights* was an assignment for my sophomore English class, but the story did not hold my interest. So after reading about seventy pages, I skipped to the end, read that part, and wrote the book report. My report, shy on details, not surprisingly received only a mediocre grade. The impact of this deceitful activity left an indelible impression on me. *Wuthering Heights*, in a class by itself, is the one title I recall from high school. I no longer remember the titles of other books I read for book reports in high school, but I can't forget this one. I'm still ashamed of my cheating; the impact it had on me was profound and long-lasting. Since this assignment haunted me, I didn't skimp on future assignments.

Each new generation feels it is the first to discover life's many facets—joy, manipulation, secrets, puppy love, nostalgia, pain, cheating. History may not repeat itself when it comes to cheating but students in each new generation think they can successfully hide their subterfuge from others, especially adults.

My students thought I was blind to their deceptions. Thankfully, most came ill-prepared to match wits with my experience, naively overlooking that I had once attended junior high and was exposed to many of the same techniques they tried in my class. Seeing me only as an adult, they failed to recognize how I had arrived at this stage of life—by first passing through all of the other stages. The naïveté of their limited experiences convinced them that their cheating ways were fresh, crafty, and undetectable by most adults. They did have some new techniques, but they were not as savvy about covering their deceptions as they believed.

Each year without fail, the cheating discussion surfaced in my classroom during the first month of school. It was precipitated by a reported or suspected cheating incident by one of the students. Sometimes cheating on a test was obvious to adults when students had exactly the same wrong answer, but other times the offense was copying someone else's homework, once again displaying identical work.

Students seemed shocked to find out that I was often aware of their cheating, especially when they felt they had concealed it so well. They underestimated how observant adults can be.

To open a discussion on cheating, I shared a story about one of my classmates when I was a junior high school student. Good time Charlie, one of the cutest and most popular boys in school, was the undisputed master at cheating. I did not know if the teachers were aware of his skillful stealth, but most of his classmates were. It seemed that Charlie could see another student's work halfway across a room, especially when he needed an answer on a quiz or a test. He also may have devised secret communication with other classmates who desired to be part of his in-crowd.

It was obvious to his peers that Charlie was a goof-off. Plenty of us wondered how he passed his classes with his lackadaisical attitude. The semester he sat next to me in English, Charlie spent most of his time on a countdown waiting for the arrival of his family's new car, a sharp-looking bright red convertible sports car. If you wanted to see Charlie come alive, ask about the new car and you had his full attention.

Over time I lost track of Charlie but learned of his fate some years after graduation. Fast forward through Charlie's cheating days of high school, graduation, and into his adult life when he eventually did time in the state penitentiary for dealing drugs.

Students form and practice their life skills—honesty, punctuality, determination, kindness, generosity, charity—on a daily basis in school. When students depend on cheating to complete their work, the stage is set for a future where cheaters won't be able to rely on their own knowledge and skills because they didn't develop them. Charlie was the most experienced and proficient cheater I knew from my school days; he's also the only classmate I knew who served time in the state penitentiary.

Honest students, who resent it when classmates cheat, have asked me how they could foil a cheater. One of the suggestions I offered was a story from my sister when she was in fourth grade. Judy realized a neighbor was copying answers from her test. Upset by this, she decided that the next time she would fool him. When that test arrived, Judy wrote the wrong answers on her paper. Her neighbor was all too eager to help himself to her work. Judy merely waited until he finished copying her answers and turned in his paper before correcting her own test. After that, he never used her answers again.

The underlying causes of the cheating problem can be hard to cure. Whether it is low self-esteem, laziness, ignorance, lack of moral fiber, or unrealistic expectations to be perfect or achieve high scores consistently, cheating happens in most American schools, and much more often than it used to, based on studies by researchers such as Don McCabe and David Callahan.

Students underestimate the difference they can make when they refuse to let others cheat off of their work or resist their own urge to cheat. They've told themselves that they are helping their friends when they share answers, but what they really should consider is how to help those around them understand the consequences of cheating and support their friends in making better choices.

I was all for students working together and helping each other. I encouraged students in my room to share their knowledge. Two benefits came from this. A student who was struggling might finally understand the concept when it was presented one more time in his language by a friend. Also, students who share their knowledge reinforce skills and understanding in their own minds. The important distinction for students was that they needed to know and understand the difference between explaining answers and giving answers. I recommended they *show* a friend how to work a math problem, as I did during class instruction or when individuals came to me for extra help.

In more recent years, students witnessed cheating among their peers in such epidemic proportions that I feared they viewed cheating as normal. To provide a new perspective, I translated how their cheating might look if the adults around them were doing those same things.

"What would happen if I decided to cheat?" I asked them. "You know I'm kind of busy, and getting my lesson plans together just takes too much time. Mr. Thompson, across the hall, has his all done. Why shouldn't I just use his? If I can't convince him to hand them over, maybe I could sneak a copy from his desk. Better yet, I could get them from the school's web site where they are posted. After all, I don't have lesson plans and I need them."

The students first looked at me as if I had lost my mind. After the initial silence, they glanced furtively at their classmates, and some even began murmuring to their neighbors. Then they mustered enough courage to criticize my approach.

"You can't use Mr. Thompson's plans. He teaches social studies, not math."

"The principal would notice."

"My parents would call the school and want to know why I have so much social studies homework and no math to do."

"How can I pass the graduation test if I don't learn math?"

I knew our discussion might not cause a student to stop cheating, but I was hopeful that it would offer me insight into my students' individual values and behaviors. Perhaps when they were next tempted to cheat, a new resolve or a new thought process would encourage them to reconsider.

Another topic we discussed was the double standard students had about cheating. Students often excused or rationalized their behavior when it came to dishonesty. This small deception was acceptable in their minds since they would tell themselves that they weren't capable of finishing their work. Poor things, they rationalized about themselves; if they didn't understand how to do their assignments, it was because no one would teach them. It wasn't their fault, they would say, trying to reframe the situation as beyond their control. On the other hand, they certainly weren't going to permit that same unethical behavior from their teachers or from other adults.

"Who wants their doctor or dentist to have cheated through medical school?" I asked. "The day you need her expertise, you find out, through your botched procedure, that she relied on a friend to do her learning."

In contrast to my classmate Charlie, I also went to school with Peter. He was a friend who enjoyed a good time, but he was diligent and conscientious when it came to his studies. And a good thing for me too! Twenty years after high school, I needed a competent doctor to perform a complicated surgery to correct a broken vertebra. By the time Peter fused my spine, he had become one of the best orthopedic surgeons in the Midwest. In an arduous six-hour surgery, he skillfully repaired my broken vertebra with C clamps, screws, and bone grafts. I was thankful that Peter was a highly ethical and skilled doctor who had done his own studying.

We can't ignore cheating just because it won't go away. I knew I couldn't stop it, but I wanted to prevent it as much as possible.

One of my tactics was to set aside approximately twenty minutes of every ninety-minute class for in-class work time. This gave students time to seek extra help from me before the end of class. I also left my teaching notes from the lesson on the overhead projector so students could refer to them while they practiced working the newly introduced math concepts. Students who were struggling could seek more instruction at my desk. Before class ended, I would also check answers for anyone unsure about their progress.

However, in my last few years in the classroom, many students adopted a troubling behavior that eliminated the need to cheat. That required too much effort on their part. But what replaced cheating was much worse. Instead of cheating on homework, many of them no longer bothered to do their homework assignments at all, mostly because the school and the parents enforced very few consequences on students who did not turn in their work. Without disciplinary consequences, teachers were powerless and the students knew it.

Another technique I used to reduce temptation and cheating in my classroom was to pass out two forms of the in-class test. Form A and Form B each covered the same concepts, had the same number of problems, and involved the same difficulty level. Students had equal opportunities to show their knowledge without the distraction of other people copying answers from their papers. I came up with this idea when I was teaching in a very small room filled wall to wall with students. We were packed in so tightly that it was difficult for me to squeeze between the rows of desks when the students were seated in their chairs. The closer they sat to each other, the more opportunity that existed for roaming eyes and cheating.

Even with this dual test system, I couldn't prevent all cheating. One crafty student had answers on his Test B that perfectly matched the correct responses from Test A. I met with him after class to discuss his test. Not bothered at all by his apparent cheating, he looked at me as if to say, "So?" Next, I called his mother to discuss my concerns since she had declined an earlier request for a face-to-face parent-teacher conference. During our conversation, she, like her son, refused to acknowledge that he had cheated despite the overwhelming evidence. I was dismayed with her reaction. Consequently, it came as no surprise to hear from a colleague a few years later that this boy was "the most cheating student I ever taught."

That same year, another junior high math student approached me quietly after class. Susie was struggling and afraid she was going to fail. The first thing we did was schedule a tutoring session during study hall to see what was causing her the most trouble. After doing a few problems, Susie noticed that she was making many little mistakes. Frustrated, she asked, "How will I ever pull up my D if I can't see my little mistakes, which make me miss the entire algebra problem?"

"Let me think about this tonight and let's see what I can come up with," I said. "See me tomorrow morning."

The following day, I suggested that Susie leave her finished homework on my desk first thing each morning when she visited her locker outside my room. I would then check her work and leave a small dot in pencil on any line where she had a calculation error. After first block, when Susie stopped by her locker, she would pick up her homework, which was waiting on a cabinet near the door.

Daily, Susie dropped off her work and returned before second block to quietly retrieve it. In study hall, she could find the mistakes and correct them. On occasion, Susie would require further explanation, but most of the time, she figured out the errors and corrected them on her own. Her grade steadily began to improve along with her understanding. While Susie continued to leave homework assignments on my desk, the frequency diminished as she grew more accurate and gained confidence. I was quite pleased that she was growing in math knowledge, improving her grade, and not cheating off a classmate's paper. Less motivated students often chose the easier path of cheating.

Not surprisingly, a few students also reverted to forging parent signatures as their choice of underhanded behavior. Other than being annoyed that I would then have to deal with this mischief on top of the original offense, there were times when it provided comical relief. The parents' signatures on the enrollment papers, such as medical forms, were available in the office. Usually checking a suspicious-looking signature required a trip to the office, but not always. Students assigned to detention might already possess previously signed forms in the detention folder from an earlier episode. Not wanting to alert their parents to another infraction so close to the previous one, students simply would enlist the assistance of a good friend to copy a parent's signature, or failing that, they resorted to forging the signatures themselves after a few practice runs. I've seen parents' signatures that were spelled wrong, as well as ones that looked as though a first grader had forged the name on the bumpy bus ride to school.

One particular question I asked when trying to get to the bottom of student deception often produced the best results. "What was your mother doing when you asked her to sign this form?" I would ask. Telling a lie, without conjuring specific elements of a story in advance or practicing relevant "justifications," was much harder to pull off.

Body language often helped me ferret out the truth more than students' words did. But this skill only came with practice, lots of practice. Being able to read small changes in a student's physical reaction often provided large clues. This ability even came in handy outside of the classroom.

One Christmas morning, for example, our pastor-in-training asked available church members to join her after the morning service at a nearby home for wayward boys. Ten of us parishioners joined the pastor that morning and spread throughout the room. The pastor and I were together seated at a table with five boys, and all of us were enjoying a lighthearted conversation when she asked for their names. As we went around the table, each boy gave his name, but as the last two boys said their names, I sensed a small, almost imperceptible change. After a few more minutes of talking, I called the last two boys by the names they had used on each other. The gig was up; I had seen through their trick. We all enjoyed a laugh at their innocent prank. That morning offered us a wonderful opportunity to share breakfast, laughter, and Christmas carols, but it also gave me an opportunity to sharpen my radar.

Later, as we were leaving, my pastor asked how I had known that the last two boys had switched names. I told her that I spent hour after hour on a daily basis with this age group, and it was an extra sense one develops after that much one-on-one contact. I suspect there were many small clues that day, although I can't list them. But my survival in the classroom was improved on some level because I got it; I had caught on. Mostly, I used this ability in my classroom, so I was surprised to see how beneficial it could be in other situations.

Lighthearted tricks are harmless, but cheating can have serious consequences. Generally, when dealing with cheating, I met in private with the offenders. But I had one incident where it was important that I discuss cheating with my entire class. However, it appeared that most of my eighth graders were already aware of the situation, at least on some level. Lenny, a very weak math student, had scored in the highest category on the state-mandated tests the students took in the spring. Together with his fellow students and the school counselor, we all wondered how this had happened. How did a student who had such an obvious lack of mathematical understanding score so well on such a challenging exam?

The school counselor decided to investigate the situation and, after some digging, discovered the problem. A fellow classmate, who was gifted in math, had devised a plan to pass Lenny the answers during the test for a price. The cheating may have been done quietly, but it didn't remain quiet. The test became a big deal when the exam results became public. If Lenny had done only a little cheating, it might have gone undetected. But to cheat on such a grand scale led to a grand number of people learning about it.

That year I had prepared a statistical correlation using my eighth graders' class scores compared with their scores from the state proficiency mathematics exam. I had wanted to show my students how their class grades could predict their results on the state-mandated test. As expected, the A students received high scores, often in the accelerated category; B students landed well within the safe zone; C students were split precisely down the middle, half passed and half failed; while D and F students had all failed, with one exception. Only one failing grade from my entire eighth math class fell outside of the expected category, landing in the accelerated category. I knew this particular student had never passed a standardized math test during his entire school career, yet here he was listed among our school's best on the state's proficiency exam. In my room, Lenny's seatwork, homework, verbal responses, and class tests revealed very little understanding.

A few days after the exam results were released, I shared my correlation study with the students. That one score stood out from all the others. "How could that happen? How could someone with an F in class score in the accelerated category?" one student asked. Instead of answering, I let the other students offer their thoughts. They discussed the results for a few minutes, zeroing in on the problem while I simply listened. They shared their views, which also happened to echo my view: someone had cheated on the proficiency test. In the end, I didn't have to explain anything. Seeing the results in a mathematical way had a greater impact on my students than anything I could have said. Did the students figure out who had cheated? Most likely they knew before they even came to class that day, although I never implicated the guilty one. I found that students often knew what was going on at school before the teachers did. Their news network may not always have been 100 percent accurate, but it was sophisticated and swift.

Cheating is an unfortunate fact of life, but that doesn't mean teachers have to accept it or pretend it doesn't exist. Even if we cannot cure cheating, we must ensure that we have done all we can to prevent it. In addition to removing as much temptation and opportunity as possible, it is important to discuss cheating, its effects, and its consequences. Whether those consequences are immediate or far in the future, it is important to help students realize that their choices will shape their futures.

> *Be kind and compassionate to one another, forgiving each other, just as in Christ God forgave you.*
>
> *—Ephesians 4:32,* NIV

Many Happy Returns

Blessed are those who find wisdom, those who gain understanding.

—Proverbs 3:13, NIV

When my students experienced problems that overwhelmed them, I was often called into service to help them solve these complications. My students showed their gratitude in many different ways.

Take Billy, for example. He was capable enough, but Billy failed to turn in completed work. Maybe he was indeed lazy or he believed the unkind things others said about him or he experienced a chaotic home life. I never saw his classmates treat him unkindly, but students usually kept those kinds of behavior out of my sight. Billy's low performance indicated that not all was well in his life. The source and frequency of his problems were elusive to me. Occasionally, it even appeared that Billy had set himself up for these complications. But whatever the source, or sources, Billy's struggle with personal obstacles affected his school achievement, and he completed junior high school with a failing grade in math.

When he returned to school the next fall to start ninth grade, Billy and his classmates took a standard achievement test in math. Immediately after taking that exam, Billy stopped by my room to talk about an exam problem that he had found challenging: 20 divided by 4/5. Describing the situation he said, "This was one hard problem, I told myself. I thought it was impossible—it had no answer. But then I remembered what you said in class. 'We never divide by a fraction. Mine is not to reason why, it's to invert and multiply.' And suddenly I got it!"

Billy worked the problem on his calculator right there in front of me to show that he did indeed understand. Then he added,

"But that choice wasn't given on my proficiency exam. So I felt good marking 'Answer not given' since I knew the right response and it wasn't there." The excitement I heard in Billy's voice that day surprised me. After all, he had spent both seventh and eighth grades in my math class—and he had not shown that enthusiasm even once. But still, it seemed the math concepts I had taught during those two years had somehow penetrated Billy's brain during class—and stuck—even if his grade hadn't reflected it.

Despite outward appearances, which indicate that students like Billy are not learning, it's important to just continue to teach. Billy had regularly embarrassed himself in my room: bringing sloppy work on the occasional times when he did his assignment, goofing off and paying little attention to the lessons, and distracting those around him who wanted to learn. Yet here he was, even after all of that, sharing his math knowledge with me. Billy's gift that day was showing me that he understood that I cared about him and why I persevered, even though we had spent a challenging two years together in math.

Through the years, many other former students also have stopped by my room to ask a question or to share how things are in their lives. After I joined the junior high staff, where my room was now part of the senior high school building, these visits increased. Close physical proximity fostered an increased—and often wonderful—opportunity for sharing. The students' stories warmed my heart and reminded me why God had led me to the classroom.

Billy's return was one of the quickest returns on record. He'd been in ninth grade just two months when he had to take the math achievement test. Danny, however, won the award for the most consistent, frequent, and eventually the most extended returns.

Danny would tell you without hesitation that I was a firm teacher—caring, but firm. However, that had not scared him away. He returned each year until he graduated to visit his former elementary teachers, Pat Nelson and me. The year that Pat and I taught Danny, our two sixth-grade classrooms were entwined in many ways—location, class time, field trips, activities, lunchtime, and recesses. Pat's and my teaching styles were so similar that this arrangement was a natural. Danny confirmed that during one of his visits when he said, "You two double-teamed us. What one didn't think of, the other did. You didn't let us walk all over you guys." The stability in our rooms provided security and a consistent learning environment, one where students could count on their teachers to be fair as well as challenging.

Regular visits from Danny slowed after he graduated from high school. I would see him occasionally when his job brought him to my neighborhood. These visits were rare because he was busy working, but I clearly recall his excitement during the visit when he announced he was getting married. I had the pleasure of attending his wedding about eight years after his graduation.

Still, Danny caught me off guard one summer afternoon when I was reading in my backyard. A voice broke the silence startling me. "I can see why you didn't answer your doorbell," Danny hollered over the fence. Overcoming my surprise, I greeted Danny and invited him to join me at the picnic table.

The first thing Danny shared that day was an update on his family. Then he admitted that he had a problem he thought I could help him solve. Danny had wanted to be a firefighter for a long time, but he hadn't been able to pass the math section on the entrance exam. "Could you tutor me?" he asked.

I offered to get my calendar from the house to schedule a meeting. With a quick grin, he admitted that he had all the materials we would need in his truck. Since there was no time like the present, we began right then.

Danny started the tutoring session by apologizing. "I am sorry I didn't pay more attention throughout my years in school. I didn't think I'd need all that math stuff." Now that he realized that he needed the math skills, I had his complete attention, and together, we cleared up his confusion so he could pass the math section he needed for firefighting. We only worked a couple of hours that afternoon, but by the time Danny left, he assured me he was ready.

I often wondered how he had performed on his entrance exam after our tutoring session that summer day. However, three years would pass before I heard from Danny again.

When I answered the phone one Saturday afternoon, the caller asked, "Is this the home of Jeanne Nordstrom?" Yes. "I've had the hardest time finding you," the caller said. By then I had recognized Danny's voice.

Since our summer tutoring three years earlier, I had moved and didn't realize I might be difficult to find. After all, I still taught in the same district where Danny had attended school. In an effort to locate me, Danny had stopped by my former house but didn't find anyone home. Next, he stopped by my classroom looking for me. However, I was gone to a meeting that entire day, and he only found a sub in my room.

Finally, with the help of the school secretary, he got my home phone number and then called. "Can I come by for a visit?" he asked. I explained how to find my new house, and he arrived within fifteen minutes. After sharing his tale of how he located me, he announced, "I am a firefighter." He had passed the math exam shortly after our tutoring session three years earlier, had taken the fire department's training, and was then hired as a firefighter.

After Danny's visit that April afternoon, the sun shone more brightly for me. Few things were more satisfying in my career than seeing a former student achieve his dreams while also being an asset to society.

Through the years, Danny has continued to stop by for the occasional visit. The last time I saw him, he stopped by my class-room with his son who was a junior in a neighboring high school. Each time Danny came back, he shared his friendship, a hug, and a smile with me.

I haven't heard from Danny recently, but I know one of these days when my doorbell or phone rings, I'll be treated to another visit and an update on his life.

A few students have returned for help in English over the years, but most have come back to ask math questions. Less than half of my career was devoted solely to math instruction, but that is where former students seem to need the most help. I also believe that math questions are the hardest ones to figure out on your own. Math explanations, particularly those delivered in textbooks, read like Greek when there is no human to translate them.

Denise is a prime example of a sixth grader who returned as a high school sophomore needing math instruction. Her rookie high school math teacher thought his accelerated class could, and should, pick up the complex concepts without his help. After all, his students each had a textbook. But Denise, accustomed to earning As in math, had a solid D when she called me for help. The situation at home had gotten pretty tense once she maxed out her mom's math skills. Throwing up her hands, Denise asked her mom, "Can we call Jeanne? Maybe she can help." Her mother agreed.

Since math classes are usually fast-paced, it's a good idea to begin tutoring as quickly as possible when a student starts to lag behind. This prevents the situation from spiraling out of control and a loss of confidence for the student.

Denise and I met the next evening. I noticed she had some correct answers on her paper as I studied the concepts she was required to learn. "Can you explain how to work these first ten questions, which are scored as correct on your paper?" I asked her.

With a discouraged look, she said, "I can't."

Denise had been unusually good at explanations when I taught her, so I asked, "Why not?"

"Do you want the truth?" she asked.

"The truth would help me teach you better," I said.

With disappointment in her voice, she said, "I cheated. We all cheated. One of my classmates got the answers from the teacher and shared them with the rest of us."

I thanked her for her honesty and started my explanation at the very beginning of the lesson. Denise had always been a quick study, and in a short while, she was successfully working the problems on her own.

She headed back to school the following morning to share her new knowledge with her friends. Teaching others strengthens one's own knowledge. It worked that way for Denise too. She returned to me for help until she felt confident, and she finished the class with a B+, much to her relief. Denise learned more than math lessons in solving this dilemma.

Another opportunity to help Denise followed three years later when she was in college. Her college math problems started out much harder and quickly grew too difficult. So I tutored her in college math as far as my knowledge carried me. Eventually, I had to suggest that Denise find a more advanced tutor. As we finished, I told Denise that I might be coming to her for math help in the future.

Approaching a teacher to ask for help can be scary for a student. I took my tutoring sessions seriously. If my students had gathered enough courage to seek my help, I wanted them to understand how willing I was to tutor them.

Later that same summer, another student from Denise's class needed tutoring for his college math class. He had delayed his education following high school and now couldn't pass the entrance exam to his technical school. Denise encouraged him to call me for help. Mostly, this student needed a refresher on the rules of math that grow rusty without use. Distributive property comes in pretty handy when figuring algebra problems, but otherwise has little use in solving problems for most people in daily life. After a few tutoring sessions, he passed his entrance exam and no longer needed my help.

I can say without any hesitation that some days in the class-room were discouraging for me. Students came to class day after day without even trying to do their assigned homework. Even worse, some disregarded my math instruction mistakenly believing that it held no practical use for them. I noticed how, on some of those dark days, God would send some sunshine my way in the form of students who actually wanted to learn and appreciated help.

It was on one of these discouraging days when two girls from a high school algebra class brought sunshine during my second-block class. Their teacher had been absent for a week due to illness, and their class was falling behind because the substitute was unable to explain algebra. So they requested a pass to my room.

They knocked on my classroom door, arriving in the middle of my instruction. I invited them in and explained that I would need fifteen minutes to complete the lesson I was teaching my eighth graders. After that, I would be available to help them.

When my eighth graders started their seatwork, the high school girls and I got busy with algebra. After working a couple of problems, I discovered that they needed to review the distributive and identity properties. These two properties are critical in algebra, but oh so easy to forget. After succeeding on a few practice problems, they headed back to their room ready and eager to explain the process to their classmates. It was rare to have emergencies like this one. But my day was brighter because I was given the gift of assisting eager students—past and present.

I knew that students from my classes also sought help from other teachers, fellow classmates, or parents. Sometimes it takes a different person or a different approach to help students understand complex math concepts.

Occasionally, students stopped by my classroom after school with the "I just need a little help" plea. Jane had remembered to keep her apples with apples and oranges with oranges when organizing "like terms" in algebra, but she was unable to finish the problems on her own. "What have I forgotten?" she asked. "I know we worked on these in your room."

I reviewed the identity property of multiplication with her. "Now I remember," she said, "but let me show you the next one to prove I can do them correctly." Since I had taught students these very rules in junior high, it was often easy for them to spot their mistakes. Sometimes all I needed to do was begin reciting the rule we had learned together. They often interrupted and finished my sentence. A few students even told me they could hear my voice reminding them how to work a problem we'd learned in eighth grade.

Like Jane, most students who returned for tutoring needed only a little assistance to get them back on the right path. But Aaron came for a completely different reason. Aaron was a former sixth grader who was talented, but his tutoring needs had little to do with academics.

The unthinkable had happened in his sophomore year—his mother had died instantly of a heart attack. Aaron and his mom, Lisa, were very close. Lisa had been my student years earlier when she was in fifth grade. It had been joyful reconnecting with her when her son, Aaron, was assigned to my sixth-grade classroom.

During our unit on careers that year, Aaron invited his mom to share her expertise in respiratory therapy with our class. What fun for me to have her back in my classroom, this time standing in front of her son's classmates and sharing her knowledge. The students learned much from Lisa, but I think they got the most from hearing about her on-the-job experiences and trying out the respiratory equipment she brought. Lisa extended her time with us that day because everyone was so fascinated by her career. Four years later, we were all shocked and saddened by her untimely death.

At the funeral calling, I offered to help Aaron in any way I could. A few weeks later, he stopped by my classroom during my planning block. "Could you help me with my algebra?" he asked.

Aaron was doing extra-credit work and wanted me to check it. I realized, as we sat there reviewing his math problems, that he was doing fine in math and truly didn't need my help. More than anything, Aaron just needed to be near someone he knew had cared about his mother and understood what a struggle it was for him. I was feeling sad too. It helped both of us to have Aaron spend time in my room sharing his work and his thoughts.

During trying times, God has blessed me with patches of sunlight to lift my spirits. These visitors from my past also reminded me how the connections I built daily in my classroom turned into the warm memories I got to savor over time.

I could never have guessed the large variety of opportunities I would get to experience in my career: tutoring students in high school and even those who had graduated, having former students make the effort to locate me just to share exciting news from their lives, and simply remembering their former teacher with a card or visit.

Whichever way it works, God will not lead us where He cannot keep us.

> *If God is for us, who can be against us?*
>
> —*Romans 8:31b*, NIV

Teacher's Pet

Since you are precious and honored in my sight, and because I
love you...Do not be afraid, for I am with you.

—*Isaiah 43:4–5a*, NIV

Some students were bold enough to ask if I had teacher's pets, while others just assumed I did—a few even thought they were the chosen ones. I had a ready reply whenever students asked, "Do you have a teacher's pet?" "Yes," I said, "at least one." When I paused, they often pressed the point and began guessing. But then I continued, "I have two teacher's pets, but they are furry, four-footed, and eat dog food."

In my passing parade of pets, Snuffy was the first. This handsome, semi-curly, charcoal gray dog had standard poodle and cocker spaniel parents. Tall and slender, he weighed about forty pounds. Even people who weren't dog lovers were drawn to his gentle nature and his warm, shoe-button eyes.

Snuffy came into my life the summer before I began my first teaching position. I was part of the staff for a small, remote junior high school located in the Appalachian Mountains. This private school, situated in a picturesque valley, was a residential facility isolated by its geography, and Snuffy loved living there.

I was a houseparent to five boys in one of the school's six houses where faculty and students lived. Snuffy became an important part of the household. Students felt it was a lucky day when Snuffy escorted them down the mountain path to school. During the day while I taught, did office work, or cooked in the school's kitchen, Snuffy scouted critters in the woods surrounding the schoolhouse or napped outside the building where I worked. For students who were far from their families, Snuffy was a comforting presence.

Part of the school's curriculum was designed to educate the students about the natural science of the mountains just beyond our doorstep. The school's remote location was more than a mile of rutted gravel road off the two-lane highway. Students spent much time outside: taking science classes, trekking up and down the nearby mountain paths, or helping repair the gravel access road. So being outside was a normal part of everyday activities for these students.

Our first all-day excursion up the mountainous trail was scheduled on a sunny day in September when the blueberries were ripe. We divided the twenty-five students into three groups for our initial hike and climbed a great distance up the mountain to an area called Bowman's Gap.

This style of learning was Snuffy's idea of a great day. The blueberry trip was not his first jaunt up the mountain; at the age of four, he was a seasoned veteran who loved hiking. He would scramble up the mountain and race forward, run back to me, and then rush back up the trail. While he climbed the path multiple times, I was satisfied to make the trek once. Surging ahead, but never too far, Snuffy returned frequently to check my progress. Everyone knew exactly where I was in the line of hikers because Snuffy came just far enough to find me. If I was first, he would barely check in with any other hikers before hurrying back to his exploring. Students liked it when I was near the end so they could have a chance to pet Snuffy as he ran past. While Snuffy enjoyed racing up and down the steep mountain path, some of the teenagers did not share his enthusiasm. His eagerness, however, became contagious, inspiring the less motivated students who struggled with the steep path.

During our two-hour climb, conversation among the hikers centered on the ripe berries awaiting us at the top. Student excitement peaked when we reached our destination and found the blueberry patch. Dropping their day packs, the students ran to the short bushes, eager to taste the wild berries we'd spent the morning reaching. The shrieks of joy grew as students found bushes loaded with ripe blueberries and stuffed them into their mouths.

Caught up in the excitement, Snuffy wanted to try whatever it was these tired hikers were popping into their mouths with such zeal. I figured once Snuffy tasted a blueberry, his curiosity would be satisfied, and he'd go back to his hobby of hunting for small wildlife. I offered him a blueberry. Snuffy tasted it and liked it. Remember those shoe-button eyes? He turned them on me, begging for more. What I picked, I shared. Snuffy was a gentle eater, careful to get every blueberry I offered.

Wild blueberries grown on a chilly mountaintop are small but rich in flavor. Students ran from one blueberry bush to another sampling the delicious treats, filling themselves with the tiny delicacies before turning their attentions and efforts to collecting berries for yummy cobbler back at school.

Snuffy was enjoying the blueberries so much that I didn't seem to be picking them fast enough to please him. Looking down at him, I announced, "I'm not going to do all of the work here. If you like these so much, you can pick your own." I bent a branch over so he could reach it. He seemed to like the idea and gingerly began picking his own, one by one, from the branch. Students who saw this couldn't believe it and called the others over to catch a glimpse of the shortest "helper."

The trail hike, great weather, and our four-footed berry picker made a sweet memory for all of us to savor. To this day, blueberries continue to remind me of special students and an exceptional day when Snuffy's antics entertained us all.

When I took a position in public school the following year, Snuffy went into semi-retirement. After he had spent twenty-four hours a day with my junior high school students, he adjusted well to the change of visiting school only occasionally. Snuffy was a true friend who traveled to four different states with me while I taught third through ninth grades. I was thankful and blessed that Snuffy lived to the wonderful age of sixteen. After his death and a period of adjustment, I decided to share life with another pet.

I was teaching elementary school when a fluffy, white standard poodle entered my life. I named her Channing. She was an elegant companion, with impeccable posture, who possessed a heart filled with patience and love.

When I told my students about my new pet, they begged to meet her. After Channing settled into life's routine at my house, she came to school to spend the day with my students. I lived half an hour from school, so whenever Channing came with me, she had to spend the entire day in the classroom.

My students were as enchanted by Channing as she was by them. After lunch that first day, I found her snuggled up with one of my students on the comforter behind my desk. "Shush," Rochelle said softly. "Channing's tired and I'm going to help her nap." Thirty-five minutes later, after reading circle, I checked on my "nappers." Rochelle was wrapped around Channing fast asleep, while Channing kept a silent vigil over her new friend.

Visits from Channing were occasional but often followed a big success in my room—as a reward. My students knew when it had been too long since they had seen Channing and would say, "We've been really good. Can Channing come to visit?"

At the end of one of these visits, I noticed James cuddling Channing. James had been seriously injured during a tornado when he was just five years old. A two-by-four wooden post had hit him in the head and had left him with lifelong learning problems, so school was challenging for James. As he hugged Channing, I heard him whispering things to her that he had never revealed in the classroom. He squeezed her tight and said, "I know the day is almost over and you'll go home soon, but I already miss you."

Channing's visits became a highlight for James. Sometimes when school work had been particularly frustrating for him, the two of us would take a break and discuss her latest antics at home. James was always ready to talk about Channing. Her occasional presence in my room opened doors for me that I am sure I wouldn't have been able to open on my own. James was one of those doors. His growth, although slow, could be attributed more to Channing's ability to love than any teaching ability I possessed. Channing's last visit for James's class came two days before the end of the school year. It touched me to witness the heartfelt good-bye he shared with her.

Whenever she came to class, Channing naturally became a part of the lesson. Saying she was intelligent seemed like an understatement to my students. They were fascinated by the diversity of words she knew: sit, stay, down, quiet—common terms from her obedience class—mixed with other not-so-common words like ball, penguin, Grover, Moose, Rudy, names of her toys and dog friends.

One warm, breezy late spring day when Channing was visiting, we all sat outside under a shade tree sharing our reading circle book. Students clustered around Channing while I read from *A Wrinkle in Time*. After I had read a few pages, Scott interrupted, "What does *shadow* mean to Channing? Every time you say it, she perks up her ears and tilts her head."

"Oh, she has a black lab puppy friend named Shadow. She loves to romp in the yard with him. They're great pals," I said. Scott shook his head in disbelief, and I went back to reading our story.

My class respected two rules when Channing visited:

1. After the initial greeting, our studies had to proceed as usual or Channing would be assigned a spot on her blanket by my desk.

2. Our classroom door had to be kept closed throughout the day.

My students took these rules to heart and did all they could to make her visits special. They would settle into the classroom activities and then wait quietly in hopes that Channing would come by so they could pet her. After the first half hour, I'd ask if Channing had been around to visit everyone. The answer was always yes. We never did understand how she accomplished this, but she did.

One morning in the middle of our math lesson, the classroom door opened while I worked with four students at my desk. I saw the principal enter our room and approach my group. He had left the door standing open. Before I could ask a student nearby to close it, the whole class turned and announced in unison, "Shut the door!" Firm in their request and wanting to protect Channing made them fearless. Channing's safety outranked deference to the principal. Their loyalty to Channing was a reflection of her affection for them.

When students graduated from my class and moved to the next grade level, I often received letters from them. I realized where I stood in some personal hierarchies when I received notes like the following one from Samantha.

Dear Mrs. Nordstrom,

I like junior high. The work is harder but I am doing okay. Volleyball was fun and our season just ended. I'm ready to start basketball practice. I got three A's and two B's on my report card.

How is Channing? Is she still playing with Grover? I really liked spending time with her. She's a cool dog. I know she really liked me because she spent so much time sitting by me. Well, I gotta go.

Love,

Samantha

P.S. Are you doing okay?

When computers first came into use in the classroom, my computer-savvy former students would e-mail me short notes. The one that stands out most for me was written in the last year of Channing's life.

> Gosh, Mrs. Nordstrom, I was sorry to hear about Channing. We sure loved her and missed her when we went on to the junior high and didn't get to see her any more. What's your new dog's name?
>
> Love, Rebecca

Word had reached my former students that I had brought a new pet to school. Rebecca was sure this meant I had lost Channing. My reply assured her that Channing was still among the living and that I now also had Maggie, a black standard poodle and the newest member of my family. Maggie took up the mantle of school visits, which allowed Channing to retire from the classroom.

During Rebecca's senior year, we held our time capsule party to share the memories we had packed away when they were sixth graders. By then sweet Channing had died, but the memories they found and shared from their journals again showed me the power a pet has in a child's life.

Each of my pets has responded differently with my students. Channing pulled back when she was around two or more adults, but never minded a room full of children crowding around to pet her. Maggie, however, was more bashful and eased into the classroom slowly. She was skittish when too many students circled her at one time but she still relished visits to school. The collective response of my students when my pets came to school reminded me how mundane my class must have looked on other days. The company of a trusted canine brightened even blustery November days.

I kept a rubber stamp of a standard poodle in my desk—the Maggie Stamp. On difficult assignments, I would circulate among my students to check their progress. After they had had time to complete a few problems, I would check their work and put the Maggie stamp on their paper indicating that their answers were correct. For those students who didn't have correct answers, I would reteach the concept showing them the mistake. The following day in class when we graded their work, papers that had the Maggie stamp each received five extra points. Those students who had needed more instruction often got their problems done correctly and received full credit for their work, a bonus in itself. Sometimes, when the entire class had shown exceptional effort, or it was Maggie's birthday, everyone would receive a stamp. My students also reminded me whenever they felt it was time to get the Maggie stamp out again.

Maggie made solo trips to my classroom during her first three years. But when she was four years old, she gave birth to five roly-poly, wavy-haired poodle puppies. Cozy, one of Maggie's puppies, later joined Maggie in the classroom. Cozy, the smallest puppy in the litter, required special feedings just to survive her first few weeks of life, but she became a willing visitor to the classroom as soon as she was old enough.

No one would have suspected after her fragile beginning that Cozy would become such a rambunctious, playful pup. Cozy was shy like Maggie. She was happy to meet the students a few at a time, but she never ventured far from me. On the days she visited my class, I had plenty of requests to, "come stand near my desk to teach, please." It had not taken long for my kids to recognize that wherever I went Cozy followed. Who could blame them for that simple request? They wanted to get the bubbly, bouncy Cozy close to their desks so they could enjoy petting her.

Alone, Maggie or Cozy was noticeable, but together they were eye-catching, creating excitement wherever they went. A ripple of anticipation spread throughout my room and overflowed into the halls on the days they came to visit. Former students—from freshmen to seniors—slipped into my room throughout the day to greet their canine friends.

Over the years, my students and I have discussed many topics concerning pet responsibility: care and feeding, training, rules and respect, and favorite dog stories. We've used my puppies' birth weights and compared them with their adult weights to study proportions. Studying unit rates and final costs was more fun when the topic was related to dogs. I can't count the number of dog stories or pet pictures my students shared with me during my teaching career. But one thing is for sure: the best smiles and happiest laughter accompanied these conversations.

My teacher's pets were trustworthy, unfailingly cordial, and eager to please. For me, it was no accident that the word for my favorite kind of pet is *God* spelled backwards. Their loyalty and love have always been beyond question. Never have I come as close to the unconditional love we know God offers as when I was in the company of my canine companions. These pets also opened the hearts and minds of my students, helping me achieve a level of teaching success I would not have experienced on my own.

Sammy said it best when he sat on the floor and pulled Channing into a hug. "I like collies the most, but I go great with any dog!"

Every good and perfect gift is from above, coming down from the Father of the heavenly lights, who does not change like shifting shadows.

—James 1:17, NIV

Irrepressible

Ah, Sovereign Lord, you have made the heavens and the earth by your great power and outstretched arm. Nothing is too hard for you.

—Jeremiah 32:17, NIV

Although I already knew who Kathryn was, the first time we met face to face was at a teacher workshop. With friends in common, particularly her husband, Jim, we didn't feel like strangers. Jim, my former landlord, had met and married Kathryn two years after I moved out of state to my next job. So for me, connecting with Kathryn felt like a homecoming with my past.

Kathryn (not an alias) had endured several personal tragedies before we met. Many years earlier, her first husband had been fatally crushed by a farm tractor, and she was the one who discovered the accident. She then had raised their three small children alone. Before meeting Jim (not an alias), Kathryn had also survived two separate bouts of breast cancer. Her faith had been tried under harsh circumstances. Through her trust in God, she still found the joy in daily living.

Jim himself was well acquainted with grief. While he and his first wife were garden shopping, she was abducted, raped, and murdered by a garden center employee. Her tragic death became a widely reported media frenzy, making it even more difficult for Jim and their three children to find relief from the ever-present nightmare.

Both Kathryn and Jim had had their faith tested deeply, and somehow each had managed to rebuild a new life from the tattered remnants. Eventually their paths crossed when a mutual friend introduced them. It was apparent to those around them that Kathryn and Jim were good for each other in so many ways.

Understandably, they were both cautious at first, but they did start dating each other and ultimately got married.

While Kathryn and I taught in the same school system, we were assigned to different buildings in neighboring rural communities, and so we rarely saw each other. However, one summer, we roomed together during a weeklong workshop. Looking back, the "new" technique we studied never amounted to much, but a blossoming friendship took hold as we shared about our lives and teaching experiences. The bond that began that summer deepened and became surprisingly invaluable for both of us in the coming years.

About two years after our friendship started, it became increasingly apparent that the principal in my building had decided to target me as part of his draconian management style. Each spring, this principal used contract renewal as a way to intimidate teachers, selecting one teacher to fire at the end of the year. I had noticed this pattern ever since I had first arrived at this school. Other teachers also were wise to this devastating tactic. In fact for the past three years, the principal had fired a teacher each year for what appeared to be trivial reasons. Exactly how he got away with this action or selected his next target was unclear to most of us teachers. Some staff speculated that he was going after teachers he thought were weak, uncooperative, or perhaps too independent and, thus, threatening his authority. Others wondered if he was in cahoots with the superintendent.

One thing was clear: I was in his crosshairs that whole year.

At the beginning of the year, for example, the principal unexpectedly sent a substitute teacher to my room, who informed me that I was to report to Room 311. The window in that classroom door that day had been blocked out with construction paper so that no one could see in or out of the room. When I opened the door, I saw the principal, the superintendent, and the school board president sitting at a table with a solitary chair facing them; the room was set up interrogation style. Until I opened that door,

I had no clue that this was a summons or that I was going to be accused of anything. For the next forty-five minutes, I sat facing my accusers, answering questions about a recent Meet the Teacher Night and why four of us elementary teachers, including me, had elected to sit with high school teachers, who were allowed to sit wherever they pleased. Traditionally, the elementary teachers had assigned seating, but that year, the elementary principal had told all of us at a staff meeting that we could sit wherever we pleased, and so four of us had. The questions the interrogators lobbed at me were bizarre: "Who is leading this power struggle? Why did you teachers rebel and not sit in the assigned seats with the other elementary teachers? What do you know about the discontent over the new teaching style this administration is trying to implement [based on the expensive, weeklong teacher workshop where Kathryn and I had roomed together]?"

I had no satisfactory answers; indeed, I was not aware of any power struggle, much less any subversive undercurrents among the teachers aimed at the administrators. So finally, they dismissed me, severely warning me not to mention this secret interrogation to anyone. As I was leaving, they also instructed me to have the substitute send the next hapless teacher in for questioning.

Failing to find any substance to their suspicions, they appeared to let the matter drop.

Another clue that I was in the principal's line of fire that year came two months later when he used a parental misunderstanding to try to intimidate me. He had found a parent that he believed was upset over a student incident that had supposedly happened in my classroom. I was unaware of any problem, much less one that had escalated to the point that required an immediate parent-teacher-principal intervention. In a rush to capitalize on this situation, however, the principal scheduled a conference for all of us to be held at seven fifteen the very next morning. It seemed the principal was rather smug when he told me that my attendance was mandatory.

But the meeting was not to be: heavy fog caused a two-hour delay the next morning. And although I never found out what the "problem" was, it obviously had been resolved at home between the mother and her son. The principal seemed almost disappointed to tell me that the conference would not be rescheduled because the problem no longer existed.

My relationship with the principal continued to deteriorate for the rest of the year. I knew things were seriously wrong when he told me in March that there was a problem with my contract. He refused to discuss it with me, and instead ordered me to attend the next school board meeting where my contract would be reviewed. Word spread as rapidly as a brush fire through the teacher network that my contract renewal was on the board's agenda.

It was standard procedure for the school board to review contract issues at the March meeting. When I arrived at school that night, the parking lot was jammed with cars. Inside, the cafeteria was crowded to overflowing and people were spilling into the hallways. Everyone had heard that the coach was going to be "released" from his contract that night. Even though he had support from the community, he was causing friction in the school district. Many parents had come to the meeting anticipating a spectacle.

Two of my closest teacher friends met me there to offer their support. We found three seats together where we quietly sat down. Fortunately for me, the school board elections had occurred the previous November. The board president who had been a part of the September interrogation had been voted off the board. He was replaced by a capable, caring community member who had grown up in this town, had raised his children here, had taught nearby, and was currently the superintendent in a neighboring school district. He was well-prepared to lead the board when they chose him to be their new president two months earlier.

As scared as I was that evening sitting in our crowded cafeteria awaiting my fate, I also held fast to the hope that my contract renewal would receive a fair, impartial review. Regardless of problems the principal had decided to use against me, my performance in the classroom was solid, and my students' performance provided the proof. I had, after all, taught children from most all the school board members' families, so they too were well acquainted with me and my teaching style.

Shortly after the meeting started, the board president asked the superintendent if there were any contract renewal problems. "Yes," he responded, "one teacher."

"Has that teacher been notified? And if so, is that teacher in attendance here tonight?" the president asked.

"Yes, and yes," came the reply.

"And who is that teacher?"

When the superintendent announced my name, these two words sent gasps throughout the room. One school board member even jerked his head around to stare at the superintendent in disbelief.

Abruptly, the president announced that the board would go into executive session and invited only the superintendent, the principal, and me to join the executive board members. As soon as I took a seat in the small meeting room, the president informed me that my teaching contract for next year was in jeopardy. At this moment, I felt the full force of the principal's false accusations, which had been accumulating throughout the year. My future in the classroom was now in the hands of the school board, which decided to postpone my contract decision until they had time to investigate the validity of the principal's charges.

One thing was working in my favor as the school board dug for the truth. The district had seven specific rules that guided teacher performance evaluations, and these rules had the power of law. During the course of that year, the principal had violated six of the seven procedures in preparing my evaluation. In April, as the investigation continued, I was again summoned to attend an executive session; this time the principal also accused me of being uncooperative and having difficulty getting along with other staff members.

In preparing to defend myself from the mounting erroneous charges, I consulted an official representative at the state level whose job was to assist teachers who were experiencing contract problems. He suggested that I visit each coworker in my building, accompanied by the local teacher association president, and ask my colleagues to assess my abilities as a team player and a staff member. All but one teacher gave me high marks and signed a paper to that effect. The one who abstained stated that she didn't find me difficult to work with, but she said she was afraid to sign her name on a document the principal would see.

At the next meeting, I submitted the signed documents from my fellow teachers to the board. Thwarted by this new development, the principal tried to refocus the board's attention by dismissing these documents and declaring that I couldn't get along with even the kindest of teachers, specifically naming Kathryn. Realizing his fabricated evaluation was losing credibility, the principal was looking for other ways to defend his position.

Surprised by this new tactic, I asked the board members to question Kathryn directly. I didn't need to talk to Kathryn about this because I was confident that her character would withstand this test of integrity and that she would clear up these fraudulent claims.

Thankfully, the school board was willing to investigate the principal's accusations even if it did mean that I had to appear before them in six separate sessions that year. Kathryn stayed strong and true, adhering to her principle of integrity, just as I trusted she would. In the end, the board members unraveled the principal's deceit and renewed my contract for two years. They told the principal that he had one year left on his contract, and that he needed to find a new job elsewhere. They also directed him to stay away from me, to stay out of my classroom, and to do no more evaluations of my teaching.

Only through the passage of time and personal reflection have I begun to see the numerous blessings God granted me through that yearlong nightmare. Many days were dark and threatening. Unclear as to whether I would even remain in the teaching profession, I still reported for duty each day with a cheerful, determined spirit, knowing in my heart that my true boss was God, and that He would direct my footsteps and enable me to deliver my daily lesson plans effectively.

The last vestige of this problem was resolved during the summer when I learned that the superintendent was now considering punishing me by moving me to another building. Again I contacted my teacher's representative, and this time, he enlisted the aid of a lawyer. Finally, with a directive from the lawyer, the superintendent was forced to remove all the paperwork from my personnel file that detailed this ugly incident. A new principal had been hired for the fall and I would start off with a clean slate.

God is ever faithful whether we can see it or deserve it. Yet when I saw the intricate mosaic picture God created from the broken pieces of my life during that challenging year, I gained a stronger faith in His plan and a deeper gratitude for His Grace.

God's permission to teach that particular year came not only from students but also from attentive school board members who were objective and thorough in fulfilling their duties.

During the next six-year span, the superintendent retired and the school board hired a new one. Some aspects of the new superintendent's management style were not all that different from his predecessor as we teachers were soon to find out.

At the start of the seventh year, Kathryn was transferred to my building. The new superintendent had decided to discipline her for reasons I never knew, and so she was sent to our "outpost" as punishment. He assigned her a room on the third floor of our aging building where she would teach remedial reading. This transfer illustrated what a mentor once told me: "If you teach long enough and have any opinions, your chances increase for being at odds with the powers that be."

It was now Kathryn's turn to be chastised. But she and I both knew that what others intend for harm, God employs for good, and Kathryn's "punishment" became a true blessing to her new colleagues and students.

The year before her transfer, Kathryn learned that her cancer had reappeared in her bones, and by the time she moved to our building, the cancer was affecting her hips. Our 1927 three-story building had high ceilings and no elevators. The bathrooms, cafeteria, and other essentials, including the teachers' entrance, were on the basement floor. Although knowledgeable of Kathryn's failing health, the new superintendent ignored her plea for a classroom on the ground floor. He answered her request with the terse reply, "That is your problem."

A teacher whose classroom was on the basement level heard about Kathryn's plight. This brave teacher skirted the superintendent, asking the principal to approve the room switch. The request was granted by the building principal without involving the superintendent.

Our students needed a dedicated, talented educator like Kathryn. The previous reading teacher spent class time entertaining the children with games and food. Everyone on the staff knew these students were being shortchanged, and Kathryn was a perfect solution to student reading problems. Her understanding of the reading process and her ability to communicate with students dramatically improved the atmosphere in the remedial reading program along with the student's enhanced chances for success. All the students noticed the difference immediately, but some didn't like it.

As Kathryn described her classroom procedure to students that first day, one boy clamored for attention. She called on him and he asked, "When do we get to play games and watch videos?"

Her no-nonsense answer set him back: "We're learning to read in this class."

"No games or videos!" he protested loudly.

"Our goal here is to improve reading skills," she said.

Unable to engage Kathryn in a debate, he finally asked, "How do I get out of this class?"

Kathryn calmly answered, "You pass the reading test, which shows you no longer need extra help."

And he did.

Most students in Kathryn's room responded to both her teaching ability and her kindness. Other staff noticed the difference that Kathryn's tutoring was making in their classrooms. Students also grew fond of Kathryn as time passed and enthusiastically showed their appreciation. But those of us who worked with Kathryn were also becoming more aware of the toll the bone cancer was exacting.

One of the more noticeable changes occurred the next fall when she returned to school on crutches. Her cheerful approach to this latest development eased but did not erase the concern we felt. Her classroom location required her to negotiate eight stair steps between her room and the cafeteria, a manageable task the previous year but now more difficult with each passing week. Eventually, her students and fellow staff ran all her teaching errands, allowing her to focus all her energy on helping children learn to read better.

Everyone in our building watched over her. When our cooks noticed the difficulty she had maneuvering her crutches in the cafeteria, they began "serving" her lunch. No waiting in line for this special colleague. Kathryn humbly accepted and greatly appreciated the first-class treatment they lavished on her.

As her health continued to decline, Kathryn adjusted to each new challenge with determined resolve. When her husband, Jim, retired from his teaching job, he became her chauffeur, escorting Kathryn to her desk each day. No one recalls when she began spending the entire day in her room. Finally, she ate lunch there as well. When possible, teachers brought their meals and shared lunchtime with her.

Small changes crept into her conversations, and the subject matter now turned occasionally to retirement. Since Jim had already retired, Kathryn began wondering if she should too. Jim supported her choice no matter what she decided, but Kathryn was just not sure what to do. She feared losing her reason to force herself out of bed, despite the pain, each morning. She was afraid her pain, without the strong incentive of her job, would rob her of her motivation.

Managing the agony of weakening bones was a challenge that made it easier for Kathryn to decide to retire. After she submitted the paperwork, she informed her colleagues of her decision. During the last few weeks of school, a small group of teachers quietly planned a surprise retirement party to honor her career and service to our district.

The customary gift for retiring staff had been a silver platter. No one thought that was appropriate for Kathryn. Considering the unusual circumstances, the committee chose to honor her favorite pastime, baseball. We all chipped in for a getaway weekend for Kathryn and Jim to watch their favorite players from days gone by in a Cincinnati Reds Old-Timers' game.

Even though she had adjusted to the idea of retirement and was anticipating more time with Jim, Kathryn talked about the difficulty of saying good-bye and cleaning out her desk. Her retirement party was scheduled for the first Tuesday in May to put some emotional distance between the celebration and her final week, a difficult time even under normal circumstances. Invitations were quietly extended to her family, close friends, and the staff.

On the afternoon of the surprise party, I dropped by to visit Kathryn and was rewarded by seeing her resilient spirit on display. We began talking about her pain. Just a year earlier, I had undergone spinal fusion surgery and had my own experience with pain management. My recovery gave me a tiny sample of the pain Kathryn endured daily. Although she hid the pain most days, it consumed much of her energy. As we talked, she quietly admitted that the back pain was getting the best of her. Realizing that her celebration was only two hours away, I asked if she had taken any of her prescribed painkiller.

"No," she answered with hesitation. "I haven't been using much of that medication because of the report I heard on the news. Did you hear the research news report about how that pain reliever might shorten your life?"

This was so typical of Kathryn. Even the pain of advancing bone cancer had difficulty dampening her hopes of a long life.

I nodded in affirmation, replying, "Your pain seems to be particularly intense this afternoon. Maybe your prescribed painkiller could help bring you relief today." This small encouragement was all it took for Kathryn to request a glass of water.

At her party that afternoon, Kathryn was in good spirits—her prescribed pain reliever had taken effect. She was overwhelmed to find her family, dear friends, and staff gathered in the school library to honor her retirement.

We couldn't tell which excited her more—the wonderful gathering with favorite people or the promise of a special weekend in Cincinnati with Jim. And we hardly remembered a day when Kathryn radiated such joy. With the help of painkillers, Kathryn was able to revel in a circle of warmth and love.

Just two days after this celebration, a colleague and friend of ours had an unexpected run-in with the principal during her annual evaluation. Again, a principal was using a transfer as a means to punish a teacher. While Kathryn and I were not surprised by this tactic, we were caught off guard when this particular teacher had come under attack. Many of us knew that this twenty-five-year veteran excelled in the classroom. But her success and experience were no impediment for this principal's power.

Immediately following her evaluation, this teacher came to my room to tell me what had happened and seek my perspective. Together, we headed to Kathryn's room, knowing that she, too, had faced and overcome similar difficulties.

The details of the conflict spilled out while Kathryn quietly listened: after observing this teacher in her classroom, the principal was quite pleased and offered high praise, but then just hours later in an about-face gave the teacher failing marks on the annual evaluation. After hearing this, Kathryn's advice was simple—something she had learned from her first husband who had died many years earlier. "Kill them with kindness," she said. This is exactly what she had done during her ordeals with the administration. "No matter what they do, *you* be kind."

What an internal conflict such advice creates; the natural response is to strike back. It takes much greater effort and faith to turn the other cheek. Kathryn's words resonated in her friend that day and for many days to come. Although difficult to implement, she knew it would be best if she could behave just as Kathryn had advised.

But before she could even begin practicing Kathryn's wise counsel, the whole school received sad news that changed everything. Kathryn had died in the wee hours of the morning. In the middle of the night, she had had trouble breathing and had awakened Jim who called the emergency squad. Kathryn was rushed to the hospital, but nothing could be done to reverse the effects of a massive heart attack.

Neither my friend nor I had any idea during our conversation the previous day that Kathryn's advice would be her last to us. She would have been delighted to know how these simple, yet powerful, words have continued to bolster us during trying times. Over the ensuing years, we have reflected on the timing of the last week of Kathryn's life, counting our blessings that she was placed in our building as a living model of faith in the flesh.

Kathryn died on Friday and her funeral was held the following Monday, a school day. The only sensible way to accommodate all the teachers and students who wanted to attend was to close school for the afternoon. This was the only time in my long career that school was suspended to honor a teacher.

Adjusting to our loss was difficult. But our sadness was eased as we acknowledged Kathryn's final blessing: her natural death shortened her terrible suffering from bone cancer. Instead, we found reasons to be thankful that she never had to deal with empty days separated from the students she loved. She never had to say good-bye or clean out her desk.

God works in many ways, and He worked through Kathryn, a dear friend and wise colleague.

I thank my God every time I remember you.

—Philippians 1:3, NIV

Help! I Need a Geek

How great are your works, Lord,
how profound your thoughts!

—*Psalm 92:5,* NIV

Computer, server, media center, PowerPoint, flash drives, VCR, DVD, CD, IM, Facebook, texting, Twitter, tweet, Instagram. Everyday language? Not even in the lexicon when I accepted my first teaching post. The digital age was in some far-off, unimagined future. A spiral-bound lesson plan book, a grade book, and chalk were standard issue for teachers in the 1970s. Today, those tools look like prehistoric relics. A teacher unwilling to grow in this digital era might soon resemble a *Tyrannosaurus rex.*

Immense technological changes, mostly improvements, have come swiftly to the classroom in recent decades. Even with the wide adoption of personal computers, however, these kinds of advancements were slow to arrive in my school. That all changed in 1996, when my school became a prototype for our state, and we began our digital transformation in earnest. That year, we learned to use an intraschool communication link. And by the late 1990s, our district had transitioned to computer gradebooks.

In the early 1980s, our school had experienced an unsuccessful attempt to incorporate computers into the daily routine of the classroom. That training disaster required us to learn DOS (digital operating system) and write many lines of computer programming code just to create a classroom review or an educational game to enhance our curriculum. This learning was both frustrating and infuriating. I didn't need to write a textbook in order to teach from a textbook any more than I needed to become a computer programmer to use computer-based review games in my classroom. And I certainly didn't need to waste my time learning such a complicated system and its concomitant language when there was only one computer available for my entire class to use. To top that, the administrators of this experimental program spanned the digital spectrum from "very competent" to "couldn't turn on the computer" without assistance from the school's only computer techie.

My very first classroom looked quite primitive when viewed through the lens of the digital age. I used chalk on a blackboard, calculated percentages for student homework either in my head or with the assistance from the standard conversion percent E-Z Grader, and listed each score, by hand, in my grade book. Then I averaged all of these grades for each student, in each subject, for each grading period. I spent much time performing this task, something my computer would later complete in a flash once I had entered the data.

In my early teaching days, the main office had only two ways to contact me: the principal or secretary could interrupt my class using the public address system (PA), or someone could walk down the hall and speak directly to me. Without phones in the classroom, teachers often sent a student to the office to transmit a message. But before I retired, office staff and fellow teachers had many ways to communicate with each other without ever leaving their offices or classrooms: landline phones (which are becoming a relict for some), cell phones, Twitter, e-mail, the countywide intraschool web link, IM, Skype, and FaceTime to name a few. Of course, the main office could still choose the PA or a personal visit, but the digital era completely transformed communication in my school.

Even tech-savvy administrators, however, can be too cautious when it comes to taking full advantage of technology in classrooms. For example, one superintendent did not believe that voicemail had any place in the classroom, so he directed that the message lights be disabled on the classroom phones. When I retired, the message lights were still not connected even though I had worked for other administrators during the intervening years. Without message lights, we teachers had no visual clues to alert us to new voicemail, and that led to some awkward moments and missteps. Sometimes I only discovered messages when I picked up the receiver to place a call and heard the distinctive *buzz, buzz, buzz* that signaled a waiting message. More than once I had to apologize to a parent for failing to return a call in a timely fashion.

Technological tweaks and updates became routine for teachers and staff who tolerated many inconvenient fixes and accommodated many needed technology updates that usually meant learning new software. One particular update to the phone system enhanced the multiline phones located in the main office and in other high-traffic phone locations, but the single-line phones in our classrooms remained unaffected. These updated multiline phones functioned as quasi switchboards, and the enhancement included a button that enabled the speaker phone. When the modification was installed, it changed the way incoming calls were received on the multiline phones. Whenever the office phone rang, the caller could instantly hear conversations through the speaker button on the phone before the receiver was even lifted. It doesn't take much creativity to imagine the difficulties that this situation could cause with sometimes sensitive office communications. A simple fix—just pressing the feature button followed by the number sixty-five—corrected the situation, preventing larger, stickier problems.

Educators certainly didn't need rules for phone usage, much less phone etiquette, when I began teaching, but the following excerpt from the Student Discipline Code #27 shows just how much things had changed. The school board adopted this code a few years before I retired, and each student received a copy:

> Use of cell phones—Students' cell phones are to be turned off, kept out of sight and not used from the time a student arrives at school until the dismissal bell at the end of the day. First violation of this rule will result in confisca-

tion of the cell phone. A confiscated cell phone will be returned to the owner at the end of the day with a letter to parents explaining future consequences, provided there are not concerns with the contents of the phone. Contents of cell phones may be searched if there exists a reasonable suspicion that it may have been used in an activity prohibited by the Code of Conduct. On a second violation, the cell phone will be confiscated and kept by the administration until the student's parent claims it from the office. Further violations will follow progressive steps outlined in the consequences section of the student code of conduct.

In the predigital "dark ages" at the beginning of my career, I rarely thought about how my classroom was cut off from the rest of the world. After all, it was a continuum of the way education had been when I was a student. But once schools began to gain access to the many and varied digital resources, teachers quickly adapted and became dependent on them. If the computer server or phone lines went down and the system crashed, everyone was annoyed by the inconvenience. "Is your computer working?" "I can't enter my grades in preparation for the grade cards next week." "Did we have a message from the office about a time change on the assembly today?"

Most technological advancements were implemented gradually—which was helpful since many of us needed time to study, absorb, and incorporate each new innovation. With each new upgrade, the rhythm of the classroom would be temporarily disrupted. Daily I assimilated and applied concepts, words, or equipment that weren't a part of my wildest imagination—or society's mainstream vocabulary—when I became a teacher. Retooling my classroom to incorporate this steady flow of innovations and changes may have thrown me off my game slightly, but not for long. I might not have embraced all of the new techniques as they came along, but I did master them. Over time I learned to appreciate and depend on them. Some became so vital in how I managed my classroom—access to the internet, the speed of computing and entering grades, and using e-mail to respond quickly to parents, to name a few—that I would not willingly relinquish any one of them for even a day.

In the beginning of my career, classroom equipment needs were simple. School libraries offered the use of 8mm film projectors, record players, film strip projectors, audio tape recorders, and perhaps one old-fashioned opaque projector. These items were available if a teacher signed up in advance, or experienced a rare streak of luck. The old-fashioned sign-up system worked well most of the time. However, problems could be expected when numerous teachers shared limited resources. Most scheduling troubles occurred near the holidays when children were restless and teachers were eager to calm them with a film that just might also be educational.

Most schools owned a limited selection of filmstrips—often outdated—covering the basic topics in science and social studies, and perhaps a literature story. Films were expensive but could be ordered, usually, a couple of months in advance from a regional library. Popular titles had to be requested well ahead of the scheduled show date, and the few available films often passed through many classrooms while they were in the building.

Arranging for films to coincide with teaching units was a challenge because the films had to be ordered so far ahead of time, and even then, there was no guarantee they would arrive in a timely fashion. Once a film had arrived, it was normally available for only two or three days. The shipping cost was usually covered by the school, but if the film was returned after the due date, the teacher had to pay a late fee.

Ordering films early through the mail, arranging for the curriculum to match, remembering to sign up for the projector, and ensuring that the film was returned on time was a restrictive, archaic system, but it was the only system we had. When video-cassette recorders (VCRs) hit the classroom, teachers were quick to find ways to enhance their instruction using this new invention. VCRs allowed teachers to record programs (from television) that could supplement their curriculum with up-to-date information.

When it comes to technology skills, teachers are not created equal and never have been. Rather, this discrepancy has become more apparent with time since technology continues to play a larger, more important role in school life. But for most tech-challenged teachers, help is usually close by. For instance, during my second year of teaching, Eleanor Custard taught third grade just across the hall from me. Eleanor had been my supervising instructor earlier during my student teaching, and I welcomed the opportunity to work again with this gifted educator. Her gifts, however, did not include running classroom equipment. One afternoon, Eleanor slipped into my room and quietly whispered, "I've got a problem across the hall, and I'm hoping you can fix it." I asked what was wrong, and she answered, "I think you'd better come and see."

Following Eleanor across the hall, I discovered that she had shown over thirty minutes of a film without the assistance of a take-up reel. On the floor behind the projector was a small mountain of costly and easily broken celluloid tape.

These films were loaned to schools because the films were too expensive for most schools to purchase. An average cost was in the hundreds of dollars, and most teachers earned well under ten thousand dollars per year at that time. Judging from the length of the film and the large pile on the floor, I guessed the cost of this film was 10 to 15 percent of Eleanor's gross annual pay—a stiff price to pay to educate third graders about volcanoes.

All teachers were well aware of the delicate nature of film, if for no other reason than the number of splices we found where broken pieces or bad spots had been repaired. Afraid to touch this expensive, fragile pile of celluloid, I had only one suggestion.

"Just wait, I'll go get my children," I told Eleanor. "Once we have them involved in an activity, we'll fix this problem." When my students entered her room, there were many wide-eyed looks from the children, but not one impolite comment from any student about this situation. Our impromptu visit was a welcome break from the regular day's work. And our students received an added bonus that day, a firsthand lesson in teamwork and problem solving.

For the next half hour, our students played board games together while Eleanor and I ran the film projector backward. We kept vigil as the front reel pulled the precious film off the floor, loop by loop. No long-term damage was done, and I can still see the relief on Eleanor's face when the last loop lifted from the floor.

Emergencies of this type no longer happen because of improvements in technology. But some of the interesting situations from the early days can still make me chuckle. It's easy to picture the elation, especially for the technologically impaired, when the older loop projector was upgraded to an automatic feed. The preautomatic machines were temperamental beasts. If the film loop did not feed just right, the audio didn't match the action, so spoken words didn't match the onscreen lip movements. This was so entertaining for some students that the teacher could count on them missing most of the reasons for showing the film in the first place. And if the loop wasn't feeding smoothly through the machine, the projected frames leaped up and down on the screen, often creating hilarious jerky motions.

Since these film projectors moved around the building with great regularity, important pieces would get mislaid or lost. Ingenious teachers wouldn't let a take-up reel too small for the film prevent them from showing the movie. They carefully monitored the amount of film accumulating on the too-small take-up reel and gently added a few playing cards as film began to edge close to the reel's capacity. The trick was to accurately guess how far out to place the cards—not far enough for them to fall out, yet spaced close enough that they would remain in place and still hold as much film as a larger take-up reel. Home remedies like this no longer have value in the classroom.

The sophistication of technology often requires teachers to seek the help of a techie. Some techies are high school juniors or seniors who are dispatched to classrooms to solve technology problems. Now and then, I was blessed with a techie from my own seventh- and eighth-grade classes too.

In the digital age, libraries have been renamed—sometimes even removed. Media centers house the library's reading materials, and their focus is now directed toward computers, given the unlimited resources of the internet. Today's students probably wouldn't even recognize a film projector, much less a film strip.

One of my favorite improvements was Elmo, a hybrid of the overhead projector and the old-fashioned opaque projector. I had spent many years working with the harsh reflection of the overhead projector's high-intensity light, which was both distracting and painful. The opaque projector, however, was an ancient machine limited to one function—enlarging. But Elmo incorporated the best of both of these machines, modernizing and enriching my classroom presentations. Everyone in my classroom, including me, appreciated the flexibility and clarity of Elmo. Elmo allowed me to enlarge graphs or math problems to clarify my class instruction, and seeing work displayed in color also made it easier for students to comprehend. The projected image from Elmo appeared both on the TV and the projector screen at the front of my room, making it easy for all of my students to see.

Whenever Elmo was broken, my students found that learning new math concepts was much more challenging. Technology had become such an integral part of the classroom for them that they begged the principal to help repair or replace Elmo.

Most incoming teachers nowadays would not be familiar with the mimeograph machine, an old-fashioned device used to make multiple copies of assignments and tests. The blue-purple of the mimeographed page with its distinctive aroma eventually was replaced by the crisp, clean black lines of copying machines.

The first mimeograph machine I used was a manual one. We hand cranked each copy we prepared. Eventually, we used Thermofax machines to create the master to run these copies. But preparing the master for the Thermofax required attention to detail or the result was a useless, smeared indigo-blue master. When it was time to prepare a set of papers, you hoped it was your lucky day—Thermofax masters were plentiful, the mimeograph machine was not jammed, and you came away without the tale-tale blue stains on your hands or clothes.

Over my career, I experienced and adapted to many changes. Phonographs and tape recorders were replaced by CDs; films gave way to videos, then DVDs; overhead projectors morphed into Elmos; and old-fashioned grade books, lesson plans, and attendance pads became computer files. A phone extension in each room became common place, but even that was changing with the innovation of cell phone technology.

Might new and unimagined high-tech developments replace teachers some day? Not soon. Technological equipment cannot compete with the qualities of a good teacher—compassion, understanding, knowledge, kindness, encouragement, and empathy, to name a few differences. One of the most powerful statements I could make to my students was, "I understand your struggle because I myself once fought a similar battle." I entered the classroom each day as a human, capable of making and learning from mistakes. Students want, and need, knowledgeable, empathetic teachers whose human qualities and experiences add depth and authenticity to their instruction.

Teachers have a decided advantage over machines because of their real-life experiences—creativity, imagination, the ability to overcome frustration and other obstacles, and understanding challenges all because they battled similar problems. Machines increase the variety of ways we reach our students, but a machine has yet to be invented that offers the variety of gifts a good teacher possesses—patience, joy, encouragement, kindness, warmth, sensitivity, understanding, and experience.

> *For from him and through him and for him are all things. To him be the glory forever! Amen.*
>
> —*Romans 11:36,* NIV

Construction Daze

*He gives strength to the weary and increases the power
of the weak.*

—*Isaiah 40:29*, NIV

Everything was a big, big mess in my school district. Our rural community was composed of three small towns, each with its own school building. Primary students attended classes in the oldest school building. Grades three through six were housed in a nearby town in a structure almost as old. And the junior-senior high school students were bused to the third town's aging facility. The most recent state inspection classified the primary building as substandard: The boiler exploded and belched soot everywhere. High levels of asbestos were detected. Cracks in the foundation led to structural problems. The roof leaked. Commodes in the restrooms were broken. The old water pipes resembled clogged arteries.

The staff of the primary school didn't think conditions could get any worse, but they were mistaken. The school board was forced to close the building so that meant the students attending the district's three schools now would be crammed into the remaining two buildings, both more than eighty years old and each with aging problems.

The state had a long list of public schools applying for aid to renovate old, dilapidated buildings. Our district ranked near the bottom of a list of almost three hundred schools. So it came as a real surprise when our district was notified that assistance was available if the local taxpayers would fund their part of the construction costs. After years of rejecting school tax building funds, voters from the local district finally passed a levy. When added to state funding, this levy allowed our district to make plans for much-needed renovation and construction. The junior-senior high building, dating from the mid 1920s, was in the best shape of the three and also met the requirement of being located on a state highway. The board voted to renovate this building and attach an elementary wing with plans ultimately to accommodate all grade levels on the same campus. Nobody could have known this process would take more than four years.

During the construction phase, primary-aged students whose building had been closed were crammed into the building that housed the intermediate grades. What had been a snug fit before now became jam-packed. This resulting overcrowding was somewhat relieved by temporarily moving the sixth-grade classes to the high school building for one year. Four modular classrooms were also set up at the elementary school to temporarily house students during the transition.

Accommodations were tight in the two remaining facilities, but the elementary students endured the most overcrowding; five grade levels were now housed in a space previously occupied by only three levels. A fellow teacher quipped that we needed to "grease each little body before it enters the building each morning to prevent logjams in the hallways." I had taught fifth and sixth grades in that structure for sixteen years before the levy passed, and knew firsthand how tight those passageways already were. No space was wasted in that building—even the garage/service area, locker rooms, and all available storage areas were converted into makeshift classrooms.

Schools are rich with human interest stories any day of the week, but these construction conditions inspired unforgettable tales.

When this renovation started, I was among the three sixth-grade teachers whose classrooms had been moved to the junior-senior high school. When the sixth grade later returned to the elementary building, I accepted the job as junior high math teacher. With all the modifications to accommodate construction, I had to pack my room down to the last paperclip and move it for six consecutive years. By that last move, my classroom materials were pared down to the bare essentials only, and I was one of the quickest to finish packing. In my case, however, the bare essentials included not only my files and textbooks for 130 students, but also twelve copy paper boxes filled with time capsule materials for the next six classes of graduating seniors. And all this packing and moving of boxes was completed without the comfort of air-conditioning.

During the two years of heavy construction, my junior high classes had front row seats to view the countless exciting happenings. The construction job began right outside my room with the new parking area and the new entrance to the building. My usually quiet, tree-shaded view became a beehive of construction activity and a source of continual distractions, as well as an opportunity to expand my usual curriculum. Most of the time we focused on math, but the action outside was stiff competition for the instruction going on inside. Many times we gave in to our curiosity and pressed our noses against the glass.

The pan moving dirt during construction.

A bulldozer used in construction.

My former classroom that was located on the top floor.

Demolition of the old school building.

The first tools of construction to appear were chainsaws. Bye-bye, shade trees. Hello, noise. Students, naturally curious creatures, buzzed with excitement over the constant construction activity on the side lawn. We learned about heavy-duty equipment: bull-dozers, packers, pans, concrete saws, drills, and jackhammers.

The packer offered the most interesting stimulus; it was not the biggest device, but it did have the greatest power to disrupt. When it rumbled through the area, this machine suspended teaching and thinking. Everything on both sides of the hallway shook—fluorescent lights, desks, chairs, overhead projectors, even Mr. Wright's belly, which became our in-house seismo-graph. When his belly reading hit an eight, he would cross the hall to my room, greet my students, and peer out the window to get a firsthand look. I taught in one of only two classrooms in the entire building that looked out onto the construction site, a mixed blessing.

During the second year, construction reached a fevered pitch throughout the whole building. Over the previous summer, every tile from all three floors had been removed in the asbestos-abatement sweep. The construction workers also had taken down the acoustical tiles from suspended ceilings on every floor. So all of the classrooms looked and sounded like warehouses. But this final preparation stage didn't stop until the interior walls of each classroom had huge holes cut into them. These holes provided access for new wiring, as well as pipes for the heating and cooling ducts.

With the warehouse effect complete, sound bounced off the rough concrete floors and exposed metal rafters. But worse, it also echoed from neighboring rooms through the gaping holes. Now that the sound barrier between the floors was gone, noise ricocheted everywhere. We could hear the sound of a pencil drop on the floor above us, but sometimes during quiet seatwork, we even heard a paperclip hit. The deafening roar from the class above when they changed seats temporarily suspended teaching and learning in my room. We even traded rooms with that class one day so they could experience the rumble of moving chairs and desks. When the upstairs class sat at our desks, one of the students exclaimed, "It was so much louder than I expected!" Over time, we all became much more aware of the curriculum being taught in neighboring rooms.

On a cognitive level, the teachers and staff knew the construction was putting a strain on our teaching. After all, we had been living on the frontlines of renovation for a full year. But, a harbinger of the difficulties we would face during the second phase emerged on a hot summer day during our opening staff meeting that second year. The computer lab and a few other classrooms (but not mine) were air–conditioned, so staff gathered there, seeking relief from the stifling humidity and heat that permeated our building. The large window air conditioner unit labored to cool the space and the closed door only helped a little.

Halfway through this meeting, the principal noticed one teacher was missing and asked if anyone had seen Mr. Hanes.

Before anyone could answer, a voice outside the room piped up, "I'm out here in the hall. I looked through the classroom door window and saw how crowded the computer lab was. However, I have heard every word you've said." Even though the classroom door was closed and the air conditioner hummed loudly, we could hear Mr. Hanes clearly. Nobody had illusions about the sound levels and privacy we would have in our rooms that upcoming year.

These working conditions strained all of us—teachers, custodians, cafeteria workers, and students. The construction crew—and who knows who else—had access to our rooms on a nightly basis. Extra vigilance was required at the end of each day to secure student records and curricular materials.

Much of the structural change in our classrooms was accomplished by the overnight workforce. And each morning, we found new evidence of progress, such as a fresh layer of dirt and grit coating our desks, chairs, computers, and anything left uncovered. Some days we even found spare parts like screws, bolts, washers, and nails; forgotten artifacts from the infrastructure these workers were incorporating into our new rooms. During the overnight shift, workers customized heating ducts with elbows and "runs," so metal also became a part of the construction debris we encountered daily.

I unexpectedly found some of these metal shavings one Friday afternoon in early October. My classroom clock required a new battery every month, and I was often the one who performed this chore. The difference this day was that I had never changed the battery in a construction zone. Between lunch and my afternoon math class, I climbed up on a chair to install the new battery.

As I pulled the clock from the wall, something landed in my eye. Unable to dislodge it, I hurried downstairs to the office to see if one of the secretaries could help. Neither of them could find the object causing the sharp, stabbing pain. But they did offer to find someone to cover my classes while I headed to my eye doctor's office thirty minutes away.

My optometrist found a small piece of metal lodged in my cornea. He numbed my eye and removed the metal sliver. Then he prescribed antibiotic drops and sent me home to rest my eyes for at least twenty-four hours in a semidarkened room. By Monday, I was back on the job. And the next time I prepared to change that battery, my students made sure I was wearing my reading glasses to protect my eyes.

Everyone—students, staff, custodians, administrators, and even substitute teachers—was aware of the need for hard hats and protective eyewear for the workers during the overnight construction. But some of us even began to consider these for our own daywear too. If given a choice, teachers and students gladly would have donned hard hats most days just to avoid plaster fallout from the ceilings. Plaster bits and chunks showered most rooms daily. The intensity of these plaster showers increased when the workers on the third floor began constructing the new science labs.

Substitute teachers reporting for duty were told to expect a wide variety of working conditions. For example, temperatures varied greatly from room to room even on the same day. A comfortable temperature was quite a challenge to maintain in our aging building under regular conditions, but it became nearly impossible when most of the school's furnace system was removed that fall. That September and October, we had chilly days when it would have felt good to have heat. But the temporary furnace did not become functional until November, long after killing frosts had set in. This provisional heating unit was installed on the front lawn and large heating ducts pumped warm air into our building.

Experience taught us the discomfort, and then the headaches, of a temporary construction furnace. During the second year of construction, we evacuated the school three times—twice during school hours, and once during after-school sports practice—

because of actual fires related to the renovation. These were in addition to the regularly scheduled fire drill practice each month. On one frosty October morning, the entire school population was standing outside the building waiting for the fire trucks to arrive because of a construction-related fire in the basement. This episode drew the attention of the television news team from a large city forty miles away. The news editor sent a helicopter to cover the incident, and our small community led the evening news that night.

This evacuation happened because workers were installing the temporary furnace on the school's front lawn, and part of the installation involved modifying an old air shaft that required a blow torch. No one realized that papers had collected in the bottom of that airshaft many years earlier. The papers ignited, but the fire was quickly contained. However, the fire department wanted to clear the smoke from the building and thoroughly inspect the facility before giving the all clear.

That morning when I arrived, my room, one of the colder ones during the construction process had registered fifty-one degrees. We thought our room was cold until we spent fifty minutes standing outside in forty-three-degree temperatures with a stiff breeze and without coats. I wanted to reassure my students that we'd be okay, but our goose bumps were hard to ignore. Our fifty-one-degree room and our jackets felt mighty toasty by comparison when we were eventually allowed back into the building.

By the beginning of November, our temporary furnace was up and running, but then a thermostat malfunctioned. This caused connecting ducts to overheat and glow red, and once again we got another visit from our volunteer fire department. We endured another invigorating morning break outside while the firefighters made our building safe again.

Calibrating a temporary furnace must be a challenge. Those of us in the school community grew to believe and understand this through experience. On any given day, room temperatures varied greatly up to an unbelievable fifty-degree difference from one room to another. For example, the temperature in my room often registered on the cool side, usually somewhere in the fifties. Yet, just one floor up and across the hall in Mrs. Green's room, the temperature might soar to a sweltering 105 degrees. I began to dread the mornings when I spied Mrs. Green's windows already open as I drove into the parking lot. That usually forecast an unpleasant, cold day in my room. We could count on it being chilly or downright cold on one side of the building if the opposite side felt comfortable.

Sometimes the temporary furnace produced gas fumes but no heat. On those days, the monster was shut off for repairs, and we were glad we had learned the key to survival—dressing in layers, at least three. For more days than I care to count, my outermost layer was a winter coat.

Despite the cold temperatures, I was fortunate to have a classroom on the north end of the building, a fact I discovered after a rainy weekend. The construction crew had cut a large hole in the outside wall on the east side of the third floor and had tried to protect the opening in that classroom using heavy-duty plastic. The storm was much stronger than predicted, and when the heaviest rain arrived, one room on the third floor was inundated. The rain created its own cascading waterfall with rainwater spilling over a four-drawer file cabinet and then pooling in the boxes of teaching materials stacked on the floor nearby. The custodial crew, always willing to assist, pitched in to salvage as much as possible.

By the time finals for first semester arrived in January, we were all wiser about managing the construction challenges and disasters. All through the fall and winter, our window view provided plenty of distractions with the heavy-equipment activity. I learned how useful this extracurricular training was on the morning of final exams. Exam day restrictions were enacted to provide an extra measure of quiet throughout the building. Before finals that January, all teachers received the following memo.

> Tomorrow is *finals day*. Once students arrive in your classrooms, *no one* is allowed in the hall during the class period. Please instruct students to use the restroom during passing time. Once the finals period has begun, there should be no students in the hall for any reason.

Maybe this memo should have been forwarded to the construction crew chief.

Ten minutes into our ninety-minute exam, a deafening roar brought the students' concentration to an abrupt halt. Opening the window and leaning out for a better view, I saw the construction workers one floor below me drilling a large hole in the concrete foundation. I called the principal and held the phone by the window. "I know you don't control the construction schedule," I shouted over the noise, "but I wanted you to be aware of the adverse conditions these eighth graders have for their final exam." This was all I could do for my students.

The drilling lasted less than ten more minutes, and I suspect my principal interceded on the students' behalf. They were troupers despite the stressful conditions. I encouraged them to focus on the exams, reminding them that they had prepared all semester for this final exam, and not with just the math concepts but also with the construction noise component. Their high scores on the final exam reflected their progress and preparation as well as their ability to concentrate despite distractions.

In late February, staff members attended an afterschool in-service training. The presenter, surprised by our construction zone, tried to adjust to the disheveled conditions in our building. We could hear the annoyance in her voice as she began her demonstration. Frustrated by the noisy reverberations due to the bare concrete floors and exposed ceiling rafters, she asked a teacher near the back of the room to close the door. Under normal conditions, shutting the door would have solved the problem. Under these circumstances, it had little effect.

Having worked under these unpleasant conditions for many months, the teachers knew doors served no useful purpose in reducing noise levels. Rather than explain this though, the teacher closed the door as requested. Shortly, it was obvious how futile this effort was when a custodian started a vacuum cleaner one floor down. The vacuuming nearly drowned out the presenter's speech. The disbelief her face registered when the disturbance continued unabated reinforced that we teachers were construction veterans and that we had been managing these conditions quite well day after day.

The strain of construction, however, was also wearing on my students. I realized I needed to help my students envision a brighter future in our new facility, something to encourage them during this cold, grungy chaos. I decided to take my students on an in-house field trip to show them where their new classes would be. Even though we visited as much of the building as we were allowed to, and tried diligently to envision the changes, the finished facility was difficult to imagine under the current conditions, which resembled a bombed-out war zone.

During the previous summer, some interior walls had been ripped out in preparation for the new floor plan. Because of this demolition, we all agreed that the science room took first place for the worst-looking class in the building. Walls that had separated two smaller, adjacent rooms were now gone, leaving chipped blocks, exposed lathe, and crumbling walls. Many different wall finishes greeted all who entered this room. The paint colors included intense blue to light blue on one wall, while other walls displayed three shades of tan. Another wall section featured remnants of wallpaper and border shredded along the edges.

A large, open area contained both the high school math room and the CAD computer lab. This space won the noisiest award. It had less to do with the students and teachers and more to do with the temporary pressboard wall divider that was eight feet high in a room with a twelve-foot ceiling. The pressboard deadened some sound, but most of the noise sailed right over the divide. The computer instructor, who stood six feet, eight inches tall, gave the high school math teacher, who stood five feet, five inches tall, a run for her money. Most days it was a draw in this contest of dueling lessons mainly because both these teachers were good-natured about the challenge of trying to educate their students under adverse conditions. When the math teacher retired a few years later, she shared this in her farewell thank-you note: "Remember when the computer teacher had to try to teach his class while I was teaching algebra almost in the same room. Don't ask him who has the biggest mouth."

Even restrooms were not immune from construction complications. One day during her break, a substitute teacher headed to the ladies room. Imagine her surprise when she heard the male English teacher from the adjacent classroom reviewing parts of speech in the middle of her restroom visit. Looking up, she spied the reason—large holes where vents had been. She figured the English class had heard her too. Even in the restrooms, privacy became conspicuously absent.

This substitute understood the physics of sound, and on her next trip to the restroom, she avoided walking past the English classroom with the large window in its door. She might not have been able to suppress echoing noises, but at least she could remain anonymous.

Other than the construction entertainment outside of my classroom window, I was one of the lucky teachers because I was in a newer wing of the school. The older section sported bigger construction openings and that brought bigger problems. All of these rooms had extra holes along the exterior walls. When the false ceilings were removed, more openings were exposed, which doubled the opportunity for sound to travel horizontally between rooms and vertically between floors. In short, awkward situations resulted. For example, the high school family life teacher showed a Dr. Phil video on teen sexual behavior while the eighth-grade students were taking the state-mandated achievement test in math at that same time—one floor up. After rereading a question and still not absorbing its meaning, a talented, yet exasperated eighth grader approached his teacher. "I have read this question three times and still don't know what it says. How am I supposed to think? All I can concentrate on is Dr. Phil's talk about sex in the family life class."

Any room unfortunate enough to be sandwiched between the top and bottom floors where active teaching was in progress received the full brunt of cacophony from above and below. An irritated student blurted out his annoyance when he had had all he could take. The booming voice of the teacher upstairs kept drowning out his own instructor. He quietly muttered, "That dude needs to calm down."

Most of us agreed that our nerves suffered the largest toll from construction. Many times, normal coping skills were insufficient to sustain us, and occasionally the pressure grew to be too much for a few staff members.

One instructor, for example, hit his limit when the megaphone voice of the teacher on the floor above him became overpowering. Retaliation replaced diplomacy for a couple of weeks when the offended teacher brought an air horn to class and blew it each time the booming voice from above overpowered his own lecture. Meanwhile, the innocent English class next door to the air horn, now caught in the crossfire, happened to be studying conflict between the protagonist and antagonist in novels. The teacher knew her students understood the concept when one student said, "You mean the tension in the story is like what we're hearing next door?"

Frayed nerves led to a variety of reactions, and we learned much about our fellow staff members throughout this nerve-racking process. One teacher, normally a polite colleague, became overheated one cold December day because of the strain of continuous disruptions. In quick succession, she verbally dismantled three colleagues eliciting three very different responses.

The first teacher she encountered showed true composure. After being yelled at, this teacher calmly replied, "If you have a problem with the way things are done here, take it to the office." That said, teacher number one went about his business. The second teacher in the path of this irate educator imagined her as the Mad Hatter, and she feigned insanity by miming, "I'm late, I'm late, I'm late, for a very important date," as she scurried down the hall in the opposite direction. The third and final attack happened outside the principal's office. This target, who happened to be the newest teacher on staff and the least prepared for such outbursts, disintegrated into tears after the tirade, which ended with the attacker's pronouncement, "And you don't know how to handle students or teach!"

At this point, the principal overheard and interceded. Despite the principal's youth, he handled this challenging situation with maturity and effectiveness by allowing the teacher to have time away from the stress to regain her compose and equilibrium.

Respiratory complaints to area doctors from our staff rose in proportion to the intensity of construction. Before it was over, one teacher had missed more than two weeks of school because of respiratory problems, another had nasal surgery, and many other staff members visited allergists.

Dirt, pervasive dirt, was a daily fact of life. The superintendent had welcomed all of us back to school during the opening day meeting with two large yellow dusting cloths for each teacher distributed by the custodians. We chuckled then as expected. But few of us were still laughing when the end of the year arrived. The custodians gallantly fought the grime and dust, but most days, dirt won the battle.

Under these adverse conditions, it was surprising more staff didn't melt down in more ways. But the end of the year finally did arrive and every room was stripped clean for the final phase of construction. All desks, chairs, books, and supplies were carried to the rental pods that had sprouted on our front lawn like giant mushrooms that May. The final phase of construction required completely empty rooms for the new floors, ceilings, and walls. I felt sorry for my tired students that final day. They no longer had chairs by lunchtime and had to sit on the concrete floor where their chairs had been. But another part of me was filled with hope knowing we'd find unbelievable improvements when we returned in the fall.

Weary, worn-down, and ready for the summer break, the staff and students shuffled out that last day of school. As we walked out, the full construction crew walked in, and the final phase began in earnest.

Consider it pure joy, my brothers and sisters, whenever you face trials of many kinds, because you know that the testing of your faith produces perseverance.

—*James 1:2–3*, NIV

Movin' In, Movin' On

The Lord will guide you always; he will satisfy your needs in a sun-scorched land and will strengthen your frame. You will be like a well-watered garden, like a spring whose waters never fail.

—Isaiah 58:11, NIV

Even though school started three weeks late because of construction, not all of the rooms were ready when teachers, staff, and students reported to our new building in our new school year. The classrooms on the main floor and the upper level were ready for students, but the lower hall had five rooms that were still not finished. The preschool students, whose classrooms were on that lower level, continued to meet at a nearby church until their space was finished. The other classes and teachers from that unfinished section were spread throughout the building, sharing whatever space was available those first few weeks of school.

Settling in that fall, I couldn't help but reflect on the conditions we had faced the previous year during our final phase of construction. Perhaps the change can best be seen in comparing my two desks—the old metal one and the new, pecan-finished contemporary style, which looked right at home in my renovated room.

My old desk, government surplus, symbolized conditions before the construction. The metal monstrosity was a castoff from earlier service in the army. No one knows in which battle my desk may have served, but the ravages of war had left their marks. What the army sells, schools buy.

Over time, the edging of the drab green relict had worked loose and snagged any item of clothing that came close enough for it to catch. The lower left file drawer was bent and hung open at an odd angle. The top right drawer no longer had working stops. I sometimes forgot this and wasn't careful when opening the drawer. When that happened, the contents crashed to the floor with a startling clatter. With nothing to stop it, the drawer just kept moving, spilling pencils, pens, gradebook, and papers on the floor.

The desk's ragged edges snagged three sweaters before I decided there must be something I could do for my war-torn, weary desk. Perhaps the large, clear tape used to repair book bindings would cover the rough edges and save my sweaters. Our school library, the source for this sturdy tape, had been closed more than a year because of construction, so I inquired about this special tape in the high school office. "You'll need to check at the central office since we don't have any here," the secretary said.

I headed across the parking lot to the superintendent's office in my quest to repair my desk. The central office secretary greeted me and asked how she could help. I explained I needed strong tape to hold my desk together. To her, my words were a foreign language, needing a translator. She was seated behind a well-appointed new desk, three times the size of my broken-down army reject. Not quite understanding my request, she asked me to explain how I planned to use tape to repair a desk.

As I described the problem, the other two secretaries in central office joined the conversation. My predicament grew funnier with the retelling as the audience expanded. None of these women could picture the conditions I described. All their desks were new with color-coordinated laminate tops and lovely pecan wood bases—large and in mint condition. Mine, however, resembled a junkyard castoff.

An outsider might think it logical for teachers to have furniture comparable to that of the district secretaries. That was not necessarily so while we struggled through reconstruction. I had worked in this school district longer than any of the secretaries in the central office. One of them was a former student, while the other two had children who had passed through my room. Yet, here I was begging for tape to hold my desk together.

The irony of the situation caused me to chuckle as I crossed the parking lot and headed back to my classroom. The heavy tape was tucked under my arm, and I was ready to do battle with my battered desk. The tape was no match for the lower file drawer, which still hung open at an odd angle, and the upper right drawer, which continued to fall out. But at least my desk no longer snagged my sweaters.

The end of construction ushered in a new era for our local school district. As part of the state mandate that accompanied the funding for our facility, we were required to replace all of the old equipment. None of the old furniture was allowed to be placed in the new rooms. So during the previous summer, two auctions were held to clear out the old equipment—file cabinets, tables, chairs, bookshelves, and my old desk, which garnered all of five dollars for the district. The replacement desk waiting in my room that September looked like something from a new era in comparison.

Settling in to the building with new rooms for some classes and renovated ones for others held an excitement for me similar to moving into my new home a few years earlier. I studied my fresh classroom surroundings and wasn't sure where I should start unpacking. The innovative L-shaped desk won. I was eager to unpack my teaching materials, put my supplies in their proper place, and savor the excitement of my updated teaching quarters.

Unlike the previous furnishings in our school where few items coordinated, all the teachers' desks now matched. These work centers were designed to accommodate the contemporary class-room's technology, unimagined when my former desk was built. One end of the L was an enlarged circle, providing a tutoring site for small groups of students. The warm honey-brown wood lami-nate matched the new storage cabinets perfectly. As I scooted up to my new desk, I noticed the edging was secure and smooth, sans tape.

The complete transformation of our old building required more time than the summer break allotted, so vacation that year was extended. Payment for those extra weeks of vacation was collected at the end of the year, when school stretched longer into June than usual, to satisfy the official 184 days required.

However, bits and pieces of construction stretched on for months. Even with the delayed start of school, the lower hall in our building—art rooms, classrooms for the disabled, the family life kitchens, a tutoring space, and the talented-and-gifted classroom—was not finished. Construction tools, ladders, hard hats, and noise still coexisted with our instruction. Flooring was still being cut and laid, wiring cables run, heating and cooling systems completed, and an untold number of punch list problems managed. These unfinished classrooms were occupied slowly, one by one, as the inspector signed off on each individual room.

Even though some of us were still dealing with construction, the fact that school was able to open in fresh, new surroundings that fall was cause for celebration. All students from K-12 reported to the same building for the first time in the district's history.

The worst was now over, and the finished sections of our facilities were handsome. Teachers and students had survived the trials of construction. We weren't too annoyed by the occasional electrical problems that accompanied the finishing work. We all had walls, doors, ceilings, floors, and storage cabinets like we'd never known, but most importantly, we all had quiet. Presentation units were suspended from the ceilings in the corner of each classroom. No longer called TVs, these units had VCRs and DVDs built right in. New wiring connected our work centers on one end of the room with the presentation units on the other. From my desk, I could display charts and graphs on the TV screen using my computer or Elmo, the updated opaque projector.

Updated bell tones were a vast improvement over the former bell system that startled students into action when it signaled the time to change classes. This new sophisticated system could be set for more than forty different programs. The ninety-seven-page instructional manual was daunting. Our principal needed time and practice to set the pass bells for the high school with a second set for the elementary.

Most of the staff members were saying, "Pinch me. I can't believe it is true." We had dreamed of a facility like this most of our careers.

Other changes weren't as apparent, at first anyway. During construction, my room registered between fifty and sixty degrees in the winter. So we were surprised during our balmy September to find our room at fifty-eight degrees. The electrical workers tried unsuccessfully to calibrate my room, but it was a couple of months before my students and I could enjoy the new heating and air-conditioning system. It was nice and warm outside, but we were forbidden to open our windows since that would interfere with the air exchange required by our heating system. The air exchange in my room was certainly effective. My students and I endured ten straight days of such cold temperatures that we wanted to issue a frost alert. Finally, our problem rose to the top of the construction punch list.

One of the inspectors came to check my room while I was grading papers. "Hmm," he said, "the air exchange in here is very good." I shrugged my shoulders and said that my students were complaining that they didn't want to wear coats on these lovely late summer days. He smiled and offered, "It is much too cold in here, but we still have a couple of weeks' work, then it should be better." The next day, I told my students to come prepared for chilly days. After talking with the inspector, I knew it might be a few more weeks before these conditions were corrected.

Each day, it seemed to grow colder, and the student moaning and grumbling became louder until the third week when it reached a fevered pitch. The outside temperature was still a comfortable seventy-two degrees. Not so in my room. We had gone from freezing to overheating and would have enjoyed a cool breeze from outside. My students begged to have the windows opened and responded in disbelief when I once again explained we weren't allowed to "crack" them even a little.

Our heat wave lasted only a few days before the big chill returned. But there was no quick fix for this problem. In late November, we received this e-mail from the superintendent:

> There are several issues. The simple one is that the north end of the high school is short on heat. Apparently there are two things causing this. 1) The pump went down over the weekend and it didn't send the proper alarm so it wasn't discovered until this morning, at which time it was reset. 2) The heating water lines have yet to be balanced. The hot water getting to the high school isn't getting to the North end of the second and third floors. Only one heat pump is currently working, and it shuts down due to overheating. A technician has been called.

Locating the problem that plagued the north end of the third floor took a procession of heating specialists. One expert finally discovered the waterlines had never been opened and purged. He assured me that we'd have heat once that job was done. It took a couple more experts before it was learned that the main valve, tucked away in the ceiling of the room across the hall, had never been opened, so heat was not getting to my room. Since temperatures in my room registered cold, the blowers were running most of the time calling for more heat, but my room never got warm. After much time and patience and many adjustments, the right technician finally found a way to make my classroom comfortable.

Even though we had settled into our remodeled facility, we logged two more construction-related fire evacuations that fall, in addition to the three from the previous year. Our first evacuation happened when a welding project in the basement caused a small fire, and it couldn't have come at a worse time. The lunch room was packed with the noontime crowd, and we were stuck outside for fifteen minutes while lunches got cold. It was chaotic trying to find lunches and finish cold meals when we returned.

The second fire evacuation emptied the new building because of a water leak in the furnace room. The firehouse is only four blocks from school, but the volunteer firefighters have to get to their station before the trucks can leave. On a nice day, a non-threatening evacuation simply allowed us to enjoy an outdoor break. In inclement weather, however, teachers and administrators had to scramble to find shelter for the entire school population.

Despite the lack of heat, troublesome fire evacuations, unfinished rooms, and startup headaches, we daily enjoyed our new surroundings and our new conveniences.

Four years after the renovations began and two years to the day after the groundbreaking ceremony was held for the elementary wing, the community celebrated with a dedication and ribbon-cutting commemoration. The last Sunday in September dawned with a cerulean sky and balmy temperature, perfect weather following the rainiest September on record. Students, teachers, board members, administrators, parents, grandparents, alumni, and interested taxpayers gathered to dedicate the new facility and appreciate the remarkable changes.

Our celebration began with the Pledge of Allegiance led by the student council president. A local minister whose children had graduated from our district gave the invocation. Our superintendent, who guided us through this entire process, addressed the audience and expressed appreciation to all who helped make this dream a reality. Flags that had flown over the old buildings were now sealed in commemorative boxes and presented by the building principals to be displayed in the conference room. Our high school choral ensemble delighted the crowd with their rendition of "The Star-Spangled Banner." Officials cut the construction-yellow ribbon as the choral ensemble and community belted out our school song. Then everyone flooded into the new facility to have a look around. The open house turned into an old-fashioned reunion in our new building.

I heard many people remark that it was one of the brightest moments they could recall for our local district. Former schoolmates, seasoned teachers, and neighbors greeted one another with laughter and reminiscing. Excitement spread throughout the entire building. Oohs and aahs rang out on every floor and in every classroom. Most of us had not anticipated just how much joy this day would hold. When the open house came to a close three hours later, people still lingered savoring the newness and the history.

And of his fullness have all we received, and grace for grace.

—John 1:16, KJV

Time Travel

Be still before the Lord and wait patiently for him.

—Psalm 37:7a, NIV

Effective teaching requires total attention to the moment. Educators may have to juggle past, present, and future simultaneously in the classroom, but most of the teacher's energy is devoted to the present.

This is typically how past, present, and future looked for me in my classroom. Past: How many lessons does Johnny need to finish in order to catch up from his three days' absence? Present: What *are* we doing in math today? What is going on in that study group over there? Future: Have the items for next week's science experiment arrived yet? What plans do I need to complete so the entire junior high can attend the symphony concert in six months?

Although I was mindful of the past and future, the present was usually uppermost in my thoughts. Except, that is, when it came to our time capsules: ordinary boxes stacked high atop the six-foot-tall antique wooden bookcase that ran the width of our room. Packed inside those boxes were special memories and mementos from each of my former sixth-grade classes.

For most of my years teaching sixth grade, I taught in a self-contained classroom—a particular favorite of mine. During the nine-month school year together, my students and I became a family, and we packed our special mementos into the time capsule boxes on our last school day together. The boxes were to be opened six years later when they were seniors.

Teaching my students every subject except physical education and music provided all of us an abundance of memorable moments. I enjoyed the students' developmental level (mostly), their eagerness to learn (mostly), and the subjects we studied in our curriculum (mostly). I had the privilege of opening their minds to many new ideas: faraway places and distant times in social studies, challenging new concepts in math, wide-ranging experiences through the books we shared, increased awareness of the English language, a variety of art projects, and firsthand experiments in science.

But then one day, my district superintendent offered me the junior high math position. And since the elementary school was moving to a departmentalized curriculum anyway, I felt this change offered a good opportunity for me to explore new territory.

Even though I was changing grade levels, I still had wonderful memories of teaching sixth grade. And many of these memories were bundled up in those time capsules right alongside my students' memories of being twelve-year-olds. Once I got the inspiration for these memory boxes, each of my sixth-grade classes thereafter packed its own special collection of souvenirs. The contents of these precious cartons connected the students to their past, and to each other.

Just how meaningful these keepsakes were became apparent when an English teacher, who taught the high school seniors, shared with me the effect these prized cardboard boxes had on the students she taught. One aspect she described was the lively class discussions she had with her seniors about the contents of their time capsule. They buzzed about the journals that had required so much effort, the art projects they could remember, and the various individual items they had chosen to include. There was much speculation about what all they would find once they opened their time capsule at the party.

For these seniors, their journals were the most important items packed in our cartons. Yet, I can still recall the daily struggle that journal writing posed for twelve-year-olds. Some days it required a Herculean effort on my part just to get them to put pencil to paper. To make matters more challenging, my initial attempts to teach journaling were disorganized, which increased student resistance. But with practice, my techniques improved, and so did their writing. However, their resistance remained a daily struggle for us all. I did not delude myself into thinking my students enjoyed this daily regimen; there was just too much grumbling about it. But they saw, or sensed, my resolve and so tolerated the assignment.

Active twelve-year-olds, in general, were not at all interested in settling down to write. Most of them felt their life experiences lacked significance. Many whined, "I have nothing to say!" I might have helped them overcome some hurdles, but I never completely cured their motivation problems.

To encourage my students, I wrote a short piece on the board each day for them to copy into their notebooks. These selections covered current events, enrichment material on one of our current topics, insightful quotes, or interesting trivia, such as the following selections.

> Louis Braille was born on this day in 1809 near Paris, France. When he was twenty, he published a special system for writing he adapted from an army captain whose soldiers sent messages at night. Helen Keller later benefited from this writing system.
>
> Today we're halfway through the school year and Channing [my poodle] came to help us celebrate.
>
> This month's name comes from the Latin Januarius, after Janus the two-faced Roman god who was able to look back into the past with one face and into the future with the other.
>
> The story of Judah Ben-Hur was written by General Lew Wallace, a flamboyant hero of the Civil War. He could have written about his Civil War battles or even his contact with Billy the Kid. But this man of war chose to write about the Prince of Peace.
>
> It's impossible to feel an emotion no one else has ever felt.

This was the season for the Romans to wage war. They named this month March after Mars, their god of war.

One of the best ways to dominate a society is to control thinking and learning. Hitler wanted to do this to bring about his Nazi state. On this day in 1933 the first Nazi book burning was held. Twenty-five thousand books were burned in Berlin by Hitler and his army.

Students who claimed they had nothing to write at least had a starting point to get their pencils moving—something to help them overcome their writing block. This method helped many students, but for others, it merely delayed their brick wall experiences.

The sophistication level of my sixth graders did not include the ability or willingness to conceal their discontent. I knew writing was agony for some students. But I could see a reward for their efforts that they couldn't begin to imagine, so I forged ahead. My students' resistance manifested itself in many ways. I was not blind to their tricks.

Some students could stretch the letters of two or three words to fill an entire line while others wrote their words as if they were using their large primary crayons from kindergarten instead of sharpened pencils. Still others, who had difficulty remembering to indent for English assignments, miraculously remembered to indent three-fourths of the way across the page for journal writing. A few students described the outfits they wore to school or went into great detail on their dinners from the previous night. But the classic attempt to beat the system came from the writers who left enough space between words to stretch across county lines, deluding themselves into thinking I might not notice.

As with many life lessons, the value of the exercise would not become clear for many years—six in this case. By the time they were graduating seniors and ready to open the time capsule, they understood more clearly why I had encouraged, cajoled, and demanded that they write more.

The keepsakes students chose to include in the time capsule varied from year to year, reflecting their personalities. But some items showed up regularly: art activities, social studies projects, current newspapers and magazines, homework and test samples, field trip booklets they had written, pictures of each class member I had taken on the first day of sixth grade, memorable events caught in photos or videos, and carefully chosen (in most cases) objects that reflected something meaningful. However, the most unusual item I remember packing was a pair of gym shoes—not because this sixth-grade boy was a star athlete, but because he was eager to know how much his feet would grow by his senior year.

We clearly labeled and carefully taped our boxes shut on that final day of sixth grade and stored them on the top of the antique bookshelf. They eagerly added their class memory box, in chronological order, with the graduation year clearly marked to the procession of time capsules lined up neatly.

When I began this activity, I was unaware of how much impact these simple cardboard boxes would have on my students. But I could tell that each new class was excited by the way they studied the boxes packed by previous classes, and the way they talked about how their time capsule would eventually be added to the collection.

When I moved to the high school building, former sixth graders stopped by to inquire about their time capsules. They wanted to know where I was storing them. They also wanted to have a peek at their special carton. Mostly, they wanted to make sure the time capsules were still safe.

When we packed those boxes, I had no idea that I would eventually be moving classrooms six times. Each time I moved, these boxes received preferential treatment because I had witnessed their magic. After a couple of years, however, I grew weary of moving them, so I took them home and stored them in my garage where I was sure they would be safe. I would not have to lug them around anymore.

During that first year in the newly renovated facility, a senior stopped me in the hall and recounted this conversation from her English class.

> We were discussing our time capsule in class yesterday—wondering where it is, what we each put in it, and when we'd have our party to open it. I told the others I was certain you had it in a safe place. We even got to discussing how many time capsules you still have since you no longer teach sixth grade. We figured there were two left—ours and the one for the juniors. Were we right?

Her calculations were correct. Much to my disappointment, only two precious boxes and two time capsule parties were left. Packing and then later sharing these memories had spanned fifteen years of my career. Those journals that had caused such struggles for this senior and her classmates would now provide quite a treasure.

The first year we opened our time capsule, I was simply feeling my way through the process with no road map to guide me. At that time, the high school was in a neighboring town; I rarely saw my former students. I felt awkward organizing that first party, working around the busy schedules of young men and women about to graduate from high school. The students and I settled on a meeting right after school in my classroom, complete with homemade cookies. The enthusiasm of my guinea pig group encouraged me to be bolder in the parties that followed.

For many years, my sixth graders and I ended our last field trip with a visit to my favorite sandwich shop. The first class I took there was a test run. Restaurants, for good reasons, can be timid about allowing a full class of elementary students to join their lunch crowd. But my students were so well-behaved that my classes were invited back year after year, a tradition that continued with each sixth-grade class.

Consequently, I was not surprised when a graduating senior requested a gathering at our special sandwich shop to open our time capsule. They all had fond memories of our wonderful meal there, complete with the restaurant's specialty, Monster Brownies. The restaurant staff once again opened their arms and their door to us.

All of us noticed many differences from the first time we had eaten there. Now, students drove themselves instead of arriving en mass on the big school bus. Poised young women and self-assured young men walked into the restaurant that day—confident in ways I could have only imagined for them six years earlier—and now were ready to take that next step. Wiser in the ways of the world, they no longer needed me to explain such things as tipping and restaurant etiquette.

One of the more remarkable changes I witnessed at that party was the use of technology—conveniences not even imagined when these students were twelve-year-olds. Before dinner, one of the seniors took a call from her friend who was seeking directions to the restaurant. This sandwich shop was located in a town twenty miles from our school district, so some students were unfamiliar with the territory. Unsure how to clearly describe our location, the senior passed her phone to me so I could direct her friend. That was the first time I had used a cell phone to give directions. So many changes had taken place since this class had packed their time capsule.

However, some things remained constant over the years we were apart, especially the laughter and joy my students shared. They were excited to gather in this special place and revisit their history. These students were a testimony to the other patrons in the diner, an explanation of sorts, as to why teachers like me willingly devote their lives to developing young minds. My students' enthusiasm was as contagious this time around as it had been on their first visit to this restaurant. I was delighted to hear some of the other patrons' positive comments about the seniors and their conduct.

Throughout the years, I taught my classes that others' impression of our school and town rested on their behavior. When we went places and met people, it might be the only time that other people would meet someone from our school. Our large yellow school bus had our school name emblazoned on both sides announcing to all where we were from. In our many field trips throughout the years, my students honored my request by showing respect for others.

Students aren't the only ones who learned in my classroom. I myself gained some helpful knowledge during our first time capsule party that I used in all the subsequent parties. The journals that had caused so much consternation among my students when they were writing them became the most important items in the time capsule box. During that first party, I passed out the contents as I came to them. But once my students had their journals in their hands, all talking ceased as they read their own personal histories. The importance of these journals overshadowed all of the other items we had packed away. From that initial experience, I learned to share all of the other memories first.

We began the journey back to their sixth-grade year by remembering the first day of school. I had taken a photo of each student the first morning they were in sixth grade. These pictures got the laughter, conversation, and memories flowing. Next, we sorted through the art, homework papers, social studies projects, and individual items we had packed. Then, surprisingly, a hush descended on the group as they realized it was time to pass out the journals, those dreaded daily assignments we had struggled with all those years ago. But now they became the piéce de resistance of our celebration.

Eager to cross the great time divide, my students began poring over their writing. Most of them turned to the last page first, eager to read their Dear Senior letter written on their final day in sixth grade. Then, impatient to reconnect with other happenings from their youth, they thumbed through their books looking for special days and events.

As they began reading their daily entries, everything became significant: handwriting, spelling, grammar, paragraph structure or lack thereof, and the many places they had made short cuts by stretching out their writing. But most of all, they enjoyed the intimate connections they found with their younger selves.

Their comments both surprised and touched me. They had really cared about each other, and still did. We all enjoyed the entertaining stories and even the blunders they shared.

> I can't believe I wrote, in such detail, about a family trip to Texas to visit cousins. We have no relatives there, never have. And I've never even been to Texas.
>
> I wish I would have written more about myself. I spent most of my time focusing on Amy—what she wore, what she said, what she did, who she liked—and next to nothing about my life.
>
> I guess it's okay to come clean now, Mrs. Nordstrom. We were playing around in the classroom one day at recess and knocked over everything on your desk. We were able to fix it all and put fresh water in the flower vase before you found out anything was wrong. I told all about it here in my journal. Listen to this.

Students who discovered gems they wanted to share in their own stories found it difficult to tear their classmates away from reading their own journals. Most were busy skipping around in their journals, finding special days and memorable events to savor. By and large, the memories were bright spots from their lives. Some wishes and dreams had come true; others had faded in importance or had been replaced with new visions.

Not all the reflections they shared from their journals brought joy. Their lives had the predictable, as well as the unpredictable, the ups and downs. But the most difficult story I recall was from a student whose older brother had died in a car accident during her seventh-grade year. Combing through those memories that she had innocently included in her journal of his last year must have brought a real melancholy to her reading. I held out the hope that her journal also brought comfort, with reminders of typical days spent as a family during her brother's last year. I knew it was difficult to relive the sadness of losing a beloved brother. Her family was caring and loving, and I felt confident that they would work through these reminders of joy and grief the way they had when her brother had died.

Occasionally I received feedback from parents, especially mothers. What an added blessing it was for me to hear their remarks.

> When our daughter Sarah came home with her journal, we got so excited reading we couldn't go to bed until we had finished. We were up until 1:00 the night she came home from the party—sharing, reliving many special moments from her sixth-grade year.

> Jenny brought her notebook home and her sisters all wanted to read it. So we sat down together to share and before we were done Jenny had to revise her opinion of her abilities. She had been giving her younger sister, currently a sixth grader, a difficult time about her spelling and grammar. In comparison, the younger sister is doing better than Jenny did when she wrote her journal. I think her piece of humble pie was big enough she will no longer give her sister such a hard time.

> Thank you for the gift of memories. When my son shared his journal, it reminded us of long-forgotten events. We shared the laughter all over again.

Journals have a way of bringing to life one's past, strengths and weaknesses alike.

Had I handed out their journals at the end of sixth grade, as I did the first year we had written journals, the students would have been denied these insights. Many journals would have been lost along the way or even discarded. Instead, my students' memories were safe with me until it was time to revisit being twelve years old again.

When reading from their journals, my students could see why I pushed them so hard to write every day. Those who had concentrated and worked diligently found a wonderful reward when reading their personal history books. Some of them were natural journalists, using words to paint pictures with rich colors, while other students scratched their way through journaling by dabbling only in black-and-white stick figures. Whichever writing style they used, I know my students, and their families, gained insights into their past from this daily writing activity.

In teaching these journaling activities, I endured some hecklers, but I am glad I didn't let them derail me. Positive feedback from many students inspired me to continue teaching journaling. Some students even saw the benefit of writing daily while still in my classroom, but their rare perceptions only surfaced in late May as the year drew to a close.

> I've learned that writing things down every day helps me understand how I've grown from my past happenings.
>
> Looking back over this year, I see I've learned a lot. Overall, this year in English has been great.
>
> Even though these journal entries were hard at times, they have still helped me with my writing. This journal has not only helped my writing, but it has also increased my organization skills.
>
> More importantly, I learned more about myself. I learned I'm smarter than I made myself feel. I learned that I can't rely on other people to help me with understanding things—I have to ask the teacher. I realized that if I don't work hard, I won't succeed. By the way, not succeeding, it scares me. I also learned that I love English! It comes easily to me. I learned that this year went far too fast and I'm really gonna miss it.

One former student sent me this note following her graduation and our time capsule party.

> I just wanted to thank you for all the effort you put into the time capsule. It really meant a lot to me to see all those things I had worked on—especially my journal! As I start this new chapter in my life, I know I will never forget all the ways you helped me and forever impacted my life. You are a great teacher and a beautiful person. Your kindness to me will never be forgotten. Thanks for everything!

Throughout my time in the classroom, I used silent prayer on a regular basis. Initially, I prayed, "Heavenly Father, please sustain me and help me to make a positive difference in someone's life today." But after experiencing a time capsule party where I heard my students' hopes and plans for their futures, I extended my prayer to include: "Thank you, Heavenly Father, for the many blessings you have shared with me through these students' lives."

> *And we know that in all things God works for the good of those who love him, who have been called according to his purpose.*
>
> —*Romans 8:28*, NIV

Tutoring the Teacher

Take delight in the Lord, and he will give you the desires of your heart.

—Psalm 37:4, NIV

Most of my expertise in education originated from my experiences in the classroom, pure and simple. Typically, my students provided the instruction, but occasionally, their parents also educated me.

One of my lessons came on a field trip. That beautiful autumn day, we visited a museum that contained ancient Egyptian artifacts to enhance our social studies unit. And as a part of our study of careers, we also toured the local newspaper. Then, before heading back to school, we enjoyed a picnic and playtime in the park.

One boy got a real surprise when we passed out the packed lunches that day, and he didn't have one. Thinking about his missing lunch, Andy could describe exactly where it sat on the kitchen counter back at his house. But now it was too late to get another lunch. My sandwich, potato chips, carrot sticks, and cookies looked substantial enough to feed two, so I divided my lunch in half and shared it with Andy. He might not have been full, but he was not hungry either.

Here is the thoughtful note I received from Andy's mom once she learned of the situation.

> Dear Mrs. Nordstrom,
>
> I want to thank you for helping Andy out on Friday by sharing your lunch. He said that sandwich was really good! But most of all I wanted you to know that he seemed really excited about the field trip because you had him so well prepared. He told me all about things he was going

to see before he went. I really appreciate your teaching enthusiasm!

Sincerely,

Jill Hamilton

From then on, I added one small change to my morning attendance ritual on field trip days. Before leaving the classroom and boarding the school buses, all students had to hold up their packed lunches when I called their names. Then they could put them in one of the coolers. Andy stands out as a reminder that we all have times when we forget, and I am indebted to him for adding to my repertoire.

Jack also added to my skillset. His negative attitude brought a positive improvement in my teaching style. Throughout his year in sixth grade, Jack frequently whined that I was cheating him out of credit. "Go ahead and give me an F, you're going to anyway. It doesn't matter what I do," he would complain. Circumstances like Jack's had shown me that it was *oh, so much* easier for some students to accept failure when they blamed it on someone else, anyone else.

By the time we began our last project in English, I was exhausted from a full year of listening to Jack grumble. His low grades revealed his lack of effort, not his intelligence. Jack was as lazy as he was bright. And it appeared that he had support from home for his *guaranteed to fail* choices, dominated by a poor attitude and lousy work habits. At the one and only conference I had with his father that year, the two of us made no progress on helping Jack grow and start reaching his potential. His father excused, even dismissed, Jack's discipline problems and lack of academic effort and growth. Jack's dad, too, had also found excuses for his son's poor performance: former teachers had already warned me that Jack's parents would blame me for his shortcomings. By now, this was a well-established pattern.

In May, we began our research reports to practice the skills we'd studied throughout the year in English. I had scheduled four weeks for this assignment, allowing much class time so I could help. The students would each select a topic, gather data, take notes, organize the information into a rough draft, and then proofread, correct, and write or type a final copy. Since this was their first experience with such a large undertaking, I wanted to break it down into sequential order and teach each required element in this process.

We spent time in the library looking for subjects they would enjoy studying. After they selected individual topics, I showed the class how to take notes without copying from their resources. I explained that encyclopedias and suitable web sites would provide good facts. But no one wanted to read an encyclopedia as a sixth-grade research project, especially me, the one who would be grading their work. I also introduced them to the concept of plagiarism, stealing another's words and using them as your own. If they read a passage in their resource material, closed the source and wrote what they had just learned in their own words, then they would not be plagiarizing. Later, when I checked their note cards, it would read more like an elementary student's work rather than a dry entry from an encyclopedia.

Eventually, when they were ready to use their notes to write their reports, the words they used would be on their level and in their own voice. I also explained that if they found words they did not understand that they should see me so I could help translate those fancy words into concepts they understood. Or they could use the dictionary to locate a synonym, a word they understood with the same meaning.

Before they used their notes to organize their material into a rough draft, I needed to teach them how to use an outline. Because outlining had not been one of my strengths in writing, I debated how I could teach this skill so that it would be a useful tool. First, I listed five zones from the grocery store: fresh produce, bakery, dairy, meat, and canned goods. I then wrote down names of a few items found in each category. Next, I mixed up these words and created a list. Finally, I made an outline template titled The Grocery Store for my students to complete using the word list. The five outline topics were labeled with letters that corresponded to the five zones from the grocery. Under each letter, I indented and numbered the spaces to fit exactly the number of foods in that category from their master list. At first, some of the students were puzzled by the assignment, but soon discovered how food items matched grocery store zones and plunged into the outline assignment with enthusiasm.

The next component in preparing a research paper was learning to use an outline to organize and write paragraphs. For this session, I compiled a vocabulary list from a biography of Helen Keller, a book we had shared earlier that year. The students looked over the words and helped select three broad topics we could use to group the vocabulary. Together, we prepared an outline using the word list and topics we'd chosen to cover the specific ideas. Finally, I sat down at the overhead projector and showed them how I would use the first section from our outline to compose a paragraph.

The Miracle Worker

I. Helen's illness
  A. Acute congestion
    1. High fever
    2. Respiratory problems
  B. Doctor's opinion
  C. Age
    1. 18 months
    2. Wah-wah
  D. Deaf and blind
  E. Talent

The outline prepared for the Helen Keller story from the class vocabulary list.

The Miracle Worker

Helen Keller's illness changed her life completely. Her high fever and respiratory problems were diagnosed as acute congestion by the family doctor. This physician felt that Helen would be fine in a few days! However, her serious illness at eighteen months left her both deaf and blind. Lucky for Helen she had already learned to say wah-wah for water. Anne Sullivan, the miracle worker, would need Helen's natural talent and the word wah-wah to help her reach her potential.

The finished paragraph to accompany the outline.

After that exercise, each student selected five possible topics from their research and wrote them at the top of a fresh sheet of paper. They were now ready to prepare their outlines. They chose a different highlight color for each topic. Next, I asked the students to find information on their note cards to describe each topic and highlight any of those notes using that same color.

As we progressed from one level of research to the next, I saw Jack avoiding any real work on his research topic. I offered help, but he resisted my encouragement. When I saw that he had copied notes straight from the encyclopedia, I urged him to rewrite those notes in his own words. But there is a limit to how much a teacher can do.

The recent conference with Jack's father about his son's lack of progress still resonated in my thoughts. His father had made it abundantly clear that there was nothing wrong with his son's effort at school. His son's problem could only have been the fault of the teacher. Case closed.

As the due date for our research reports approached, I could see a big difference in the preparation Jack showed in class when compared with his classmates. However, Jack's poor preparation didn't appear to bother him—not a new notion for me, as this is how Jack had treated his work throughout that entire year.

Pondering Jack's situation, it struck me: Jack did not understand that he was responsible for the failing grades he'd been receiving for some time. In his mind, the blame belonged to someone else; according to his family, it was usually his teachers' fault.

Before my students prepared their final drafts for their research projects, they had one last step to complete. They were to find an editor who would read and markup their rough draft, making suggestions and corrections. This editor could be anyone except me: parents, grandparents, older siblings, neighbors, and even other teachers. And this editor was to mark the corrections with a special colored pen and then sign the report.

When I collected the research reports on that last day of our projects, I had quite a mountain of folders filled with the various requirements. I explained that it would be more than a week before I could grade all of the work, but I would begin that weekend by looking over their notes, outlines, rough drafts, and final copies.

Jack's packet stood out from the others because it was so thin. The note cards were still the ones he had copied directly from the resources; there was no outline; the rough draft was missing; and the final copy had words and concepts that were obviously not his.

An idea hit me that following Monday morning as I was driving to work. Since my grading was going to require more than a week, perhaps I could let my students evaluate their own projects, giving them some advance insight into their achievement. Even though I had not spelled out the different weights I gave each category on these research reports, my students understood the requirements for their projects because we had discussed them and had spent so much class time working on them together. No one questioned the essential parts to these research reports. Students whose projects contained all the required elements could count on scoring at least a C. Then the quality of their research notes, outlines, rough drafts, and final copies would determine if they earned an A, B, or high C.

Since I decided to let them evaluate their own work, I needed a rubric, a guideline to assess each part and assign a value to it. During my planning period that morning, I created a work page with the various elements from the project: notes, topics with highlighting, the outline, a rough draft with corrections that matched the outline, an editor's corrections and signature, and the final copy. I assigned percentages to all of these topics with each percentage reflecting its overall importance.

After I passed out the evaluation rubric in English class that day, students focused on assessing their individual projects. I was eager to compare their opinions of their work with what I had observed when grading their projects. These project evaluations were complete only after they had included an insight from their research experience that they thought I would find interesting. Here are some comments they included.

> Well I actually had to ride my bike to the library so that I could add to my notes.
> I did even more research to make a better ending for my final copy.
> It can be easy if it's organized.
> When I was preparing, I went online to dictionary.com and I found other words.
> I learned that there are several steps to preparing research.
> I had to do a lot of work changing the facts from my rough draft to my final copy because I did not write them in the correct order.
> This topic really interested me so I would look at a lot of websites, and I would look in the books that we had at our house.
> I learned to jump right into the topic of each paragraph.
> I worked on it whenever I had free time instead of the last minute.
> I should have started on it when I was given the assignment, instead of waiting until the last minute.

I recall clearly Jack's retort when I collected the rubric papers that day. "It doesn't matter what I put on this evaluation because you're gonna flunk me anyway." I noticed Jack's evaluation on his rubric totaled 33 percent. If I had graded these papers with my other system, Jack would have received an F, normally a 50 percent in the grade book for me, but the percentage I wrote that day was 33 percent. Paradoxically, Jack scored himself lower than I would have. And all because he claimed I would cheat him if I graded his work in the usual fashion.

That rubric idea became a useful tool in my classroom. One of the biggest changes I made after that original effort was to introduce the rubric when I initially gave the assignment. Then students would know where the bar was and how much effort they would need to achieve the grade they wanted.

I appreciated how Jack helped me become a better communicator.

Some lessons have come directly from the parents. This was the case with Dwight who entered sixth grade with weak skills. His low grades foretold a struggle with the increased mastery required during the upcoming year when we teachers would be preparing our students for the independence required in junior high school.

Our classes were departmentalized that year, so three teachers shared the responsibilities for all the academic subjects: English, math, social studies, spelling, science, handwriting, and reading.

At the first conference with Dwight's mother, the three teachers spoke about the difficulties he was having with the academic material in sixth grade. It didn't take much for his mother to convince us that he had barely squeaked by in fifth grade. She said she had wondered last year if he ought to be retained, but his fifth-grade teachers assured her that he didn't need to be held back, that he would be fine.

At that time, some students in our school district attended church in old order religious denominations. We teachers found that children from these homes were outstanding students, without exception. These families had no TVs or radios, and they were committed to academic excellence. Reading was second nature for most of these students. So it was a bit of a shock to find Dwight, from a family of one of these religious orders, struggling with great difficulty in his academic pursuits. We used the standard techniques for helping him: extra instruction, the chance to correct difficult work and resubmit it for a better grade, communication with his parents explaining the challenges, and one-on-

one tutoring. Yet none of these procedures seemed to improve Dwight's achievement or his failing grades.

In early March, all three of Dwight's teachers met as a team to discuss his progress and possible placement the following year. The consensus of that meeting was that he lacked the skills and maturity to be successful in seventh grade. Checking his cumulative record, we teachers noticed that Dwight had struggled in his previous years with low grades. We wondered if former teachers had considered retention as a possibility in his earlier school experience.

We knew we would need a conference with Dwight's mother to discuss next year's options. In preparation, we consulted a couple of his former teachers to find out why Dwight had never repeated a grade level when his marks had been marginal the past three years in elementary school.

We learned that Dwight's fifth-grade teacher had indeed recommended that he repeat fifth grade, but his mother would have none of it. She convinced his teacher that he would be fine; they would give him additional support at home, and he would be successful. When the fifth-grade teacher again requested that Dwight repeat fifth grade to strengthen his skills, his mother became agitated and then openly refused.

The three sixth-grade teachers thought back to the parent-teacher conference from the previous fall when Dwight's mother convinced us that she thought Dwight was not ready for sixth grade, yet his fifth-grade teacher had insisted that he needed to move on to the next level. There was a big discrepancy between the fifth-grade teacher and the mother. So we checked with the fourth-grade teachers about Dwight's progress. They also told us that they had wanted to retain Dwight, but his mother had objected so vehemently that they went ahead and placed him in fifth grade. The team of sixth-grade teachers was now getting a clear picture of Dwight's past. Each year, his mother had forced teachers to promote her son to the next grade level, and then she justified his poor performance by blaming teachers for promoting him over her better judgment.

The sixth-grade team came up with a plan that we believed would serve Dwight's best interest. Before the scheduled conference later in March, we consulted the principal about our proposal. Considering the prospect of Dwight turning in a failing performance in junior high, we recommended that he repeat sixth grade to strengthen his academic skills before he tried to manage the many classes and increased personal responsibility of the next grade level.

However, we also had gotten a clear picture of the resistance his mother would probably offer at this recommendation. Perhaps we could give her a choice in writing. This technique had worked well in other situations. In this proposal, we would list Dwight's grades in his academic subjects by percentages, noting how far below passing his grades were. Then, if his mother still wanted to have him placed in seventh grade, it would be clear that it was her choice, not our recommendation. She would be required to sign the letter and choose whether he was retained or promoted.

The principal had agreed and so signed our proposal along with all three teachers. At the bottom of the letter were two options for his mother. We asked her to read and sign the letter and check which option she wanted for her son.

> _____I am aware that Dwight has failing grades in his academic classes as listed above but I request that he be placed in seventh grade this next school year.
>
> Or
>
> _____I request that Dwight repeat sixth grade to strengthen his failing grades as listed above.

We were aware that Dwight's mother had pitted teacher against teacher in the past, but none of us had any idea of the emotional explosion this choice would ignite.

Although we did not see any actual steam pour from Dwight's mother as she read the letter presenting the choices, we did get a lesson in how an irate mother can use a cape like the red cape of a bullfighter. After reading the proposal, she grabbed the pen and signed the request for retention. Rising abruptly, Dwight's mother harrumphed, dramatically threw her cape across her body with a loud swish, and stomped out.

We got another year to help Dwight. He strengthened his skills before going off to the independence of junior high where he was also successful.

Some of my influential lessons have come packaged in quiet moments. Heather, a thirteen-year-old, was my teacher in this example.

For an eighth-grade English assignment, students were asked to explain how a quote from Helen Keller impacted their lives. Heather selected "When one door of happiness closes, another opens; but we look so long at the closed door that we do not see the one which has been opened for us."

> Now, there are many examples that relate to this. For example, let's say you got a bad grade on a test. You may be so concentrated on the bad grade, you do not see the open door that could help you, like extra credit. This example is a very simple encounter. However, this quote affects me deep in my heart.
>
> Last year my grandma passed away. I was devastated, constantly looking at that closed door. That's the only thing I thought about. I was too blinded by the loss to see the new open door. Little did I realize how my sadness was bringing others down as well. Then someone brought my attention to the new door.
>
> Just one tiny sentence she wrote on my paper got me to finally see the light. My teacher wrote, "I hope someday the good memories your grandma left you will overpower the bad." That's when I realized that my grandma hadn't disappeared, she had been in my heart and memories all

along. She wouldn't want me to be sad; she would want me to move on. I needed to give others the chance to enter the gate to my heart.

I can't say I'm completely healed, but the door that I was blinded to see before is a great start. The hole in my heart has been getting smaller and smaller as time passes. This quote will affect me every day for the rest of my life, for with every end there is a new beginning.

Heather taught me how fourteen words in a simple, heart-felt sentence can have a profound impact. She also caused me to reevaluate how I was using my influence in the classroom, and making sure I was truly heeding God's guidance.

For with God nothing shall be impossible.

—*Luke 1:37,* KJV

Shhh! She's Got Her Hands on Our Book!

*She speaks with wisdom, and faithful instruction is
on her tongue.*

—*Proverbs 31:26*, NIV

Sharing a book out loud with my students in reading circle was the best part of the elementary classroom for me. I was student teaching when I first experienced this magic. My cooperating teacher, Eleanor Custard, suggested I share a book with her third graders as part of my training. I selected a book, scheduled a time for circle, and discovered what would become one of my best teaching tools.

The students in Mrs. Custard's room were an attentive audience. Caught up in the story and their reactions, I didn't notice that Eleanor had put down her grading pen and was listening intently. Later that day, she commented, "I know I had a lot of paperwork to do while you read, but once you began, it was so engaging, all I wanted to do was enjoy it. And I did. Now I will have to find another time to finish my grading. But it was worth it." This was my first hint that reading circle would be an effective way to reach students, and the first time I realized I just might have a talent.

It was personally rewarding to share a story and have my students caught up in the tale. Everyone in the class, regardless of reading level, could enjoy the adventure. We visited foreign places, shared moral dilemmas, encountered fascinating people, experienced the world through others' perspectives, and solved mysteries, all while feeding our imaginations. Time travel, forward or backward, was exciting and educational. While expanding our horizons, we bonded through our shared literary experiences.

As students advanced through elementary school, their attention span grew, and reading circle could last longer. My sixth graders begged to stretch our thirty minutes to forty-five. When I announced it was time to stop, my class often let out a collective groan, accusing me of stopping at the exciting point. But in reality, they enjoyed the books so much that most spots were exciting once we got involved in a story.

Over time, I began creating voices for the main characters so I would not have to break the flow with "Mary said" or "John said." Characters came alive when the voice I used reflected their individuality. Students enjoyed the contrast of the deep lumbering voice of the old sheepdog from *One Hundred and One Dalmatians* when compared with the shrill, irritating whine of the enemy, Cruella de Vil.

More than once, when a substitute would read from our story, my students would request that I reread the passage. "Our sub didn't do voices, and the story wasn't as much fun," they said. One class became so protective of the book we shared in circle that they even requested I hide it whenever a sub was scheduled to teach. They didn't mind if the sub read a different story, but not the special one we were sharing.

Some books I read were of a serious nature, meant to educate and encourage. *The Lady of the Seeing Eye* was one of these. My students were so fascinated with this story we invited a guide dog, Eddie, and his blind master, Marilyn, to our third-floor classroom, and they both became our teachers that day. We witnessed firsthand the close relationship between Eddie and his companion, Marilyn. One-on-one contact with a legally blind person was a first for most of my students, as well as an inspiring lesson that enlarged their worldview.

Other books helped us prepare for field trips. And some were selected to help us explore friendship, kindness, loyalty, and forgiveness. Books enhanced our social studies and science classes. Archeologists and marine biologists "appeared" in our classroom for extended visits, along with medieval knights and one hundred and one Dalmatians.

In a typical year, we shared twelve books aloud, which added up to more than one thousand pages. Often, the first book I read was a biography of Helen Keller. Once students met Helen and learned of the obstacles she overcame to succeed in life, they saw their own lives in a new perspective. Seeing Helen triumph offered new views on their own possibilities.

When we had finished her biography, I modeled a first-person book report for my students. We borrowed Braille books from the local library and experienced "reading" with our fingertips. Next, we viewed the movie *The Miracle Worker*. Each student then selected a biography to read and bring to life in our class.

One student read about Mother Theresa and set a high standard for her classmates when she transformed herself into a Sister of the Missionaries of Charity. With her mom's help and the clever use of blue-striped dish towels, she presented quite a likeness, through her costume, to a real nun. She created an indelible memory of the day "Mother Theresa" visited our class.

During the winter doldrums, I enjoyed spicing things up with humorous books such as *Max and Me and the Time Machine*, an amusing, entertaining story of two boys who used a garage sale time machine to visit the medieval year 1250, Steve as Sir Robert Marshall and Max as his faithful horse at the start of a fierce joust with the Hampshire mauler.

My students enjoyed *Max and Me and the Time Machine* so much that I wrote the authors to share my students' reaction— true enjoyment. The authors graciously responded, and I shared their reply with my class.

November 16, 1989

Dear Ms. Nordstrom,

Thanks so much for y our nice letter about MAX AND ME AND THE TIME MACHINE. It makes us feel really good to hear that your sixth graders enjoyed hearing it read to them!

You mentioned doing more episodes with Max and Steve. We have done one other adventure already, a book titled MAX AND ME AND THE WILD WEST. In it, the boys travel to the Arizona Territory a hundred years ago and get tangled up with Gentleman John Hooten, the Rhyming Robber of the Rockies. But it _is_ about time for us to be thinking of writing _another_ Max and Steve story; and when we do think about it, we're torn between a book set in the future, in ancient Egypt, or in the age of the pirates. So it was very interesting to hear from you that you think ancient Egypt would be a good era. About three years ago we made a trip to Egypt just so we would be better qualified to write about it--and we are fascinated by Egyptian history. If we were faster writers, we would just sit down and dash off all three ideas!

Anyway...thanks for mentioning that you favor Egypt. We value the opinion of someone who has such close contact with the age we're writing for, and your vote may just tip the scales.

For the last year and a half, we've been writing chapter books for 7 to 9 year olds. We've finished two of them; both are space adventures, but with different characters. Now we have a contract to write a sequel to the second space adventure, and that's what we'll be doing until June. We travel quite a bit each year (in fact, at this point we travel pretty much all the time--we don't have a house or a car), and that slows us up a bit.on the writing front. But after we finish this space adventure, we may just sit down and do that next Max and Me.

Again, thanks for writing. We were really glad to hear that your students liked TIME MACHINE!

Sincerely,

Guy Greer & Bob Ruddick

Letter from the authors of Max and Me
and the Time Machine.

After hearing this letter, my class was off and running with the next book report idea. Each student selected a book whose author was still alive, as best as we could determine in those pre-internet days. After reading their book selections, they contacted the authors, sending personal letters that introduced themselves and described their favorite parts of the book. These letters were their book reports, which they then shared with their fellow classmates introducing them to new authors and new books. Any return correspondence was thrilling for all of us to share. Here are eight excerpts from different authors' letters to my students.

Thanks for your letter. It's always a pleasure to hear from my readers and your letter meant a lot to me...Besides, the truth is I'm better at book writing than I am at letter writing.

I sit at my desk every day, unless I'm traveling, and write. Sometimes I feel as if I haven't a single idea in my head. Other times my head is crowded with them.

You help make the immense difficulties of writing books worthwhile.

When I write I take bits and pieces of my own life and the lives of my friends and then I weave it into something that becomes new. I do think that Adam confessed when he did, because he could no longer take deceiving his parents which is the way I used to feel.

Thank you for your nice letter. I'm so glad you enjoyed my book. It's always wonderful for an author to hear from her readers!

It means a great deal to me to know that my book has a special place in your regard and in your sixth grade's response. Knowing that makes me want to start a new book just as soon as possible!

I get my ideas for my stories from lots of places. I remember things that happened when I was growing up. I listen to kids at home and to my students at school. Then I add a *whole lot* of imagination to the ideas they give me. Most of my characters are fiction. They are combinations of people I know. I take the way someone looks and put it together with the way someone else acts. Most of my settings are real places that I know. It took me ten years before a company in New York City decided to publish one of my stories.

Thanks for writing to my father. I'm his son. I have to tell you all some very sad news. My father died recently. He would have appreciated the effort you made in writing and would want to wish you all the very best. Keep reading and thanks again.

When my class now finished a book, they wanted to know more about the person who wrote it. If I had written the author and received a reply, I would share the letter. We were blessed with wonderful authors who were generous in their correspondence.

After reading *The House without a Christmas Tree* to my students, I wrote Gail Rock a letter of appreciation for the wonderful story. Through her book, my students learned much about life in Nebraska during the 1940s and the 1950s. They also begged for more of her books, so I tracked down more titles for them to read. I was delighted when she responded to my letter with a form letter as well as a personal note that she penned on the back. The form letter addressed to Ms. Favreau (my name at the time) and my students, and the personal note addressed to Jeanne follows:

June 25, 1987

Dear Ms. Favreau & Class,

Thank you very much for your nice letter about the "Addie" stories. I'm so glad you enjoyed them.

I get letters from hundreds of young readers, (and their parents and teachers too), so you will understand why I am unable to answer each person individually. However, this letter answers some of the questions I am asked most often.

About me: I am single and have no children, but I have many young friends, including Lisa Lucas, the actress who played "Addie" on television. I love pets, especially cats and dogs, but I travel too often to keep my own. I am not an artist, in fact I can't draw well at all! I have taken some acting classes, but have never worked as an actress. In my writing career I have been a newspaper reporter and movie and television critic as well as a television writer and author of books.

About the books: I have written four books about Addie; "The House Without A Christmas Tree", "The Thanksgiving Treasure", "A Dream for Addie" and "Addie and the King of Hearts", all published in hard cover by Knopf and first published in paperback by Bantam. Dell now is publishing all four books in paperback for those who wish to find them. These stories were all written as television specials first, and the books were written later.

The stories are based on my own childhood in Nebraska in the 1940's and 1950's and are essentially true. Just a few details are changed to make the stories flow more smoothly. Each book took about two months to write. It's hard work, but very rewarding — especially when your letters arrive.

I always loved reading and writing, but never planned to be a writer until I was already out of college and working. I have no plans at this time to write more "Addie" books or TV shows, but it is possible that I may do more someday. At this time I am a television producer/writer and I have several projects in development which I hope will air in the coming months.

Thank you again for your interest and kind remarks.

Sincerely yours,

Gail Rock   *(over)*

Gail Rock
Knopf, Author
201 East 50th Street
New York, New York
10022

Dear Jeanne,

Thank you for your wonderful letter. I'm not sure whether your class received one of these letters from me, as I've recently moved and my mail has been very slow in catching up with me.

I appreciated hearing about your great dog, Channing. Is he/she a golden retriever? She sounds like one. My uncle used to raise them and I thought they were the smartest dogs ever.

Your letter meant a lot to me. Thanks again, and I'm sorry the answer has taken so long.

Love to you and all your students.

Gail Rock

The class letter and the personal note from Gail Rock, respectively.

A select few books I have read out loud to my class only once. *The Incredible Journey* belongs in this group. Three pets make a long trip trying to locate their family. It's a wonderful story with a happy ending. But I made the mistake of finishing it on the last day of school. I knew the ending would tug at my emotions, so I took the book home the night before that last day. I decided if I practiced, I could get through the last chapter without tears. At home, I read the remaining pages aloud four times; maybe five would have been the lucky number.

The next day when I tried to finish reading it to my language arts class, I choked up. My students weren't surprised to see an occasional tear to a touching story, but my reaction to this was much stronger. Saying good-bye to students was often difficult for me. I should have known better than to mix these two emotions—the last day of school and a tender moment from a good book.

Caught between these feelings and unable to read the last few pages, I laid the book down and quietly left the room. While I composed myself in the hall, one of my students finished reading the story for the others. Able to face my class, I returned to find the book completed. Whew.

Later that day, I had lunch duty for all of the fifth graders. When I entered another teacher's room, Brad from my language arts class asked if I would read the last few pages of *The Incredible Journey* while they ate lunch. I smiled and told him I would fetch the book; I suspected I could manage it now.

Returning with the book, I perched on the edge of the teacher's desk and prepared to read the last few pages. Brad leaned forward and scooted the tissue box across the desk, next to me. One of his friends asked, "Why did you move the Kleenex?" Brad replied, "You've never seen her read this book!"

I was pleased, and relieved, to find that the sixth time was the charm.

Over the years I've shared many books with students. Some of their favorites have dealt with triumph over loss, something I suspect they were all too familiar with in their own lives. My one language arts group watched me grapple with it personally through *The Incredible Journey*.

I know I have touched many children through our reading circle. Some of my students might have been difficult to reach any other way.

James was one of these. He started fifth grade with the attitude that he should be in at least seventh grade, a fair assessment based on his academic achievements. His bored demeanor was obvious in most of our classroom activities, the curriculum receiving barely a sigh of tedium from him. James was an intelligent child, but the dull look in his eyes day after day haunted me. One of the most important ingredients in learning is enthusiasm, and James was running two quarts low.

Three weeks into the year, I noticed during reading circle that James had found something that caught his interest. This family of dogs from our book, along with their adventures, captured his attention. *One Hundred and One Dalmatians* is a riveting tale of good and evil. Many students who had seen the Disney video felt they knew the story. But I asked them to be patient and give the written version a chance.

Some students related to the puppies' mother who couldn't keep her directions straight or remember which paw was her left one. The lost dog, brought in as a second mother to help feed the puppies and keep them warm at night, reminded my children that even lost dogs have a chance at finding a home and belonging to a family. Most students agreed the story was not complete without the gentlemanly cocker spaniel that saved the Dalmatian parents when they were lost, cold, and hungry. When I had to stop reading for the day, my students grumbled. They had found the treasure I hoped they would.

Whenever it was reading circle time and I reached for our book, calm settled quickly over my students. I do recall a particular day when James was in my room and the class was slow to settle down. James couldn't wait for the next installment. When his fellow classmates continued to talk, he saw his chances of hearing the story fade. I was not the only one surprised when soft-spoken James piped up and said, "Shhh! She's got her hands on our book!"

> *He has told us that you always have pleasant memories of us and that you long to see us, just as we also long to see you.*
>
> *—1 Thessalonians 3:6b,* NIV

Gotta Laugh

*Clap your hands, all you nations; shout to God
with cries of joy.*

—*Psalm 47:1*, NIV

Tempting as it might be for some teachers to run down the hall, pull out their hair, and scream at the top of their lungs when faced with some of the foolish circumstances that occur in this profession, many of us often try laughter instead as a way to release the pressure. June Henry, a talented elementary teacher and a master of mirth, often focused our laughter in a delightful way that gave us a chance to laugh at ourselves for our more embarrassing blunders. Whenever June got news of a comical situation involving a fellow staff member, she reported the incident to her colleagues through her Wacko of the Week announcement on the elementary staff web site.

At first the Wacko of the Week honored only the staff who taught together in the elementary facility; June posted her announcement of the recipient and the reason for the award on the elementary staff web site. But when the high school building was renovated to include the elementary grades and all the teachers in the system were then located on the same campus, she began posting "wacko" incidents on the all-school web site. The newly expanded pool of readers and recipients included the high school staff, teachers, classroom aids, custodians, and even administrators. Most everyone experienced the humorous side of daily life with June's intermittent publishing of funny tidbits.

While these reports weren't published regularly, any week that contained a new wacko story brought added pleasure and joy, at least to the teachers who were not receiving the honor and trophy. The recipient was expected to display the actual trophy—an old bowling statuette complete with a miniature bowling ball—until a new beneficiary was named. Here is a sampling of activities that merited recognition through this "auspicious" award.

This week's winner of

Wacko of the Week

Goes to:

Connie Kendall for being viciously attacked by the toilet paper holder that jumped out and nearly tore her arm off. You have got to watch those toilet paper holders! Congratulations, Connie, for being the first Wacko of the Week for this year. There will be others.

Trisha Pawlowski for having her car doors frozen shut on Wednesday. It took Steven with all his manly strength (and wisdom) to push the unlock button to get the "frozen" doors open. Congratulations, Trisha!

Rick Reid for nearly setting off the fire alarm while making popcorn for lunch. What is this? A new dish? Popcorn flambé! Congratulations, Rick!

Carolyn Radcliff for trying to steal the school's toilet paper. (*Everyone* knows that you won't get very far stealing toilet paper when it is hanging out of your drawers!) Congratulations, Carolyn! P.S. Carolyn, will you please see the high school year book sponsor? It is something about a picture for the year book.

Brent Sorrell for wearing his sweater inside out for the second time this week. (Yes, Brent, even church counts!) I agree with Donna. I do hope this is not a new trend. Congratulations, Brent! Has the trophy made its way to the latest winner? Brent, let me know if you don't get the trophy!

Brenda Hopkins for saying, "Na-na-na-na-boo-boo" as she waves her letter of retirement in the faces of us poor teachers who are returning next fall. Congratulations, Brenda, for winning the Wacko of the Week (and on your retirement)!

Missy Fisher for identifying herself to her Secret Santa by putting signed Christmas cards in the bag with the presents. Missy, talk to another teacher and she will tell you how the game works. Congratulations, Missy! (John, now is when you pass the trophy to the next recipient. Thank you.)

Edna Campbell for predicting on Wednesday who was going to be absent on Thursday. (Man, is she good!) Congratulations, Edna!

Penny Simpson for being so efficient (or ready to retire) that she sent papers, books, folders, and pencils home yesterday so the students had nothing to write with today. Congratulations, Penny! We all know she could not leave without one last memory! (Does this earn her the Wacko for Life Award?)

Linda Chandler for getting her students to shoplift cigarettes for her on their trip uptown! Congratulations, Linda! (In Linda's defense, she had no idea her students were stealing until they arrived back at school. And more importantly, Linda never smoked.)

Jenna Taylor for locating the missing textbooks which everyone had spent weeks and weeks looking for. She found them in the closet in her room! Congratulations, Jenna!

Deanna Frame for walking in on me while I was brushing my teeth in the primary bathroom. I heard the knock and the key turning in the door, but I was powerless to do anything. The expression on her face was priceless when she saw me there. And then she tried to give me the award. Gotcha! Congratulations, Deanna!

Sandy Carter for putting a book in the microwave and turning it on. I heard melted CDs are not the tastiest treat for lunch. Yes, there was a CD in the book at the time. Congratulations, Sandy!

Carolyn Radcliff (again) for having stubbly legs after shaving them *two* times. I don't know if anyone has ever told you, but it doesn't matter how many times you shave your legs. They will still be stubbly if you don't take the cover off of the razor! Congratulations, Carolyn!

Kelly Powell for walking in the rain this morning with her umbrella inside out over her head as though everything was as it should be. Yes, Kelly, I saw you. You made my day as well as Amy Martin's. We both sat in our cars and watched the whole thing. Congratulations, Kelly!

Dean Somers for giving the morning announcements one day this week. There was only one problem, no one could hear them. Dean pressed the wrong button. Congratulations, Dean! Would the holder of the trophy please pass it to Dean?

Cathy Lewis for being the twisting queen. My source tells me that Cathy was twisting at the sock hop in her classroom where she slid across the floor. Much to her surprise, she had floor burns on her knees. She was even wearing slacks at the time. Way to show flare for your classroom. Congratulations, Cathy!

Greg Smith for making the best coffee using hot water and no coffee. Congratulations, Greg!

Carolyn Radcliff (are you noticing a pattern here?) for leaving her husband at school after a softball game. It appears she couldn't leave school fast enough, because her friend questioned her several times about taking him home, and Carolyn replied, "No, he's going home with Chuck." The poor guy was left at school in the rain with only two cars left in the parking lot. Congratulations, Carolyn!

Melissa Stengel for trying to do a strip tease in the teachers' lunchroom. Luckily, Janie Miller stopped her before things got out of hand! Did you know that Melissa's face can get as red as a red Coke bottle cap? Congratulations, Melissa! Dean or Carolyn, would you please do the honors of awarding Melissa the trophy?

Myra Baxter for trying to feed stapled papers through the top feed of the copy machine. Has Mr. Stanley been training you in the Stanley Syndrome? Congratulations, Myra, on your first time winning such a prestigious award!

And finally, Annie Randolph for the burn marks on her arm when she came to school yesterday. Her excuse was that she was in a hurry and needed to press some wrinkles out of her blouse but didn't have time to take it off first. Congratulations, Annie!

One of the more startling aspects of this award is that it was given to adults who were entrusted with educating, influencing, and caring for the next generation. Some staff felt cautious around those who frequently received this trophy, fearing that they, too, might be awarded this honor just through association, or worse through innocently revealing a similar situation.

Even the elementary principal recognized the value of shared laughter when he encouraged the purveyor of this award to continue to help all of us see and appreciate the humor in our daily lives. Mrs. Henry admitted that, over time, her sources began to dry up as fellow staff said to each other, "I'll tell you my funny story if you promise not to share it with June Henry."

However, humor was not limited to June's wacko publications. Occasionally, communications released through our school intranet site, such as a few gems that follow, also gave us cause to chuckle.

The rumor that senior Aaron Steger is incarcerated is not true…he is ill.

A memo from the principal to the junior and senior high staff arrived April ninth with the subject line "Most Wanted." It read: On Friday the local newspaper ran a picture of me at an ATM saying that the unidentified man pictured had used a stolen card to withdraw 200 dollars and if anyone could identify the man call crime stoppers. People started calling me and I met with the police. The camera and ATM were not synchronized so my picture matched up with the wrong transaction. A retraction is supposed to be in the newspaper today.

A cell phone was taken off the custodial cart during class change. We will be doing a direct connect to see if the student was smart enough to turn off the phone. If not, take the phone and call the office. We will come get the student.

The good news is we do not have to have a fire drill tomorrow unless Mr. Owens does another experiment in his lab and sets it off! We told custodian Charlie Pierce that we wanted to send him off on his last day with a parade and asked the fire trucks to come and escort him into retirement! Thanks for everyone's cooperation and hopefully Mr. Owens will let us know the next time, in advance, that he wants the fire drill on Thursday and not Friday!

The first year in our new building our third grade classes were sharing a Valentine filmstrip. Mrs. Pike had told Mrs. Cohen that she would bring the filmstrip over once her class was finished viewing the film. Mrs. Cohen asked if Mrs. Pike could set it up for her because she wasn't sure how to run a filmstrip projector. So, when Mrs. Pike's class was finished, she pushed the filmstrip projector, all set up, to Mrs. Cohen's room. As Mrs. Pike was leaving her classroom several kids asked, "Where are you going?" Mrs. Pike said, "Oh, I'm taking this filmstrip projector to Mrs. Cohen. She isn't from the "old school" and doesn't know how to work this projector." As Mrs. Pike left the room pushing the filmstrip projector, she overheard one of her kids say, "Oh, I thought Mrs. Cohen had taught at the old school building last year."

Some of you might remember this from last year. One of my little boys came to school on picture day with a button, spool of thread, and a needle and told me his mom wanted me to sew his button on before pictures. Well, I have the same little boy in my class this year. Today he came with a note on his picture packet. "Please make sure he doesn't have a silly smile." Some things you just can't fix."

My second graders write in a journal every morning. They needed to finish this sentence this morning: If I were a teacher….One of my little boys finished it this way: "I would run away." Thought you might enjoy this.

During the first months in the new facility, my students and I were struggling through forty- and fifty-degree days in my room as engineers were fine tuning the heating system. A student in my math class brought this list:

The Top Ten Signs Your Classroom Is Too Cold

10. It takes ten minutes of uncomfortable sitting each morning to defrost your chair.

9. You've been feeling blue lately, but only because that's the color of your complexion.

8. You try to put on a sweater because you're chilled, but it won't fit over the coat you're already wearing.

7. If you don't put your lunch away, it freezes on your desk.

6. Your students are petitioning to get hypothermia listed as a learning disability.

5. Your students are requesting mitten-compatible keyboards for the computer.

4. Every time you pass out worksheets, the students start a fire.

3. You've stopped bringing hot coffee to class because when you do, the steam merges with the cold air and it snows on your desk.

2. The last time you clapped the erasers, they shattered.

1. The custodian was just in to salt and sand the aisles.

Occasionally, my "gotta laugh" became "gotta giggle," especially when student artists would leave drawings on my desk. I truly enjoyed their delightful, often comical, pictures and still have a terrific collection of them in my teaching files. This particular artwork made me reconsider how I must have looked when I was teaching my students.

Portrait drawing by Chelsea Brant Phenis (not an alias).

Shenanigans in the office ramped up one casual Friday when teachers, secretaries, and classroom aids wanted to help the custodian by taking care of the office vacuuming. What would have been a simple task for the custodians took a turn for the humorous as it required four staff members to try cleaning the carpet. One worker carried the vacuum from the storage cabinet, a second one pressed the handle release, another one flipped the switch to the on position, and the fourth one started pushing the machine. But even though these were willing workers, they were not well qualified. No one had bothered to plug in the cord. Somehow they managed to avoid having their picture appear in the yearbook or the incident reported as a wacko of the week.

While e-mails from parents usually involved serious matters, now and then, parents' e-mails could evoke an unexpected giggle. Here's how it started with one of the dads from my sixth-grade class. His son, Charlie, had been goofing off in class, and his grades reflected his lack of interest in and attention at school. Because of pressure at home from his dad, Charlie had been struggling to improve his grades. And his dad was afraid if Charlie didn't change his work habits before junior high school, he never would. So Charlie, his dad, and I met in October to determine a plan of action that would lead to a new attitude. Because Charlie didn't complete his homework, he had little reason to pay attention in class. One idea from the conference we agreed to try was periodic updates on Charlie's grade average. His dad could use e-mail to contact me whenever he needed to be sure Charlie was doing his work, turning it in on time, and telling his dad the truth about his progress.

Charlie's dad and I communicated through e-mail on a regular basis, and by the end of the first semester in January, Charlie had the best grade card he had seen in a long time. In those days, students took their report cards home in envelopes. A parent then signed the envelope before returning it to the teacher.

However, instead of receiving the envelope with a signature, I got an e-mail from Charlie's father.

> Mrs. Nordstrom,
>
> Well, here I go again, I have to beg for your indulgence! We have lost Charlie's envelope for his report card. I think in all the *excitement* we must have reduced it to confetti. Hopefully you can provide us with another.
>
> I also want to say thank you again for taking such an interest in Charlie. Without you we could not have made it. Charlie is so excited about his grades, it almost brings tears to my eyes. Thanks so much.
>
> Keep up the good work. Roger

How wonderful when parents and I got to share joyful emotions and positive outcomes.

Not all parents' notes brought such joy. Some parent communications, like the one a colleague in another school received, pointed out just how extra hard a teacher may have to work to help a child attain those standards established by the state. I doubt the mom who wrote this note took the time to reread it before sending it to school. One can only guess the pressure the recent death in the family had placed on her.

> Dear Mrs. Jones
>
> Ther have been A Death in the Family.
> Scotty took it really heard. Please wash him.
> Also Will you Please help him fill out his Blue Book so he can Know all of his homework.
> Also I lost his time and day for my meeting with you can you Please write it down in his blue book.
>
> Thank You

When tensions from the stress of work built up, the junior high teachers played good-natured pranks on each other. The seventh and eighth-grade science teacher and the eighth-grade

English teacher were masters in this sport. One day during class change, the science teacher made a quick dash to the restroom. The English teacher saw this as an opportunity to play a joke. She gathered her students and quietly slipped over to the restroom where she had her class lean their weight against the door so it was impossible to open. The students were only able to stifle their laughter a few seconds before the science teacher figured out what was happening. Our students enjoyed watching and helping their teachers interact when harmless pranks and laughter were a part of it. The friendship among this staff made a pleasant atmosphere for all of us, students and teachers alike.

Sometimes a funny situation can play out unexpectedly, almost as if the comical circumstance couldn't be avoided. Late one afternoon, for instance, a few teachers were wrapping up their workday with casual conversation in the small teacher's lunchroom. Most of the staff had already left for the day, so it startled the teachers when the loud speaker sparked to life and the principal called out, "Miz Riley? Anybody there?"

Mrs. Riley wasn't there, but the sudden interruption caught the four teachers off guard. They felt dumbstruck and no one answered. Again, the principal called out, a little louder, "Miz Riley?" The staff members, now too embarrassed to speak, stifled their nervous laughter.

And then, after another few seconds, the principal called out using his southern drawl, "Yooooo hooooo. Is Miz Riley there?"

The situation had now escalated to a most uncomfortable level. Nearly rolling on the floor with laughter, the four teachers covered their mouths to smother their reaction. Caught off guard, they now felt embarrassed having let three opportunities to answer pass them by.

The teachers wanted to end this awkward incident without further embarrassment for anyone, including the principal. With hand motions, one teacher directed them to follow her. They moved en mass to the closest stairway and silently crept upstairs to avoid the principal's office, located on the lowest level. The teachers' workroom was in the middle of the second floor, so the teachers sneaked up the stairs to the top floor to avoid discovery. Moving as one without a sound, they eased down the hall to the staircase that led to the parking lot two levels below. They descended quietly, step by step, down two flights of stairs where they eased the door open, headed to their cars, and drove away as quickly as possible.

On special occasions, when teachers were laughing and visiting after school, this incident was described in hilarious detail. And the mention of yoooo hoooo, delivered with the principal's inflection, always brought gales of laughter.

Humor, when used judiciously, can often redirect inappropriate behavior—preventing small infractions from growing into larger problems. In my experience, simple, jocular interventions could diffuse large explosions before they happened.

Take lunchtime with Daphne from my sixth-grade class, for instance. The three sixth-grade classes ate in their individual classrooms because of overcrowding in the lunchroom. The teacher on duty rotated among the three rooms doing her best to keep an eye on the situation. Because the sixth-grade classes were departmentalized, each sixth-grade teacher taught each sixth-grade student at some time during the day, and those same teachers also shared sixth-grade recess and lunch room duty. So we each knew which students were likely to instigate a problem when the teacher was tending another classroom. Daphne was among those students who enjoyed irritating her classmates. They knew it, I knew it, and the other teachers knew it. We never wanted to be too far away from her in these types of situations.

One day during lunch duty, the noise level from my room caught my attention. As I entered the door, I saw Daphne's back so she didn't see me. She was stabbing her green Jell-O salad with gusto. I had seen a simple situation with Daphne escalate before, and I really didn't want a big argument over proper lunchroom etiquette. I temporarily paused in the doorway to consider my options. I chuckled softly as I entered and said, "You don't have to kill it, Daphne. It's already dead." That was all it took. Everyone got a good laugh, Daphne didn't have to feel like she was "in trouble," and I didn't have to engage in a larger problem.

One of my favorite stories came from my friend, Pat, who substituted in my room an entire week while I was attending a meeting one spring. Pat knew my students individually by name and personality, and she was both knowledgeable and qualified to instruct the subject matter. Plus the best part was that she also was very experienced in the classroom. Her teaching style was similar to mine; I felt almost as if I hadn't been gone when I returned and picked up where Pat had left off.

Seth, one of my more challenging students in that class, had enrolled at the school the previous October. He had brought failing grades from his former school and continued that pattern at our school. Throughout recent months, his teachers and the principal had held numerous conferences with Seth's mom. However, he was still failing his academic classes and his behavior had not improved. So I was concerned that in my absence Seth would test Pat's patience the same way he had been testing the junior high staff.

Apparently, Seth was not quite prepared for Pat's qualifications in teaching or her ability to direct a classroom. Most likely, he had planned a whole different set of circumstances knowing he'd have a whole week without me.

Pat liked to involve every student during class discussion. Seth seemed to have a different idea when he arrived in class that Wednesday with his usual attitude of disrespect. But each time she called on Seth, he mumbled, "Un dun't know." Pat tolerated this reply more than a half dozen times that day as Seth made it clear that he was not interested in the discussion nor was he planning on participating in class.

When Pat finally gave the assignment, Seth was not listening. As she finished, he asked her when the homework was due. Without missing a beat, she turned and answered, "Un dun't know," using Seth's inflection.

While the class savored the justice of her reply through controlled laughter, Seth was shocked into silence, a rare occurrence for him in any class. No other teacher had used his own words so effectively on him. Seth recognized, as did his classmates, that he had been bested and silenced by a substitute, no less. Perhaps the best outcome from this interaction was that Seth's insolence diminished during the rest of the week.

Another story came from a teacher whose elementary classroom was next to mine. She found herself in an unexpected situation one day while she was trying to explain to her students that they needed to slow down when going down the hall to the restroom. Starting at the back of her classroom, Mrs. Hemmer demonstrated speed walking by hurrying down the aisle between the student desks. She imitated the speed her students used when dashing to the restrooms.

"When I tell you *walk*, I don't mean like this," Mrs. Hemmer said as she hurried between the desks headed for the front of the room. Near the door, she made a big flourish by turning to head out into the hall. But she went down so fast that no one, not even Mrs. Hemmer, was prepared for the spill she took right in front of her students. Propping herself up on her left elbow, she looked at her students and finished the lesson. "And *this* is why I don't want you using that speed walk down the hall!" Then she collapsed into laughter, still lying on the floor. When her students realized she was not hurt, they joined in the amusement her impromptu lesson had created.

Mrs. Hemmer's ability to laugh at herself left a lasting impression on her students, and temporarily cured the speed walking problem. Even an unintended pratfall proved useful in the hands of a beloved teacher.

Mrs. Arnold, another cherished teacher, also ended up on the floor one day in her high school classroom. This creative, quirky teacher taught family living and used innovative methods to educate her students. However, unbeknownst to her students, Mrs. Arnold had a terrible problem with claustrophobia. This problem rarely affected her teaching. But the students inadvertently became privy to her phobia one day in early March. The whole situation started, innocently enough, with a wig.

Wigs were a fashion trend that Mrs. Arnold wanted to try. She enlisted the help of her colleague and friend, Mrs. Nelson, for this endeavor. After pricing wigs, Mrs. Arnold decided that she and Mrs. Nelson would both need part-time jobs to finance this fashion, and coincidentally, she also learned that the athletic department was hiring ticket takers for the basketball games. If the two of them could earn—and save—this supplemental income, then they could each purchase a wig at the end of basketball season.

When the season ended, they tallied their earnings and headed to the store. Each one selected a wig as close to her hairstyle and natural color as possible. The next school day, Mrs. Arnold arrived sporting her new wig. Things went well during her first class that day. But the tightness of the wig combined with her claustrophobia overpowered her as she was teaching her second period class. Right in the middle of a sentence, she fainted. As she fell to the floor, she also pulled off the wig and held it as far from her head as her arm allowed. That is the position Mrs. Arnold found herself in when she came to seconds later. Her laugh echoed down the hall when she realized what she must have looked like. And her relieved students joined in.

Sometimes we search for humor while other times it finds us. Whenever this humor is well-intentioned and kind, we all benefit.

But the fruit of the Spirit is love, joy, peace, forbearance, kindness, goodness, faithfulness, gentleness and self-control.

—*Galatians 5:22-23a*

Redemption

Restore to me the joy of your salvation and grant me
a willing spirit, to sustain me.

—*Psalm 51:12,* NIV

Feedback from students is more than useful, it's critical, but that doesn't mean it's something you always want to hear. Annie offered feedback on a regular basis when she was in my sixth-grade class. She had an opinion on every aspect of my classroom management and regularly questioned my decisions. Here's a sample of the many questions she asked on a daily basis:

> It's almost time for lunch. Shouldn't we be putting our math away?
>
> Remember our library time is a half hour earlier this week. Isn't it time to leave?
>
> Can we have more silent reading time at the end of the day?
>
> I think we need more time on our projects. Can you extend the due date one week?
>
> Have you decided where we will go on our field trip?

I got so many questions from Annie that I discussed the situation with her mother at parent-teacher conference time in the fall. Her mother told me that Annie did a fair amount of interrogating at home, also. Her mother also understood the frustration this behavior caused in a classroom full of students. During that conference, Annie's mom gave me permission to "sit on Annie" in order to curb her interference.

One of the biggest lessons Annie needed to learn was that my classroom was not a democracy. Her teachers had been honing their teaching skills for years, if not decades, before Annie walked into their classrooms. And although Annie was academically gifted, she failed to acknowledge the reservoir of experience we teachers drew on to educate her and her classmates.

I figured a gentle prodding would help Annie realize that I was not going to let her assume the position of power when I was the teacher. Getting her to understand and accept this concept was a slow process; it was a good thing I was more than her equal when it came to tenacity. Annie held tightly to her stubbornness while I persisted in trying to help her see that I was a competent classroom manager who didn't need her help. I understood the academic curriculum and was capable of teaching it.

By early December, after three months of redirecting Annie's questions and energetic outbursts, I felt I had made no measurable progress. I had corrected her numerous times, met with her mother, and even counseled Annie regularly about what was expected in my class, all to no avail. It was now time for a new approach.

Finally, I decided to give Annie a detention each time she tried to boss me by interrupting me in order to direct the class. I told her that I would give her a warning look first, then I'd pause and allow her to catch her breath and hold her tongue. At that point, if she kept going, I would assign her a detention. I wasn't having any academic problems with Annie, just bossy difficulties. Her constant interference had started to impact my instruction, and most likely, my attitude too.

Annie absolutely did not want a detention, but my resolve to mete out the correction was just as strong. And as difficult as it was for her, she managed to start holding her tongue. I could see it required quite an effort on her part. Growing into this new self-control was not easy for her, but when Annie put her mind to something, she was usually successful. By the end of the semester six weeks later, Annie and I both saw much improvement. Her new behavior was fragile at first, but as Annie practiced self-discipline, it grew stronger.

Each month Annie grew more comfortable with her newly acquired restraint, and eventually, it appeared that her self-discipline required less and less effort on her part, almost becoming second nature. The best way to describe our second semester together came in the form of a Christmas card from Annie the following year when she was in seventh grade. I found the card with homemade chocolate and candy on my desk the day before our Christmas break. The sweets were tasty, but Annie's note was the most lasting and satisfying part for me.

> Mrs. Nordstrom,
>
> I am sure by now that you know how I feel about you, but I'm going to thank you again for making a major difference in my life. Thank you for setting my head on straight, and getting me on the track that I am still following today. I will always remember you for caring!
>
> Love,
>
> Annie

With her talent, there was little question that Annie would be successful in high school—she was an excellent musician, an outstanding scholar, and a model student. One of a teacher's greatest rewards is watching a former student continue to grow, thrive, develop her natural talents, and especially to do the hard work of removing behavioral stumbling blocks.

Once again, when Annie was a junior in high school, I was blessed with a Christmas card:

> Mrs. Nordstrom,
>
> You're not my teacher, and you haven't been for some time, but I still wanted to tell you "thanks!" You taught me so much and I'll never forget it. You were my special teacher

who taught me to be me. Thanks for giving me a boost with my academics because now it's embedded in my mind.

To My All-time Favorite Teacher

Merry Christmas,

Annie

By the time graduation rolled around, Annie had been accepted to college where she would prepare for her future—teaching. She sent me her high school graduation announcement. I sent her a gift of bright yellow towels; and here's the note I received.

Mrs. Nordstrom,

Thank you so much for the towels. They will be a daily reminder to look at the bright side! Thanks for everything you've done for me. I'll try to keep in touch.

Thanks,

Annie

Annie kept that promise. She stayed in touch and eventually substituted in my room when she was between jobs. How satisfying for me to see this story come full circle. This case study from my classroom turned out better than I could have imagined those many years earlier when Annie and I had our "battle of wills" in that sixth-grade classroom.

Cathy, a junior high math student, presented a completely different and much larger challenge. Seventh-grade math seemed to be just one of many trials for Cathy. But the pressure of this class only seemed to intensify all of the other problems she was dealing with on a daily basis. The pressure inside of Cathy exploded one November day in my math class.

Because we studied complex ideas, I needed my students' full attention in class. Math is a building process, rather like a staircase, where each separate stair is required in order to climb to the top. If a student skips two or three steps, confusion and failure are certain to follow. As I guided my class through a mathematical process, I wanted to be sure that they understood each concept before I moved on to the next one.

But when I looked over at Cathy that morning, she was busy writing. Any of my students would have told you that note writing was expressly forbidden in my room, as it was in the other classrooms. But the audacity Cathy displayed by writing directly in front of me, during class instruction, was not something I could ignore. I didn't chose to fight all the battles students presented to me; I overlooked the smaller, inconsequential ones. But this was in my face and Cathy appeared not to care that I saw her ignoring class instruction while she wrote her note.

From previous episodes with other students, I knew better than to make a big deal out of confiscating a note. I simply walked over to Cathy's desk and asked her to give me the paper she was working on. She was so busy concentrating on her message to Susan that I seemed to startle her with my request. I doubt she even heard me approach her desk. (My students often told me that I walked too quietly for them to hear me coming.) I also knew, again from previous experience, not to look at the contents of the note during class. So I slipped the folded paper into my center desk drawer and continued math class.

Was I ever glad that I had waited for a private moment to read this missive. Its contents were so alarming that I immediately showed this note to the principal. I knew Cathy was upset, but I was truly stunned at the depth of her rage.

> Susan,
>
> I Hate Mrs. Nordstrom! I really hate her. I got in trouble because I was making noise in class, disturbing the others. I —— hate her, your (sic) lucky you don't have her. She needs to die. So what ya (sic) doin (sic)? She really, really

needs to die. I'm going to the office and see if I can switch to Mrs. Cox. I don't really know what to talk about exept (sic) for

The note ended abruptly because I interrupted her writing.

Death threats were taken seriously in my school. Later that day, after considering the contents of the note, the principal called Cathy to his office to discuss it. He assigned her three days of out-of-school suspension. He also told Cathy that during that time, she was to reconsider her part in this situation. I was not included in that meeting, but I did spend time that afternoon mentally reviewing Cathy's time in my room. How did I miss the opportunity to help her? How could I have missed noticing this much anger building up in a student under my care? But most importantly, how would I be able to help Cathy when she returned to my room in just three days?

My prayer was that God would step into this situation and guide me because I felt lost. I realized that students often had much more going on in their lives than we teachers could begin to guess. But how did I fail to see Cathy struggling so? Was her anger toward me warranted?

I thought about Cathy at home serving her suspension. What would I have needed if I had been caught in such a devastating (compromising) situation? Definitely forgiveness, understanding, and kindness. But what a tall order! I knew this was beyond my human capacity. So I prayed for both Cathy and me. Somehow we were both going to have to get past this because there was no way the principal would reassign her to another teacher. That would have rewarded her misbehavior. As challenging as this situation looked, I also felt that Cathy and I needed to work our way through the difficulty.

When Cathy returned on the fourth day, I taught math class as usual, and did my best to show Cathy the kindness she needed. I had to put the message she had written out of my mind for fear it would taint my interaction with her. The compassion I showed Cathy came from a higher source. If left only to my own resources, my response would have been much less generous.

Healing took time, but Cathy and I had plenty of time left in that semester. As we worked on math problems, the other problem seemed to slowly fade into the background. Focusing on math provided us with common ground. During the two months remaining in that semester, I felt blessed. A calm settled over us as Cathy and I concentrated on math. I never did come to understand what was at the root of Cathy's pronounced dislike for me. But she worked hard in math and treated me with respect, which was all I really wanted. Our situation improved day by day, and by the end of the semester, I rarely thought about the November incident.

The following school year, Cathy was again assigned to my class, eighth-grade math this time. I never would have guessed in the dark days of the previous November that Cathy would eventually compose another note, this one actually addressed to me. Her communiqué was written on the back of a colorful picture Cathy had drawn for me to display on my file cabinet.

> For Mrs. Nordstrom…The best teacher ever who was the only one to open my eyes and make me realize that I could do anything if I tryed (sic) my best! Thank you, Cathy

Our eighth-grade year together in math was a whole different story than our time in seventh-grade math. And once again, Cathy wrote me a note. She shared this message during our last week of class together. It is gratifying to see just how much some students can grow and mature during junior high school.

> Mrs. Nordstrom,
>
> I think I owe you a really big apology. I am so very sorry about last year's note thing. I realized that you are the best teacher and I'm not just telling you that. You have probably heard that a lot but I really mean it. And you are an *Amazing* person. You are the only teacher who has told

me to keep trying when I get something wrong and the only teacher who had faith in me. Oh, and you are the strongest, smartest woman I have ever met. I have had a very hard life and when I met you my life got 2x easier and better, really even if you don't believe it.

Your student,

Cathy Franklin

P.S. I will really miss you after the final tests.

Left to my own resources, I would never have received these wonderful notes, but God is faithful and answers prayer. Through trying circumstances and prayer, I often find God's blessings once I am given the gift of perspective.

> *"If you forgive anyone's sins, their sins are forgiven; if you do not forgive them, they are not forgiven."*
>
> *—John 20:23,* NIV

Monkey See, Monkey Do

For he will command his angels concerning you to guard you in all your ways.

—Psalm 91:11, NIV

Behavior is infectious in the classroom; peer pressure influences most classroom dynamics for good or bad. The force of peer pressure intensifies in junior high school, a time when students struggle with personal changes: increased responsibility; vast body changes both inside and out; amplified pressure from school, families, and friends; and their push for independence.

One example of this drive for independence, as well as an inclination to challenge authority, happened in my room at the start of a new semester in January with a new batch of eighth graders. Bradley, a leader among his peers, decided he would not participate in the annual field trip to the technology career center. Each year the eighth graders in our district visited this career center. During their sophomore year, our students then were given the choice to attend this school for their final two years of high school.

Most of my students enjoyed field trips, a free school day with no homework, as well as extra time to visit with friends. So I was surprised that Bradley refused to return his permission form. When I asked in class, Bradley boldly announced, "I won't be taking this field trip because I am not interested." I learned that day never to ask for a permission form in front of the whole class. (Who would have thought that would be a problem!) Bradley had decided he wanted a free day from school, and apparently, his folks agreed with him.

I had not experienced this level of audacity from a student before. To me, "You gotta go where you wanna go, and do what you wanna do" were just lyrics from a 1960s John Phillips song.

Not for Bradley; these were words to live by. And it appeared that he had support from his parents to make such choices. Bradley skipped school that day, missing the field trip. At the age of fourteen, he was already taking control of his life.

Student behaviors are not played out in a void. Bradley's best friend and comrade in crime, Jason, was busy studying and learning from his errant friend and mentor. It was two months before the next field trip and the opportunity for Jason to practice his own power play.

A rite of passage before starting high school, the eighth graders could opt for a three-day trip to a large city. However, only half of the students opted to take the trip that year. This time, Bradley brought back all the requisite forms and participated in the trip. Jason was among those who did not go. The teachers who remained behind, along with the three substitutes hired to replace the teachers who traveled with our students, planned projects with important lessons for those three days.

Some students didn't take the trip because of economic reasons. Due to my family's financial circumstances when I was an eighth grader, I would have been a part of the group who stayed home. So I wanted to enrich these students who remained behind with an educational, fun field trip that would only cost them the price of a lunch. Since I taught math and was friends with the firefighters from my town, I scheduled a trip to the firehouse where we could put our math into practice. Before our lesson that day at the firehouse, the students and I had a misconception of how fires were fought. We quickly learned that firefighters do not just pull up to a fire, grab the fire hoses, and aim the nozzles at the fire. The assistant fire chief showed us how the engineer on the fire truck calculates the settings required to maximize water pressure at a fire. Then this assistant fire chief gave my students an opportunity to practice with some different settings using the formula—figuring friction loss on a hose line.

After the firefighters' math lesson, the emergency medical technician (EMT) presented a forty-five-minute class on the math he used in treating accident victims. The fire department members on duty then performed a rescue training lesson on a mock car accident. My students and I witnessed the Jaws of Life as it pried open the crushed car door on the vehicle. We then saw the careful extraction of the volunteer victim from the vehicle. Our firefighter instructor explained the step-by-step techniques he and his buddies used while saving lives.

Following a full morning of instruction at the firehouse, my class and I boarded the school bus for lunch at my favorite sandwich shop. And then, before returning to school, we enjoyed forty-five minutes at the park.

Where was Jason that day? I don't know because he did not return his field trip permission form, and he skipped school on the day of the field trip. Sound familiar? This was Jason's first opportunity to practice Bradley's example. Jason had convinced his mother that our outing was nothing more than a play day—in his words a "stupid field trip." He did not show his mom the letter I had written that accompanied the permission form describing the educational opportunities planned for this outing.

A few days before the field trip, I had even called Jason's mother to ask about his permission form and the accompanying memo. "No, Jason didn't bring anything like that home," she said. "He told me that the field trip was a play day and I didn't feel like it was necessary for him to be there. So I gave him permission to stay home." When I provided details on the learning opportunity the fire department had planned for us, Jason's mom backpedaled and said she would sign the form. But that didn't change Jason's plan; he still skipped school. To the best of my knowledge, there were no follow-up consequences for him, either.

When I checked in at the office upon our return that afternoon, the school secretary told me she had talked to Jason's sister earlier in the day when his sister had run an errand to the office to pick up supplies for a teacher. While the girl was there, the secretary asked her why her brother was absent. The secretary said his sister seemed very uncomfortable with the question, fumbled for an answer, grabbed her supplies, and then hurried from the office.

All things considered, I suspect it was for the best that Jason was absent that day. He had been disrespectful during regular school activities, and I had wondered if Jason would be more disruptive outside the confines of the classroom.

The students who made the field trip and I had a terrific time meeting a great bunch of firefighters and finding out the surprising and challenging ways that math is used to save lives.

I had taken many groups of other students to the firehouse but never before had we done math while there. My teenagers, more skilled in math and calculator use than the elementary students who routinely visited a firehouse, impressed the firefighters. After this field trip when I taught formulas back in the classroom, my students remembered how real people had used real formulas doing real jobs.

This outing was one of the most relaxing field trips I ever had with junior high students. I did not have to correct one single student the entire trip, and my students sincerely appreciated everything the adults had done for them that day. Later in the school year, these students described their trip to the firehouse as their best day in eighth grade. I was thankful that I had made the effort to schedule this field trip.

Two years later, I learned another important lesson, this one from Mark, a seventh grader who moved to our district eight weeks into the semester. At that point, the math class he joined had been with me two months. In our block schedule, this class met every day for a ninety-minute period, double the class time of a traditional schedule. In his previous school, Mark had already been in seventh-grade math for six and a half months. My class had met for the equivalent of four months, and that meant Mark should have been considerably farther along than my students.

However, Mark got off to a rocky start in my room. He was not doing his homework, so it was difficult to know if he understood seventh-grade math skills. Because of his seeming confusion and lack of participation, I arranged a parent-teacher conference during his first week. Never before had I needed to schedule a conference so early in a semester.

Looking for insights into Mark's ability and understanding of math, I asked his mother to describe his experience at his other school. "Well, he struggled some, and he didn't seem interested in finishing his homework," she said. "I know he's smart, and I figured he'd snap out of this slump when we came here." Mark's mom gave me the impression that she would be willing to work with Mark, assuring me that he would do his homework. Mark, who was also at the conference, promised to do his work. But it didn't take many assignments to see that Mark wasn't intending to make good on his promise.

Mark, his mom, and I met twice more over the next couple of months. But by the end of the school year, there was no noticeable improvement in Mark's effort or his achievement in seventh-grade math; he finished the year with an average of 22 percent.

When school resumed in the fall, Mark showed up in my room. Even though he had not passed seventh grade, I now found him in my eighth-grade math class. Once again I would teach him in a ninety-minute class on a daily basis. The first day of class Mark approached me and promised that he was different, and that he was going to pass math this time. I told him I would be glad to help; he only needed to ask when he was struggling. I might as well have saved my breath.

By the end of September, Mark's grade average had fallen apart—again. Lack of interest, lack of motivation, and lack of effort. I didn't know how to change his trajectory and nothing I had tried was working. I never did discover the magic for Mark in my room. When I checked with Mark's other teachers, I found that he wasn't finishing assignments or finding success in their rooms either.

Mostly, Mark concentrated on crafting daily excuses for his missing assignments. His work habits deteriorated so much that he eventually came to class without supplies—no pencil, no paper, no calculator, and no desire. I knew from his mother's evaluation as well as Mark's cumulative record that this behavior had started much earlier in his formal education. However, my efforts to help produced no visible effect.

Mark's demands and disrespect drained my patience. And eventually, even coming without his math homework or his supplies did not satisfy Mark. His next move was to disrupt class through any means possible—mocking teachers and classmates and interrupting class at every opportunity.

Mark's downward spiral intensified throughout that fall, and by November, his problems had escalated to the point that the principal called a conference with all his teachers. Mark's failing grades, combined with his disrespect for authority, prompted the principal to temporarily assign Mark to a remedial school that dealt with behavior problems. For one week, Mark worked one on one with a staff member there who was assigned to help him improve his deteriorating grades and redirect his impertinence.

A week later, Mark returned to our building. I saw him visiting with classmates in the cafeteria before school began that Monday. Yet when it came time for math class, Mark was not in my room. I asked my students if they knew where Mark was; I've found that students were a reliable source on school news before many teachers knew.

"He's withdrawn from math class," Frankie said. "His parents don't like you and had him removed. He won't be coming back."

"Is that true?" I asked, unable to contain my surprise.

"Yup, that's what he's been telling everyone," Frankie answered.

"Where did he go for this block?" I asked.

"He's in the library playing on the computers," Tim offered.

During my next break, I checked in with the principal. "What happened to Mark in math class?" I asked. My principal confirmed the story my students had told me. Mark's parents had complained about my class and my teaching style. To resolve this situation, the principal assigned Mark to the library for the ninety-minute class to work on the computer.

My perspective was this: the principal had grown tired of the trying struggles with Mark's parents and had caved to their pressure. The monkey was off the principal's back, at least for now. And while I was concerned for Mark, I couldn't really complain because the other students in my room were no longer going to have to waste time with Mark's disruptions. Even though the decision was out of my control, I began to feel like we all had let Mark down. I hadn't been consulted about this class placement. I was, after all, only his math teacher. But it would have been a professional courtesy for the principal to at least inform me before I learned of the situation from my students during class.

The library aid was to monitor Mark while he worked on a computer in the library. Whatever played out with Mark's "math class" would not surprise me. I had witnessed his "work ethic" for many months by that time. But Mark was not done educating the principal, fellow classmates, or me even though he was no longer in my class.

It wasn't long before Mark grew tired of being alone during his free time in the library. He began inviting classmates to join him on the computer; anyone who could slip out of class or finagle a pass from the resource teacher to "work" in the library would show up. Tales of his escapades reached me through other students or even fellow staff members, but I had to overlook these reports since I no longer had any involvement where Mark was concerned.

However, Mark's pranks escalated until they eventually involved the eighth-grade social studies teacher. One particular day when Mark's friend joined him, the two of them became so engrossed in their computer activities that they totally lost track of time. When Mark and his friend did not show up for social studies class that afternoon, his teacher called the office and reported them missing.

When a student was reported missing, the office flew into action. Whoever was available—the school counselor, secretaries, or aides—fanned out to search for the missing student. That day, locating these two students took nearly an hour. By the time the students were found and had reported to class, an hour of social studies was gone, and word had reached the principal about Mark and his friend's misconduct. Before social studies class ended, the principal called the teacher and asked that these two students report to the office ASAP. Their teacher called them into the hall to tell them to report to the office and then sent them on their way. She lingered in the hall to see that they followed directions.

As the two boys headed to the principal's office, the teacher overheard Mark instruct his friend. "Once we get to the office, I want you to be quiet," Mark directed. "I know how to handle this principal. So just let me do the talking, and I'll get us out of this." On this point, I had to agree with Mark.

But not all of my lessons on peer pressure were negative. During one of my years teaching junior high, I also was a school tutor. I met regularly with small groups of eighth graders who were struggling to pass math before the school year ended. Initially, I had been assigned just three students per session, but as the weeks passed, my class enrollment increased.

My classroom was a twelve-by-twelve-foot glorified closet with no windows. The entry door to this space didn't even have a window. Tucked into a quiet corner of the building, my students and I had few outside distractions. However, my little space did share a common wall with the kitchen where one of the vent fans was located. After spending time in my little room, students rarely questioned what was for lunch.

One morning in the middle of a tutoring session, the class-room door banged open. My students and I saw Andrew, an eighth grader from another class, standing there with his friend. "See, I told you there was a classroom here with a real teacher in it. This is where I have been getting help with my math. Ask her. She might let you come here too." Andrew's friend stumbled through an awkward request to join my class because, as he said, "I'm having a terrible time in math and I really need help." I explained that I would present the request to the principal and see if he could make the arrangements. Two days later, Andrew's friend was in our tutoring class sorting out his confusion on his eighth-grade math lessons.

I wasn't aware of Andrew's influence with his classmates until I was assigned to monitor a silent, sustained reading class (SSR) later that semester. I was just in my third year of teaching and barely twenty-four years old when I joined Mrs. Becker in that long, long language arts room. Mrs. Becker was not only at the other end of this long classroom, but with more than thirty years' experience, she was also at the other end of the teaching spectrum. The sixty teenagers crammed at tables between us were supposed to read silently—for sixty long minutes. This situation looked more like a formula for disaster than an opportunity for instruction.

What could possibly go wrong here? Lots. Mrs. Becker and I were outnumbered. I hadn't yet mastered the "strict teacher" demeanor. A good many of the students also towered over me, but somehow I held my own.

One day after class, Mrs. Becker and I were discussing our situation and what it took to get sixty adolescents to read silently for an entire hour. She asked me about my background. It didn't take long for me to explain my previous two years of experience—one in junior high and the other one in third grade. Mrs. Becker offered, "Well, considering your limited experience, you really seem to be holding your own. You should be able to make it in this challenging career." I really needed to hear a veteran teacher's vote of confidence.

By what I didn't know at that moment was that God had planted a guardian angel in that SSR class. Andrew, the student from my small math tutorial, had been attending my tutoring sessions long enough to raise his D in math to a B+. I could tell that Andrew appreciated what I had done for him. What I didn't know was how much he was respected by his peers and how these two concepts—the successful tutoring sessions and his role model status—would work for my benefit.

A young teacher, loads of students, and an entire hour of silent reading was more temptation for troublemaking than one student, Stevie, could resist. He just had to test the waters. And he did that one day by creating enough noise to distract the other students. However, I had a difficult time catching him because he stopped making the sounds whenever I got near. Reading time was not productive or relaxing that day as Stevie created his disturbances. Rather than confront Stevie before I knew for sure it was him, I let the problem go that day.

When my students returned for the next class, there was no more trouble from Stevie. Yet I hadn't done anything to correct the problem. I found out from another student a few weeks later that Andrew had sent out the word among his classmates that this new teacher was all right and to leave her alone. I myself never saw any of this message firsthand, but I was happy to be the beneficiary of this kindness.

God sent a variety of messengers to assist me in my classroom. These emissaries came in many different forms and blessed me with guidance and protection. And I was truly thankful for each and every blessing.

Are not all angels ministering spirits sent to serve those who will inherit salvation?

—Hebrew 1:14, NIV

Low Tide

The Lord is good, a refuge in times of trouble. He cares for those who trust in him.

—*Nahum 1:7*, NIV

If the in-service days at the beginning of fall semester portend the type of year that lies ahead, it was looking like this next year was going to be a doozy. We teachers spent the two professional days before school started discussing formative assessments, a.k.a. standardized tests. We were told we would be collecting and using more data now than ever before. The jargon from these meetings reinforced that we had crossed into a different era: contextual, multiple discipline, student friendly, indicators, meta-analysis, data-driven learning, and learning targets, to name a few. Discussing these words was just as boring as it sounded. But the new state mandates that were driving this training would barely register on the slate of changes ahead when compared with what we were about to encounter among this year's crop of students.

I was part of a veteran, dedicated staff. We were classified as highly qualified teachers because of our education levels, years of experience, and effective involvement with the learning process. But being "highly qualified"—an official status required of educators throughout the state—didn't mean any of us would be an equal match for the lack of character we were about to encounter among the students in our junior high classes that year. The five teachers assembled at my table that morning had a grand total of 160 years of conscientious service in the classroom. The consensus in my group was that the administrators were focusing too much on data analysis while classroom discipline was unraveling. Granted, it is important to focus on interpreting the data, but without proper classroom discipline, both student learning and standardized test scores would continue to decline.

My colleagues seated around the table agreed that we were seeing more classroom behavior and discipline problems, less parental involvement, and less student motivation in recent years, all resulting in fewer As accompanied by a steady increase in missing homework assignments.

Our speaker for that workshop informed us that we needed to "adjust instruction in progress" in each of our classrooms. In other words, take our cues from students to gauge whether they were getting the concepts or we were just "talking over their heads." I silently wondered what did this presenter think we *were doing* in our classrooms instead.

At the end of the two workdays, the presenter invited a brand new teacher to describe for us how she would handle a difficult standard selected randomly from the ones we had spent the last two days studying. My problem with this request was not that we were discussing ways to redirect our energy to improve student academic growth; but rather, that an inexperienced twenty-one-year-old rookie—with no hands-on understanding beyond her student-teacher training—was asked to guide the rest of us. This new hire was schooled in theory only; she had zero years of classroom experience and lacked training in any of the academic areas evaluated by the standardized, state-mandated exams. Worse yet, she wouldn't even be teaching any subjects that required state-mandated assessments. And based on her weak response, it also appeared that she was being asked to speak off the cuff. Her answer, delivered with the aid of a microphone so all could hear, was a muddled response that caused those at my table to glance around at each other and groan silently. She didn't grasp the scope of the problems, plain and simple. But the rest of us in-service teachers maintained a polite, courteous demeanor as she gave her response.

During the dispiriting start to that year, something deeper was resonating within me. Here is the note I wrote in the margin of the printed agenda that day: Why don't they just let us teach!

I could have already retired by this time, and many of my colleagues already had. With each passing year, I could see retirement coming into clearer focus because of the increased and sometimes unrealistic curriculum pressures arising from state mandates, the increasing percentage of unruly students, the diminishing classroom time available for instruction, and the negative interference and lack of parental cooperation in support of the teaching mission.

One of my friends, who had already retired, advised me never to leave any job on a sour year. And by early October, I knew from the many disturbing events that had already happened in my classroom this particular year that I would need to teach at least one more year after this one if I were to end my career on a high note. Some of the situations I encountered that year might have been comical, if only they hadn't been such obvious precursors to more serious underlying ills. I had difficulty seeing any humor in these circumstances, given the grave consequences for students who failed to learn, my inability to effect a much-needed course correction among recalcitrant pupils, and the fact that I was trapped in the middle of the chaos and turmoil emanating from situations beyond my realm of influence. My years of experience and willingness to teach seemed insufficient to countermand the lack of character and gumption I encountered in that group of students and the denial and disinterest of many parents.

Take Bobby as a case in point. Even though the weather was fifteen degrees above average that first week in October, I was unprepared to find Bobby in my math class one warm afternoon with his pants completely down around his ankles. "What's wrong, Bobby?" I asked.

"I'm hot!" he said.

"Pull up your pants; you're in class."

Again, Bobby said with more emphasis, "I'm hot!"

"I'll give you a choice. Either pull up your pants or report to the principal's office."

Bobby chose to visit the principal and headed down to his office. Less than five minutes passed before Bobby was back in my room. I was still explaining the lesson when he returned and must admit that I was surprised to see him back so soon.

Unwilling to spend any more class time on this discipline problem, I completed my lesson and quietly called the principal out of student earshot to ask what Bobby was doing back in my room already. The principal assured me that he had spoken with Bobby about proper behavior before sending him back. I explained to my principal that I felt sexually harassed by Bobby's exposure in my classroom. Many of my students—girls and boys, alike—seemed equally upset by his conduct. Then I asked my principal what type of reaction he anticipated from parents of students in my room when students went home and described this situation. I could almost hear the conversation at their dinner tables that evening.

"What happened at school today, Amy?"

"Bobby dropped his pants in math class and just sat there with them down around his ankles. The teacher sent him to the office. He was only gone a few minutes before he was back in class, and it seemed that nothing happened to him."

I felt we owed the other students in my room more than just a "talking to" from the principal.

"Okay," the principal said. "Send Bobby back to the office with his assignment, and I'll have him work here."

Just two days after this incident, Bobby arrived late to math class. This time his pants were unzipped and slung low around his hips. Without even commenting on his lateness or condition, I went straight to the phone and again quietly called the principal. I guess the principal began to see the seriousness of the situation because he arrived a few minutes later and provided Bobby a personal escort to his office. Bobby did not return to class that day. The principal also assigned Bobby an in-school suspension, which kept him from disrupting my class one additional day.

Unless students have already developed a sense of honor or have parents and family who expect them to behave, in-school suspensions in many school districts aren't really much of a deterrent in restraining, much less redirecting, disruptive or unacceptable classroom behavior. The flaw lies mainly in the lack of consequences for students who get in-school suspensions. Their misbehavior, in our school at least, simply meant the students reported to a different location in the building where they were expected to sit and do assigned work. Teachers knew that fewer than 10 percent of suspended students in my school turned in work assigned during an in-school suspension. So while most suspended students did not derive much educational benefit from this disciplinary action, at least the students in the classroom had one less distraction, if only for a short while.

Ironically, teachers paid the biggest price for in-school suspensions. Because suspended students were absent from the classroom, they missed the lessons. To keep these students on track, teachers had to go the extra distance, preparing additional instructional and review work and delivering this to suspended students, who often didn't bother to turn in the work anyway.

While Bobby never dropped his drawers in my classroom again, he still refused to do his work. Moreover, the principal and other teaching staff didn't seem to have much effect on Bobby's work habits or academic performance either. He continued to flunk most of his classes and received numerous detentions. Seven months later, he served another two-day in-school suspension for acting out. Basically, we spent the year with Bobby nickel and diming us over discipline problems and his personal irresponsibility. Teachers I have worked with through the years have used the term "nickel and diming" to refer to lots of small, incessant misbehaviors meant to disrupt—never enough to really go after the troublemakers, but taken as a whole, the cumulative misconduct registers as a huge problem.

Randy Turner, a former education writer, classroom teacher of fourteen years, education blogger, and author of *Let Teachers Teach*, urges parents and the public to take specific actions when faced with the difficulties that arise from the current discipline philosophy in many public schools.

> Back the teachers by showing a backbone and providing discipline in their buildings. When you hear an administrator bragging about how disciplinary statistics are improving, you should always check to see if his or her nose is growing. When statistics improve dramatically, it is usually a sign that definitions have been changed so that many transgressions will not be counted against the total, or that teachers are being bullied into not writing referrals because they will be written up for lack of discipline on their evaluations. At my last school, we were required to have seven classroom referrals (which do not count on the school's discipline statistics) before we could send a student to the principal. We were given a list of things that should be handled in the classroom and that list included many things which only 10 to 15 years ago would have brought an automatic trip to the principal's office. We don't have to have zero tolerance policies, just firm, consistent discipline.[1]

Whatever you allow in September, you'll find much more of that same thing in May but with emboldened embellishments. Let's take my third block math class as an example. This group was my smallest class, only fifteen students. Students who had been struggling in math were assigned to this block in the hopes that, with extra time and attention, together we could improve their skills. But achieving this objective also required that the students themselves cooperate and invest their time, attention, and energy.

In the first nine weeks of school, their grades were pretty low, but that came as no surprise as they had been placed in this smaller class to receive extra help. My biggest disappointment that first semester was their failure to complete their assigned work. During the first grading period, these students averaged nine missing assignments each. That's a lot of missing work, and their grades reflected their lack of interest. With that much missing work, no one was surprised that nearly half of the class received Fs. I was beginning to think that the students had more of a motivation problem than a learning problem.

Failure appeared to be contagious with this particular group of students. No matter how much I tried, they resisted every tactic. They were disengaged, even openly defiant, about learning. I did what I could to reverse this downward spiral, but they appeared to have given up on themselves and were indifferent to any outside help.

Many times that year, the students and I discussed the problems they were experiencing in school. After scoring their homework and then teaching the lesson for the day, I led a discussion on how we could encourage each other. Roy, one of the few students with a passing grade, said, "I think it would help if we all would just complete the assigned work." He made a valid point, but the unmotivated students seemed to bristle at his comment. To turn the conversation in another direction, Jimmy exclaimed, "You aren't teaching us!" Now there's an interesting, self-serving perspective, I thought, but it offered confirmation of the real problem that Roy had identified: students were not accepting responsibility for their own learning. At that point in the semester, Jimmy had already failed to do 50 percent of his assignments.

"No, I don't think we're lacking in instruction," I said. There was no doubting that I had provided thorough instruction and plenty of time for questions. Each day during the lesson, I specifically included how to work the first five problems from their work assignment, which I then left available on the front table for their reference during in-class work time.

Brad, a student who relished trying to intimidate teachers, piled on with his emphatic pronouncement: "My dad wants to come talk to you."

"I'd be glad to meet with your dad," I replied. "I have a few things I want to share." Brad was carrying a 34 percent grade average in my class at that time. Over half of his assignments were missing, and he exhibited a negative, even belligerent, attitude no matter what concepts we were learning in class. A few months earlier, I had met with Brad's dad at a parent-teacher conference but had seen no improvement in Brad's attitude or effort following that meeting. Even so, I was eager to meet with his dad again. I don't think Brad appreciated my willingness to have a conference and provide his dad with additional facts about Brad's disrespectful attitude, poor grades, and lousy work habits. He seemed to think about my reply and, surprisingly, quieted down.

Some students patiently wait with vigilance in the hope they'll catch their teacher making an error. I suspect that was Brad's plan. For the rest of that classroom period, he looked more hopeful during class and appeared to listen more carefully than normal.

During class discussions, I tried to help students see new ways to increase their knowledge as well as their grade averages. Math can feel like a foreign language with all of the terminology required, so students in my class prepared vocabulary cards of the terms they needed to know. They had already used some of the words in previous math classes, so some terms weren't actually new. However, they were learning enough new terms mixed in with the familiar ones that it could be quite confusing. These vocabulary cards served many functions: a good review and reminder of the meaning of the terms; a useful reference tool for homework and tests; a way to practice learning by preparing and then using the cards to study; and a way to improve their grade averages, since one-third of their grade was based on these cards. Any students who wanted to raise their grade would simply need to write each word on the front of an index card and its definition on the back. These words were assigned a few at a time throughout the year with class time provided to complete them.

Preparing vocabulary cards was a rote-level assignment, a basic style of learning that mostly required a time commitment from my students. I graded the cards eight times in a nine-week session, and any student who made these cards and brought them to class would receive a 100 percent in the grade book each time we checked them. Students who needed a boost in their grade average could do just that by completing this simple assignment.

Brad, however, had received eight zeroes, sacrificing a total of eight hundred points for vocabulary cards in that nine-week grading period simply because he had refused to invest his time in completing this task. But sadly, he was not alone. Failing to do easy jobs had been infectious, particularly in this group. Only one-fourth of this class completed their vocabulary cards as directed, and that one-fourth received a grade of one hundred percent each of the eight times I scored these during the grading period. Conversely, the other three-quarters repeatedly chose to get a 0 percent because they elected not to complete the assignment. My intention was to help them raise their math averages by giving so much credit for simply finishing an assignment that mostly required a time commitment, but an assignment that also offered the additional benefit of a useful resource for tests and homework. They, however, seemed to have no intentions of applying themselves.

As I explained rote learning that day, I could see that my students were not familiar with the term. So, I spelled r-o-t-e for my class as I explained the concept. But for this discussion, Brad had decided he would rather argue than learn. And after my explanation, Brad added, "No, you're wrong. *Rote* is spelled w-r-o-t-e." Their class average that day for the simple rote-level assignment was 38 percent. Sometimes it's best to give the assignment quietly and firmly, and allow those who were ready to begin their homework.

A sad postscript on Brad is that he took his attitude of disrespect with him into the next school year. During the first week of that new year, Brad received a detention from his social studies teacher. The reason, as stated on the discipline report, was chronic failure to return homework. The year dragged on with Brad getting into trouble regularly, and it finally ended for Brad when he received a three-day suspension with a recommendation for expulsion because of drugs.

Another student in Brad's class acted as if she were serious about doing her homework. The first time we checked vocabulary cards, however, I found the following definition on the top of her stack of three-by-five-inch index cards.

> Algebra: Rama de las matematicas que involucre expresiones con variables

However, this student did not speak Spanish. She had simply copied from the wrong side of the glossary at the back of the textbook and hadn't bothered to check her work, much less wonder about the lack of meaning for her. I would have found copying the definition in Spanish rather than in English to be much more laborious. So I wondered why she didn't find that same challenge when she prepared that index card. Could she really be so removed from the process that she hadn't noticed?

Day by day, I began to understand why teachers would want to leave the classroom and seek employment in another line of work. An article in Reuters reported that "half of new US teachers are likely to quit within the first five years because of poor working conditions and low salaries."[2]

The students, parents, teachers, administrators, and even the courts must stand together in this effort to improve character and instill responsibility in the formative years of our pupils' lives.

Otherwise, we can expect no improvement in their behavior or their test scores as they ascend to each new grade.

As much as I enjoyed teaching, I questioned my effectiveness many times that year. I examined my teaching techniques regularly throughout that entire year and kept experimenting with different approaches in an effort to engage the students and spark their interest in math. Very few of my efforts seemed to ripple the surfaces of their distracted minds.

Much to my dismay, the two-day in-service workshop held at the beginning of the year was proving to be a reliable portent of things to come. By early December, I was so discouraged with my lack of progress with some students that I wrote the following journal entry in an attempt to sort out what was working from what was not working.

> Cheating, lying, laziness, and open defiance are in my world every single day this year.
>
> I've lowered my standards drastically in my career. In the beginning and throughout my years, I evaluated my success by the progress I could see in my students. I looked for improvement in their grades and their efforts to complete assignments. Was I giving my best and reaching more students each year?
>
> But my new standards? If everyone keeps their pants on and no one is injured, then it's a good day in my room. Sad that these would be the criteria for a successful day.
>
> Throughout my years I've relied on God's evaluation to determine success. However, I have to wonder: Does God see me doing my best to serve Him and my students? Is it getting harder for me to judge what a good day looks like?
>
> Circumstances have changed so much since I began teaching. I may well invest more time and attention dealing with discipline in one day now than I previously did in a month. I can't imagine how this affects instruction time and instruction quality.

If my class is a microcosm of the larger region, our state, or even the country, we're facing dire times. With each new grading period, my eighth graders lose more ground. At the beginning of the semester, 75% of my students were passing math, but now only 45% of my class is passing.

I'm afraid there are many causes to this decline. We seem to be losing our accountability as a society. In the discipline arena, we used to grant power to parents, teachers, administrators, and even the court system. Now we give young people the decision-making power over their every choice.

Don't want to finish your year in band? No problem. We'll let you drop it and then we'll place you in another study hall.

Don't like that teacher? No problem. We'll let you transfer to another class. Which teacher would you rather have?

Don't want to complete your homework? No problem. You can come to class any day without it and no one will say anything.

Don't feel like being to school on time? No problem. We wouldn't want you to be uncomfortable or pressured.

Normally discipline is just a small part of my job, but lately it's taking a larger amount of my time. And that is difficult to ignore. Just today I tallied the number of times I had to stop and correct a student or redirect the class. I found that I had to deal with a major discipline issue every six minutes during my instruction time. This can't be helping our students learn!

Before Christmas break, I asked my students why they weren't learning or producing homework. Robbie replied, "Well, you missed a few days this year." Did such weak excuses work at home, I wondered. Obviously, neither Robbie's fellow classmates nor I believed his feeble suggestion. Never mind that a well-qualified substitute teacher, someone I had worked with many times in the past, had taught my students the few days that I was absent, covering with great skill the same material I would have presented to this class.

When circumstances in my classroom had not improved by January, the students and I discussed the repercussions of failing to do the assignments. One idea that came from that discussion was that there were no meaningful consequences for not doing homework. I asked if they knew anyone who had repeated a grade because of failing grades. They did not. Nor could I name anyone retained in junior high for more years than these students had been in school. In fact, I could think of several students among their peers who had been "passed" on to the next grade despite failing grades. So that kind of accountability was not a part of their experience and offered no deterrent to their flagrant disregard of assignments and honest effort.

We as a society can't really expect a different outcome when students know there are no personal consequences for their deliberate misbehavior. One student summed it up well when he said, "We all know nothing serious will happen if we don't do our work, so we don't do it." Our students were watching and learning. Were we teaching them good life lessons? Were we preparing them for successful futures?

The next grading period brought me more discouragement—this class scored even lower grades in February than they had in December, and irrespective of Robbie's foolish comment about my earlier absence, I had not missed school a single day for more than two months. And to add to my low spirits, Robbie, who wanted to blame anyone but himself for his lack of work and resulting poor grades, was also caught cheating before the end of February. He had done only half of his assigned work and when the students exchanged papers to grade each other's work, Robbie asked a neighbor to lie and give him an A. Robbie didn't hold himself accountable for his behavior, and he didn't want anyone else to hold him accountable either. But he was willing to ask classmates to lie for him.

Karrie, another student in this class, was also caught cheating, but her only concern was making sure that the other student who had been cheating with her also was caught and brought to justice. Both Karrie and her accomplice received zeroes, of course. But unlike the other student, Karrie displayed no shame, embarrassment, or remorse about her cheating ways.

Failure was again a topic of discussion in my class in March when someone remarked, "I didn't think a D was a failing grade." Part of me had to agree silently because students in this classroom no longer considered even an F to be a failing grade that carried repercussions. I was saddened by my students' collective attitude toward grades and learning, and was disheartened and worried about their futures.

So much had changed in our culture's attitude toward learning since I had first taught junior high math. In those bygone days, receiving an F was an unforgiveable mark in most homes, homes where parents expected and demanded that their children complete their school assignments and master the material to the best of their abilities. Had the parents of these current students really lost sight of the value, not to mention the necessity, of a good education?

I clearly recalled two seventh graders from my early years teaching junior high. Both had flunked math and were required to take it again as eighth graders while simultaneously taking the required math courses for their eighth-grade year. As their teacher in both classes, I knew the message got through to them and they took this lesson seriously. Much to their delight and mine, both students passed the proficiency test at the end of eighth grade, demonstrating they had mastered two grade levels of material in one year. I saw improvement beyond their understanding of math, which included better self-images, more personal satisfaction, and renewed pride of effort. These characteristics would have been difficult to achieve in any other way.

Before this defiant class and I finished the discussion on failing grades that discouraging March day, I asked what would happen in the workplace for below average job performance. Would the boss tolerate that very long? Did they think I would keep my job if I didn't do what was expected or if I showed up late on a regular basis? Eventually, work would become their school, a lifelong place of assignments and deadlines. I don't think they wanted to consider this idea seriously. These students didn't want personal responsibility to encroach on their "do whatever you want" approach to life.

By late winter, my year continued on the downward spiral that had started back in September. One of my math students challenged me in class—boldly, loudly, and repeatedly. "You are trying to control my learning," he blurted out. "Yes," I answered, "I guess you could say that I am. That is my job. I'm supposed to teach you the concepts and then clear up any learning problems or questions you may still have." My answer, however, did not help him progress that day. He kept complaining and finally wrangled a pass to see the principal as a ploy to get out of doing math. After he left, our class settled down, thankfully, and the other students had a chance to start their homework in peace.

In the midst of this challenging winter, the teachers attended another in-service training. This could have been an uplifting day for the staff. I certainly needed a tonic of encouragement that year. But instead, the first handout we received at the meeting read:

ARE OUR STUDENTS:

Critical thinkers?

Problem solvers?

Good communicators?

Good collaborators?

Information and technology literate?

Flexible and adaptable?

Innovative and creative?

Globally competent?

Environmentally literate?

I'd like to focus on these higher ideals in class, I thought to myself, but my classroom situation was much more basic—I was simply trying to get junior high students to learn the eighth-grade math requirements, while most lacked rudimentary knowledge of basic multiplication tables.

My students and I were struggling with difficult concepts in junior high math: linear equations, hierarchy, and algebra, to name a few. Yet, many of them had not even mastered the prerequisites of multiplication and long division. And here I sat listening about ways to ensure that our students were "globally competent"—whatever that meant and however we were supposed to assess them for this proficiency.

I wondered how I was ever going to teach these kids higher math concepts when they hadn't memorized their multiplication tables from third grade. Schools in general are not equipped to help junior high students master proficiency math skills taught in the primary or elementary grades. That's one reason it is so important to weigh carefully the decision of whether a failing student is better served by being passed to the next grade level or by being retained one year.

In yet another discussion with this recalcitrant class, I assured them that if textbooks alone were capable of communicating math, then no one would need math teachers—anyone could get their hands on a math book, study it, and pass the proficiency test. But I have found that most subjects, and particularly math, don't work that way. My students who wanted to learn will tell you that math is much easier when a teacher explains it. And that was the case for me, too, when I was a student.

One day in the intervention class, I brought math games and prizes to encourage these students who continued to struggle in their regular math classes. The games were a fun way to reinforce the concepts we had been studying. But after all of this fun with games, chocolates, and classroom supplies as rewards, this particular group reverted to their usual inappropriate, rude, and quarrelsome behaviors. I would simply have to think up more ways to try to engage them.

While handling these challenging academic situations, I was also called to handle many dress code violations with these students. One day in February, for instance, I had a student who needed to keep her sweatshirt zipped up because of the low-cut blouse she was wearing. She had already been sent to the office by another teacher that day and was then told by the principal to keep her sweatshirt closed. Yet, I had to waste more class time on this situation, and finally, I sent her back to the office because she was so determined to keep her sweatshirt open and show off her cleavage.

Study hall that year was an extra challenge. Students who didn't want to work encouraged their classmates to join them and goof off during study time. Stephanie, an eighth grader who was struggling in most of her academic subjects, seemed happy to bring her own entertainment instead of her assignments. One day when I approached Stephanie to help with her homework, I found her drawing pictures. When I asked if I could help her with her assignments, she made the bold-faced claim that she had no homework. Even if Stephanie had completed her assignments, study hall rules required that students bring extra reading material. When I asked Stephanie about having a book to read, she shot back, "I don't like to read. I have overdue books in the library, so I'm not allowed to check out anymore. And since this school doesn't have art, I'm drawing on my own." I encouraged Stephanie to find some homework to complete as she handed over the artwork.

But Stephanie did have a valid point. Financial limitations in the school's budget had eliminated most of the art classes our school had offered in recent years. Many students had enjoyed art, but creative art classes were no longer available at the middle school. I happened to agree with Stephanie—our students, especially talented artists like Stephanie, did need art classes. But study hall was not the right time or the right place for her to make her position known. Learning is a personal choice, and I couldn't force Stephanie to learn. The most I could do was to take away her drawing supplies and encourage her to study. Because of her stubbornness, I was unable to help Stephanie with her homework. Study hall proved to be a waste of time, at least in her world.

On the other end of the spectrum were students who received auxiliary tutoring and often became dependent on that help. Occasionally, I had witnessed them abusing the situation and taking advantage of the assistance meant to improve their skills. Alisa comes to mind. She didn't like completing her assignments so she postponed doing her work as long as possible. This meant that she would be rushing during the last week of the grading period, trying to get her missing assignments from me and then hurrying to the tutoring teacher's room to dash out as many of these as time allowed.

I recall a particular grading period when Alisa skidded into my room two minutes before the final bell on the last day of the grading period and handed me a thick stack of overdue homework. She had made two other stops that day with papers for her English and social studies teachers also. Perhaps Alisa thought I wouldn't bother to score the pages since she was so late, and she had so many. I sat down at my desk to see how many missing assignments I could fill in with scores in the grade book. I found an unusual and unexpected response on the second assignment I graded. When asked to describe the type of situation where one might need to calculate an average in math, Alisa wrote on her paper, "Check teacher's notes."

Check teacher's notes? I reread Alisa's answer. Now what did she mean by that? I reached for my teacher's manual to reread the question. And there it was. The manual did not have enough space to write the entire answer under the question, so it directed the reader to consult the teacher notes where extra space was allotted for detailed examples. Alisa had made a last-ditch effort to salvage her failing math grade. I understood her panic. What I didn't understand—or endorse—was why the resource teacher had let her use the teacher's manual that included all of the answers, often listed with the instructional notes. This educator was entrusted with helping Alisa, encouraging her through extra explanations, and setting a standard. It appeared that Alisa had simply copied all of the answers from the teacher's manual and expected full credit.

Then there was Benny. Teachers are expected to set the tone of a class by treating all students with respect. But the disrespect from some students continues to grow throughout the year, adding to the challenges a teacher faces daily in the classroom. If I had dared to mirror Benny's total disregard and disrespect for me, the consequences would not have been good for me. But no matter what students do, teachers and other adults are still expected to control their emotions, take the high road, and model good behavior. As trying as all this can sometimes be for teachers confronted with the upsetting anger of persistently rude, angry, or disrespectful teenagers, we teachers are the adults, the role models, and the authority figures. We must return disrespectful behavior with composure, unruffled diplomacy, and understanding. Sometimes that can be a very tall order. And I often longed for the dynamics of my early days of teaching when respectful discourse guided both sides of a teacher-student exchange. I can't recall a student like Benny from the early years of my career.

Benny was one of my biggest challenges, and the difficulties I had with him only increased as the year progressed. Each time he was in my room, he presented a new trial for me as well as for his fellow students. Benny didn't reserve his disruptive behavior for my room alone; he usually had enough impertinence to spread throughout the day. My biggest concern, however, was the time when he was in my room. I had to be ready to curtail and redirect his disruptive behavior as well as protect the other students from the chaos he tried to create.

When Benny first walked into my classroom at the beginning of the year, he created such a commotion that I had to rearrange the seating chart after only four days. Never before had I resorted to this tactic during the first month of school. On one particular day, Benny used excessive, prolonged, derisive laughter to create a disturbance during study time. He found this so effective that he repeated it for two more days. The interventions I tried were to no avail, and while it was difficult for me to deal with his insolence for one class period, I pitied his fellow classmates who had to tolerate his rudeness class after class all day long. At least I could find relief from Benny's insubordination and bullying when he was not in my room, but his fellow students had to pick up the tab for his disruptive behavior in every class they shared with him.

Another morning, Benny disrupted the class for forty-five minutes while he made guttural sounds in his throat. I was on the other side of the room and I could still hear his noises. I felt truly sorry for his neighbors. Again, I tried to intervene and stop this behavior, but Benny denied hearing any sound. I know his fellow class members were annoyed because even they eventually began pleading with him to quit.

The principal had warned me in advance of Benny's open defiance and had cautioned me to handle him and his attention-getting disruptions carefully. Okay, I wanted to say, but how about the innocent students he was affecting? As a society, we have minimized the power teachers have to maintain a classroom environment that is conducive to learning. We have also hamstrung diligent students who must endure these disruptions.

In trying to make my classroom a safe learning haven for Benny and his classmates, I used many different approaches: verbal corrections, seating changes, assigned detentions, office referrals, and just ignoring his unruly behavior. Not one of these was more than marginally successful.

During one of Benny's bossy tirades telling me how to teach my class, a mother came to our room to collect homework for her sick child. Even that didn't slow Benny down. He was not the least bit embarrassed to have an outsider witness his outburst. Before the mom left, she whispered in my ear, "Some people may think teachers are paid too much, but they haven't seen what you have to work with on a daily basis."

One of my colleagues helped me see that other teachers were also struggling with student behavior problems. He summed it up best after he returned from a few days of vacation. "I'm going to be positive about my job," he announced to his fellow teachers on the first morning back. But at lunch, just two days later, this same colleague announced, "I hate this —— place!" Yep, we all understood what he meant.

On a Thursday in March, I wrote in my journal, "I could list fifteen major problems from today alone. Ugh." As I numbered those students one by one, I wondered how I would outlast them and the mischief they were plotting for the fourth nine-week grading period.

My principal discovered one of their shenanigans in mid-April when it came to his attention that one of my students had created a Facebook page to ask students to comment on my class. He did his best to ferret out the originator of this site and deliver fair warning if the site was maintained. He explained that the originator could be charged with slander. And if a lawyer had to be involved, then this situation might be heard in criminal or civil court. The site was gone before midnight that day; no further action was required. And I was grateful for his help.

Another student, who had earned in-school suspension, needed some assignments to keep him busy, and hopefully to improve his grade. I received a request from the principal to send missing assignments for him to do. I was also to report to the office during my preparation time to make sure this student understood his math lessons. Well, now, let me see: This student had failed to turn in sixty-two math assignments in eight months of school. Yes, perhaps I ought to drop everything I needed to do for all my other students during my prep time and instead rush right down to the office to see if I could sort out the supposed confusion this defiant learner had about math concepts.

The end of the school year came a little late for one of my troubled students I was trying to redirect that year. Lee got to finish his year with an in-school suspension during the last six days for his outright insubordination in defying the principal's direct orders. To me, this just typified the situation the teachers and principal had been struggling with, yet hadn't been able to correct that year.

Somehow I managed to finish the spring semester, and my final journal entry at the close of school summed up that challenging year.

> I feel like I've been battered and bruised this year. Some days I wondered if it would ever end. It did today—as far as the students are concerned anyway. I didn't quit trying, but I am tired and ready for summer break.

But before I closed my classroom for the year, I found this note tucked under my teacher's math manual, written by a graduating eighth-grade student.

> Dear Mrs. Nordstrom,
>
> I would just like to tell/thank you how much you mean to me! You make me love math days. You amaze me in

everything you do. Really you are my role-model. If I could choose to be like anyone in the world it would be you! You stand-up (sic) for what you believe in and take action when you see wrong doing. You are always in an (sic) happy mood and have a good attitude. The way that you teach is absolutely amazing. I know that you will do great in English next year. I know that nobody is perfect but in my eyes your (sic) perfect! Great job this year and Thank-You.

Love,

April

April, you may be the best reason I will return this coming August refreshed and ready to teach again.

Now faith is the substance of things hoped for, the evidence of things not seen.

—*Hebrews 11:1*, KJV

You Reap What You Sow

One person gives freely, yet gains even more; another with-
holds unduly, but comes to poverty.

—*Proverbs 11:24*, NIV

My teaching career spanned four decades and four states and included third- through ninth-grade students, not to mention the college classes I taught. More than 1,500 middle school students alone sat in my classroom at one time or another. In addition, most students I taught were ready to transition to the next level of their education, either moving from elementary school to junior high, or moving up from junior high school to senior high. About half the time my students transferred to another school in the system, but the rest of the time they simply changed status within the same building. Because my students were entering a new phase in their education, my main focus during the final nine weeks of school was to prepare them for this transition.

For many years, I taught eighth-grade language arts. This subject provided a wonderful opportunity to prepare my students for their upcoming transition. I required my English classes to write journals, and most of their entries described favorite sports, daily activities, special events, and life in general. But, occasionally, I asked students to reflect on a specific topic from our class discussion. So by the last nine weeks of the year, all my students had running commentaries of their activities and thoughts from their eighth-grade experience, albeit at varying levels of introspection and sophistication. One of my goals for journaling was for students to gain perspective on their skill development throughout the year. Could they see a difference between August and May in how well they wrote? Were they clearer—and more mature—in expressing their thoughts? Were they using the knowledge they had learned in eighth grade?

English composition rules were dry when I had studied them years earlier. I knew these rules weren't any more exciting for my eighth graders than they had been for me. I also knew how important and fundamental these skills were for high school success, and my objective was to help my students learn English grammar and use it correctly in their compositions.

They had applied some of these new techniques in our first research paper on World War II earlier in the year. By May, my students had learned, and many had even mastered, more complex rules of grammar, organization, and composition. I planned another project that would incorporate these recently acquired skills while also improving their critical thinking and editing abilities.

Whenever I began a multipart project like a research paper, one of my first concerns was motivating my students. Sparking interest and imagination was a focal point of my preparation. If my students didn't care about the subject matter, then my job—and theirs—got harder. Sometimes I used a video with an accompanying vocabulary list to introduce the topic and establish a starting point.

One video, *Music of the Heart*, related the true story of a school teacher's struggle to share the beauty of music with underprivileged students living in East Harlem. Another movie, *Disney's the Kid*, helped my students see how missed opportunities and individual choices affect the future.

There were, however, students I didn't reach and didn't inspire no matter what introduction I used. Still, I tried a variety of approaches in order to engage as many of my students as possible.

As the end of the year approached and summer loomed just over the horizon, both my students and I needed an extra shot in the arm to build energy and enthusiasm for the upcoming assignment. Holding students' attention and interest as summer daydreams tugged at their thoughts was challenging enough; I didn't need bored, distracted students looking for opportunities to cause trouble in my room. So I worked to create an assignment for the last nine weeks that would capture their imaginations, draw upon the skills they had developed during the semester, and tap into their interests.

To spark student interest in the final project of the year, I used two in-class presentations. The first was to have each student demonstrate a favorite hobby, a special interest, or a sports skill. I modeled a how-to speech to help them visualize this presentation. I liked cooking so I stirred up one of my favorite foods in class. My presentation would teach them the essentials of giving a how-to speech as well as foreshadow our final language arts project, researching an American who had enriched our way of life.

My second presentation would be a model for their last project, a legacy report. I had high hopes that this research project would also inspire my students to consider their academic and personal choices as they prepared to enter high school.

For my model how-to speech demonstration, I became Mrs. Ruth Wakefield. I dressed in the style of the 1930s because that was the decade that Ruth and her husband bought a Cape Cod-style toll house inn near Whitman, Massachusetts. A trained dietician, Mrs. Wakefield used her skills to prepare meals for the guests staying at the inn, but she was best known for the tasty desserts she baked. So I brought my baking supplies and demonstrated a how-to speech for my students.

While I mixed my ingredients, I shared Mrs. Wakefield's story of how she was preparing her famous chocolate butter drop do cookies one afternoon at the inn. Partway through her baking, Ruth Wakefield discovered she was out of baker's chocolate. Searching through her cupboard, she found a block of semi-sweet chocolate Andrew Nestlé had given her when he passed through the inn a few days earlier. Ruth decided to chop up this large piece of chocolate and use it as a substitute for the usual baker's cocoa thinking it would melt, permeate the cookie, and create the infused chocolate of her original chocolate butter drop do cookies.

But the chocolate she added did not melt as she had expected; the chocolate pieces simply became soft and gooey. That evening, Mrs. Wakefield served the experimental cookies to her guests who raved about how much they enjoyed this new sensation. And before long, Mrs. Wakefield's new Chocolate Crunch Cookie was the most requested dessert item at the inn.

The chocolate block that Andrew Nestlé had shared with Ruth Wakefield was an important part of her Chocolate Crunch Cookie. But because this dessert was so popular, Ruth found she was spending too much time and too much energy chopping the chocolate she needed to bake so many cookies. Eventually, she made arrangements with the Nestlé Chocolate Company to produce these small chocolate bits for her cookies. Then, in 1939, her recipe was featured on a Betty Crocker radio series,[1] where it created a large demand for the Nestlé chocolate morsels. Ultimately, the Nestlé Chocolate Company printed Mrs. Wakefield's cookie recipe on every package of their Nestlé's Toll House Chocolate Morsels—where we still find Mrs. Wakefield's recipe today. And in payment for the company's use of her recipe, Ruth Wakefield received a lifetime supply of the tasty chocolate morsels.

Ruth Wakefield became an accidental inventor of the most popular cookie ever, I told my students. In fact, by 2013, there were about "7 billion chocolate chip cookies eaten in the United States every year, with about 50% of those [being] homemade cookies" according to the web site http://www.todayifoundit.com (accessed on June 18, 2014).

Before I removed my apron, put away my baking tools, and passed out the chocolate chip cookies I made the night before, I took questions from my class. One student was so engaged in this story that he said, "Could I please have Mrs. Nordstrom back? I need to ask her a question." Sweet success! My students could now visualize how fun and imaginative their own how-to speeches could be.

My class had practiced public speaking two earlier times that year. The previous fall, each student had shared a favorite selection from their "Celebrating Me" project. Then in March, we created brackets to choose one favorite poem from the class's favorites. We drew names to start the first round of poems; we usually began with sixteen to twenty poems. After the first round, we narrowed the pool by half, then by half again until we eventually voted a class winner. By that point, they had recited many wonderful and often funny poems.

The last opportunity to practice their speech-making skills before their final project occurred in April when students presented their how-to speeches. Students spoke on a variety of topics from throwing a fastball to making puppy chow (which was really people food), and even creating "dirt," a tasty dessert with gummy worms hidden inside. This assignment was a favorite because we got to eat so many treats in class.

The end of junior high school was a wonderful opportunity for students to pause and reflect on what they had learned, what they dreamed for their futures, and what they needed to do in high school to move toward their personal goals. If my eighth graders were not pleased with their personal progress at the end of junior high school, that would be a perfect time for them to change directions. Perhaps studying the legacy of inspirational people could help my students see how hardships and difficulties had shaped and enriched other people's lives. Then my students could share their newfound knowledge and appreciation of notable Americans with their classmates, providing inspiration for my students to think about when considering their own futures. Thus, the legacy project was born.

To help my students understand what I was asking them to do for this final project, I chose Minnie Pearl for my influential person and prepared a legacy report on her life. Born Sarah Ophelia Colley in Hickman County, Tennessee, Cousin Minnie had a wonderful way of making people laugh. In her more than fifty-year career at the *Grand Ole Opry*, she delighted audiences everywhere. "Pearl's humor was often self-deprecating, and involved her unsuccessful attempts at attracting the attention of a 'feller' and, in particular in later years her age. She also told monologues involving her comical, 'ne'er-do-well' relatives..."[2] Her comedy also revealed the genuine affection she had for others. Since Minnie had passed away many years before my students were born, I was sure most of them were unaware of her story.

Dressed as Minnie Pearl, my entrance came as a real surprise to my students who were in the media center studying research skills with the librarian. Wearing a hat with the requisite $1.98 price tag, I greeted my class with Minnie's often repeated cheerful "How-*deeee*! I'm jes' so proud to be here." I then shared highlights from Minnie Pearl's life and explained the dangling price tag. Having put on her best dress, telling everyone that she is pleased to be there, she then exposes her human weakness by forgetting to remove the $1.98 price from her hat.

I closed my presentation as Minnie would have, "I love you so much it hurts!"[3] Even the challenge of cancer hadn't stopped Sarah Ophelia Cannon, a.k.a. Cousin Minnie Pearl, from bringing joy to others.

In class the next day, I described the final project for eighth-grade English and assigned each student an influential historical figure. From Dr. Virginia Apgar to Admiral Nimitz and from Dr. Jonas Salk to Meredith Willson, I included a wide variety of people and occupations for the legacy reports. In their research, my students were to learn about their person's accomplishments, challenges, family, honors, and hardships. I also asked my students to hunt for a little-known, interesting fact that would astound the rest of us.

One of my focal points during this last project was to teach my class more about editing. Teachers often direct their classes to edit their work, but many students don't know where to begin or how to improve their work through editing. So one of my activities was to demonstrate editing a paragraph word by word and sentence by sentence with my class. I needed a brave student who would volunteer to share a paragraph so we could see step by step how a bit of good editing can improve writing. Fortunately, I always had a volunteer who was willing to share so that all of us could witness the transformation. With the student's work displayed on the overhead projector, someone from class would read the paragraph out loud. Often after hearing the paragraph read, all the author could do was groan. I explained to the class that I have heard it said that many of us do not actually read what is written, but rather that we hear the words as if they are being read orally. I wanted my class to understand how important it was for them to read their work out loud since that was how their audience would experience it.

Next, the class and I then took a look at the paragraph's sentence structure, vocabulary, verb usage, content, and flow. We rewrote the paragraph one sentence at a time: correcting verbs, rearranging prepositional phrases, replacing weak words with stronger words, and ensuring parallel construction within a sentence while always checking to see that we preserved the author's original meaning. As we worked, I wrote the new paragraph with the students' suggested changes. Then we read the original paragraph followed by the revised one. Their reaction was palpable and predictable: "Oh, I can't believe how much better the paragraph sounds now. And how much easier it is to read and understand!"

Once a high school junior stopped me in the hall and said, "Could you help edit my opinion paper for my literature class? I can still remember how much we improved that paragraph we worked on together in eighth-grade English." I asked if my editorial assistance would be okay with his current English teacher.

He assured me that she encouraged her students to seek help. I told him to come to my room during my next planning period, and we'd see how we could tighten his writing and make his points stronger.

I also heard from the parent of an eighth grader on the subject of editing when he felt his son had followed my instructions to seek editing input from two sources, and yet was maligned by another teacher for doing as I had asked.

In an e-mail, Ryan's father explained that his son had spent at least five hours the previous weekend finishing his rough draft. At school that Monday, Ryan then traded his rough draft with a classmate so they both could complete the editing process. Ryan's student editor was so impressed with Ryan's writing that she shared the rough draft with a social studies teacher. Because Ryan's rough draft was so exceptional, the teacher wondered aloud if Ryan had plagiarized his report. The student editor relayed the teacher's comment to Ryan, and Ryan was very upset at the accusation.

Here is my e-mail response to Ryan's father:

> Thank you for the opportunity to discuss this with you.
>
> All of my students are to enlist the aid of two "reading" editors and one "out loud" editor to see if the paper actually sounds correct. So, this is what Ryan was doing when he asked another student to check his work. Most of us cannot see our own mistakes. Also, when people read articles they actually hear the words in their heads. That is why I ask my students to either read their work out loud or listen as someone else reads it.
>
> Ryan was apparently upset today as he brought me his paper in class so I could have a look at it. I asked him to match the words from his research notes that he had highlighted with the same words in his rough draft. This is an activity we will all do together in class before they turn in their reports Friday.

In his research folder, Ryan should have an example of how this works. Somewhere in the middle of March I prepared a word list, an outline, and a final paragraph from *The Miracle Worker* to illustrate how this worked. Perhaps Ryan could show you that to explain better what I have been teaching in class.

When Ryan left today he was attempting to match up the notes, which were highlighted, with the words in the outline. If we would have had more time, we next would have matched those with the words in a paragraph of his typed work.

I am excited to hear how hard Ryan worked. (I enjoyed the depth of his thoughts in "Celebrating Me" from earlier this year.) What I am concerned about at the moment is whether his notes and outline used the same words for his rough draft as we discussed in class. This would prove the work was actually Ryan's writing.

Has this helped you understand what I was guiding my students to do in this assignment? Do you have other questions I did not address?

Having Ryan this year has been a blessing for me. I have enjoyed working with him and seeing the kindness in his heart. Thank you for the opportunity to share what's going on in my class. Let me know if there is anything else I can answer.

The depth of insights I saw in class daily from Ryan, added to correlating vocabulary from his notes, outline, rough draft, and final copy left me comfortable that Ryan had indeed constructed his own research report.

Besides wanting to improve my students' writing skills, I also wanted to expand their vocabulary. So during our first month of school, we began learning the *100 Words Every High School Freshman Should Know*. This vocabulary list contained a variety of words students could expect to encounter in their high school curriculum. We used many different approaches to master these words. Sometimes in class we got out of our seats and acted out words such as *cower*. Occasionally, they practiced by using the words from the 100 vocabulary list in their daily journal entries or class writing assignments. Other times, they used the words in pencil drawings to illustrate the word through art. My example for them was to illustrate what I expected by using the word *yacht*, written over and over to create the lines that resembled a fancy ship, as best as I could anyway.

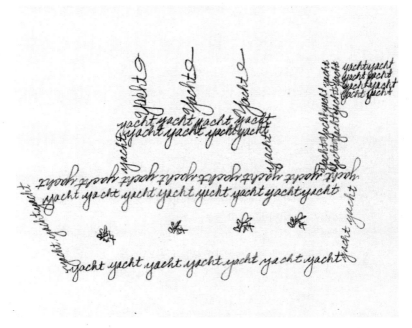

The yacht picture I drew to illustrate how students could create a picture using a word from the 100 words list.

One of our favorite ways to practice vocabulary was to play "memory," a game of concentration where teams of students matched cards; one card had the definition while the other one had the vocabulary word. Sixteen of these cards were shuffled and arranged in a four-by-four pattern on a desk, for a total of eight words and eight corresponding definitions, all face down. Teams then took turns turning over two cards at a time trying to find a pair of cards that matched. This game required both knowledge of the definitions and a good memory of each card's location when trying to match the two cards that went together. The winners got the thrill of victory, and the whole class got better at learning vocabulary while heightening their memory skills.

Throughout the year, my students had made personal dictionaries where they listed the words they had learned from our in-class reading alongside the 100 words from our yearlong vocabulary study. In these notebooks, students also included the general rules of grammar that they had learned in English the past nine months. Their final research papers presented an opportunity to use many of the words and rules we had been studying together all year.

Aspire, one of the words from our 100 list, was part of the central theme for their legacy reports. After we discussed Eugene Bell Jr.'s phrase "Aspire to inspire before you expire,"[4] I posted this saying on the board and included it on their directions sheet.

These were the guidelines for our research projects.

Legacy Paper
Due: 5/12

Use this opportunity to show your **best** research and writing skills.
GOOD LUCK!

These are items to be checked off and turned in with your final copy.

___Rough draft
___Edit notes/marks
___Signature of editor
___Signature of second editor who heard you read your writing out loud
___Length (1-3 pages)
___Use of bibliography materials
(Notes must be in your writing, organized by topic, displayed in an outline; and matching your rough draft and final copy.

Remember: Penmanship is part of Scholarship.

Aspire to inspire before you expire.

When I assigned the research paper, I also passed out this rubric for them to study because we would use it to score their research papers on the due date.

Final Copy Rubric for

Legacy Paper

Highlight and label one of each unless another amount is indicated.

____ (1) Appositive   "A"
____ (2) Adjective clause   "Adj"
____ (3) Adverb   "Adv"
____ (1) Complex Sentence   "CS"
____ (1) Compound Subject   "Com S"
____ (1) Compound Predicate   "Com P"
____ (1) Compound Sentence   "C"
____ (15) Vocabulary from your dictionary
     -no label required (just highlight them)
+++

____ (10) Introductory Paragraph
____ (20) Paragraphing-topic and details
____ (10) Wrap up paragraph
____ (10) Flow
____ (5) Title page
____ (5) Bibliography (at least 3 sources)   one has to be a book.
____ (15) Overall content

____ (100) Total

Surprisingly, when my students graded their own projects using this rubric, most scored themselves within five points of the final evaluation I arrived at when I made my assessment.

One of my favorite parts of grading these research papers was reading the backstories the students shared on their evaluations. Here are some of the comments my students wrote concerning their experiences while writing their reports.

Little known, interesting facts:

- So, my important person sold children's underwear as one of his first jobs.

- I used the font called Norman Rockwell to type my paper about Norman Rockwell.

- Juliette's childhood nickname was Daisy, and she was buried in her Girl Scout uniform.

- Clara Barton's middle name is Harlowe. This was fun to learn about someone who was very important in helping the United States.

- The biggest transmitter of disease was fleas.

- I think you didn't know that Meredith Willson who wrote *The Music Man* also wrote a musical called "1941" that never made it to Broadway. I really enjoyed trying to look for something you didn't know.

Research development:

- My guy is cool and I could have wrote (sic) a 6 page report but 3 or 4 is good.

- After putting all of my notes into three different categories, it made it a lot easier to write my report.

- I had to rewrite my rough draft about three times, redoing it, then printing, redoing it, then printing, but it was worth it in the end.

- I got my information really fast and that way I was able to get my notes, outline, rough draft, and final copy done ahead of time. It was a lot less worrysome (sic) and I knew that I could turn it in early.

- I watched *The Sound of Music*—three whole hours—just for one *great* sentence.

Families:

- My grandma helped me so much this time. This report took not very long. Also my mom helped too. [This student's mom passed away after a long battle with cancer the following year.]

- My parents learned about my person and they asked me questions about him and I liked to answer them.

- My family and my person have a lot in common—mostly the challenging things.

- I really enjoyed writing this because I not only learned about a great person, I learned how much I could relate to Itzhak [Perlman]. I love music as well as he does too. [This student related to hardship; his family was tested daily helping a disabled relative.]

- I got in a fight over this with my mom. She was going crazy screaming why didn't you do this earlyer (sic)!

Considering all of these delightful comments, one might think that I was an important factor in the success of this class. But after considering these next two students, I questioned my influence.

The difference between Marc and Janet can illustrate this point. These two students were in the same classroom being taught by the same teacher for a whole school year, yet one's failure and the other's success couldn't be explained because of my determination or my ability. Both Janet and Marc were gifted students with plenty of smarts, but that's where the similarity between them ended.

Their academic track records in my eighth-grade language arts class were complete opposites. Even though learning came easily for both of them, Janet rarely turned in homework while Marc was punctual with each assignment, working carefully as well as trying to earn any bonus points offered. Janet didn't read the books we studied together in class; Marc not only read his assignments but also participated in class discussions. Janet did not update her personal English dictionary with the words and concepts we had studied while Marc received 100 percent each time we graded these notebooks. On quizzes, their scores were at opposite ends of the spectrum, with Marc earning As while Janet refused to study and never scored higher that an F.

Consequently, the results of their final projects came as no surprise to me; once again on opposite ends of the spectrum. Janet turned in a partial bibliography, that's all. No research notes, no topics, no highlighting, no outline, no rough draft, no editors' signatures, no final copy. Just two sketchy bibliography notations. Scoring her in-class evaluation, she gave herself two of the five points allotted for the bibliography. However I couldn't agree to those two points as Janet had not bothered to capture the information required for the bibliography. When I scored the evaluation page, I had to mark her grade as 0 percent.

Janet was bright and understood how she had failed herself. In a reflection assignment at the end of the year, she wrote:

> I don't will myself to do homework unless someone supervises me or it's an in-class assignment. If someone was to describe me in one word, it would be a slacker. I have failed to live up to my potential.

Marc, however, met every requirement. Research notes, check. Highlighted topics, check. Matching outline, check. Rough draft with actual changes, check. The signatures of the editors who read his work and made suggestions, check. Terrific final copy, check. Marc even used one of our 100 words in his opening sentence describing his influential historical figure: "Irving Berlin was born to be a legendary *virtuoso*."

Marc's report was peppered with the many types of sentences they had learned. He had also incorporated the other elements the class had been studying, all the while including many fascinating facts from his research. After I read his research paper,

I felt sure Marc was well-prepared for high school. Here is the conclusion of his report: "Irving Berlin was an amazing composer who changed America's music for eternity, and will never be forgotten."

However, Marc said it best in his evaluation of this research report:

> I really enjoyed this assignment and learning more about Irving Berlin. I found it interesting that I had a family member who was also a big fan of his. I got this done in a very short amount of time, a lot faster than the way I used to write reports.

Remember when I wrote that I was not the most important factor in the classroom? The year-end assessments from these two students sounded as if they had studied under different teachers in separate schools.

Janet wrote:

> I learned that eighth grade English is just a blow to me because we have not learned a whole lot that I didn't already know. I really didn't like reading the books, either. [Nice try, Janet. I knew she didn't read the books.] I just didn't like this class much at all. I did like the how-to speeches and our poem contest because they involved good poems or good food. The dictionaries were fun at the end of the year, but I somehow always got good grades on our big tests even though I never studied. [As I said, she was bright. She was referring to the state-mandated exams because she failed every test given on in-class material].

Marc's counterpoint:

> I have learned a colossal amount of knowledge this year in your class. The 100 words have been a lot of help, and have really improved my vocabulary. Now, I make my family's jaws drop when I talk using the vocabulary words. I learned many things in English that have improved my

writing. The books we have read in class were very interesting, and I especially enjoyed *The Miracle Worker.* You also had us do a lot of activities to express ourselves, like Celebrating Me and the poems. With these projects, I not only learned more about myself, but it allowed me to find out more about others too. The most illustrious thing this year you taught us is how to properly write a research paper. Before, my work was very unorganized, and it took me forever to put all my information together. Now, it's very easy to write a report, and it doesn't take me long at all. My knowledge in Language Arts has flourished (thanks to you, Mrs. Nordstrom). You are always so enthusiastic, and I always look forward to your class.

Ditto for me on Marc's last two points: He was enthusiastic about learning. I always looked forward to teaching students like Marc who wanted to learn. My challenge was to inspire those who were reluctant to learn, or at the least to prevent them from hindering the rest of the students who were determined to participate and accomplish their goals.

In my last few years of teaching, the administration had to find cost-cutting measures to ease budget woes. One cost-saving measure was to cut by half the time allotted to junior high school language arts classes, which meant that the school could stretch the budget by having fewer language arts teachers on the payroll. Even though I wasn't in favor of this particular cost-cutting measure, I did understand that something had to be done to save money in our school district.

Because of the decrease in class time, many of my language arts projects also had to be reduced by half. Some of the lessons I cut were never missed by my students—at least that is my perception based on the complaints I had heard from former students in previous years. To my dismay and to that of many students, however, the six books we would have read together as a class were reduced to three. The time restrictions also made it impossible to teach the same amount of English as I had covered in past years. As a consequence, I taught fewer chapters in the English book, much to my disappointment and much to the detriment of students who would be less prepared in high school. And sadly, I also had to condense the research projects that had stood my students in good stead for their high school years and beyond.

Even though my teaching time was cut in half, no one indicated that it would be okay for my students to score lower on their standardized tests. I had been pleased with the progress my classes made when I was able to teach ninety-minute classes each day. I would have to adjust my schedule and keep my fingers crossed that I could still help them achieve the standards required in the state-mandated testing. As it turned out, most of the students who received fewer instructional hours in language arts were able to attain the baselevel scores required on the state exams, but consistently, these same students also produced lower scores than previous classes who often scored in the upper percentage brackets.

I liked to remind my students of two facts: that knowledge is power and that knowledge was the one gift I could share with them each day they were in my room. Teachers from my past had shared this blessing with me, and their efforts had made all the difference in the quality of my life. Even though I couldn't compel all of my students to acquire the knowledge, I could still pass this blessing on to any students who were interested in improving their understanding of the world and bettering their futures.

Over the years, I have had many students seek me out to apologize for their conduct while in junior high school. These former students have found me in the hall or slipped into my room to express regret over their behavior in my classroom. I have experienced this confession enough times that I can share the dominant points my students usually included in their apologies.

1. Believe it or not, I learned a lot in your room.
2. I don't know how you put up with me.

3. I'm sorry I was such a pain.

4. You'd be so proud of how much I've grown and how well I'm doing now.

They were so right. I was proud of how they had grown, what they had learned about English, and how they had gained a deeper knowledge about themselves. And I was thankful that they had returned to share their thoughts and insights with me. These encounters inspired me to work harder on the challenges I faced each day in my classroom. Their feedback also provided ongoing course corrections during my career, with each new class benefiting from their predecessors in unseen ways. While former students may have remained oblivious to their contributions to my honing of classroom techniques and methods, I knew just how much they had taught me, and I silently thanked them for the gifts I had received: deeper understanding, renewed inspiration, new approaches, and gentle compassion.

Remember this: Whoever sows sparingly will also reap sparingly, and whoever sows generously will also reap generously.

—*2 Corinthians 9:6*, NIV

Pass It On

*Be strong and courageous. Do not be afraid or terrified
because of them, for the Lord your God goes with you; he will
never leave you nor forsake you.*

—Deuteronomy 31:6, NIV

After eleven years in the classroom, I also became a part-time college instructor. This position started with a summer course for the third and final math requirement for education majors at the state university's regional campus. I enjoyed the change of pace and found it inspiring to help these adult students decode the mysteries of math. But they also wanted to know what the classroom was really like—from the teacher's perspective. They wanted insights about everyday experiences from someone who was currently working in their chosen field. I enjoyed sharing stories from "the front" that illustrated how the techniques they were learning in math—combined with their own ideas, experiences, insights, and inspirations—would one day be useful to them in their classrooms.

Besides sharing my perspective on daily classroom life, I drew upon my personal struggles with learning math to help them see how teachers can break down complex ideas into smaller, understandable components. To me it sounded as if some of my former math instructors were speaking in a foreign language when explaining math concepts, confusing me more. But when I finally understood a concept, I could usually explain it in a way that others would also understand. I had most likely had the same struggles they were encountering.

My motivation to help these future teachers gain confidence in their math skills came from an experience the previous fall. I had witnessed a colleague's meltdown when she learned that she had been reassigned to a sixth-grade math position just days before the school year started.

"I don't know the upper-level math concepts well enough to teach this new grade level," she worried aloud to her coworkers after hearing the news. "I don't know how I will survive this teaching assignment."

There was no time for her to take a refresher course at that late hour. This teacher had a strong English background but felt weak in math and, consequently, quite unprepared to teach it. However, student enrollment and staffing levels control teacher placement, and that year, the administration needed a sixth-grade teacher who would teach both English and math. If this seasoned coworker refused to teach math, then she would be out of a job.

At the completion of this challenging year, this colleague disclosed to me that she had learned math right along with her students. And she knew that her math students had suffered because of her limited knowledge. But with time and practice, she did garner the skills needed to instruct her math classes well.

Having witnessed this teacher's experience, I wanted the students in that summer college course to be competent enough to teach math at any grade level. Further, I wanted them to have a solid foundation in math so that they would not have to rely on the wraparound instructions provided in teacher manuals to create effective lessons.

Some of the summer college students had naïve, unrealistic teaching expectations for their careers. For example, quite a few were under the mistaken impression that they would actually get to choose their grade level as well as their subject matter in their future employment. One future educator piped up in class and said, "I don't plan to need all this math stuff. You see, I want to teach the younger grades." Most new hires, at that time, were thrilled to have a teaching job, no matter the age group or the subject.

Before I began teaching college classes, my students ranged from eight to fourteen years of age. But in my new position, the students were anywhere between the ages of nineteen and sixty. For me, one of the best assets of teaching adult students was their intrinsic motivation, driven by their desire to earn a college degree and begin a teaching career. Before these students entered my class, they had already passed through the gauntlet of college acceptance, registration, financing, and any number of other classes as education majors. So I taught many willing students each week.

Following that summer class, I was hired as the regular instructor to teach the math T series—a three-semester, yearlong course. Most college classes were completed in a semester although a few classes required two semesters, but this series was unusual because it lasted a full year. For me, this extended class time offered a wonderful opportunity to become better acquainted with my students. Most of my time on the college level was spent teaching future educators. One semester, however, I did teach a statistics class for students of any major.

The lessons I learned from my college students were very different from the lessons I learned from elementary and junior high school kids. For example, one rainy October evening, my college math students were taking a midterm exam and were free to leave when they had finished the exam and turned it in. I noticed Dianne was limping as she approached my desk to turn in her test paper. "Is everything okay?" I asked.

"Mostly," Dianne said. "But damp, cold weather like we have tonight causes the injuries from my accident to flare up. My limp comes from many broken bones, and even though the bones are mended, I doubt my limp will ever go away completely. Some days are okay, but other days aren't."

I had not known about Dianne's accident or the events that brought her to my math class. But we found an opportunity to talk a few weeks later, and she told me her story of the accident and how it changed her life.

Fourteen months earlier, she had been out to dinner with her husband, John. Their friends, another married couple, were riding in the car's backseat as the two couples returned home from their evening out. An intoxicated driver, who had just left his third bar that evening, lost control of his vehicle and smashed into the side of Dianne's vehicle. Her husband and the wife of the other couple, both sitting on the same side of the car, were killed. John died instantly of a torn aorta. Dianne and her friend's husband survived the crash, but each of them sustained severe injuries. Most of the bones on one side of Dianne's body were broken due to the force of the impact.

Eight months' pregnant at the time, Dianne went into labor at the hospital. The baby died when the force of the impact separated the placenta from the womb. Dianne's doctors explained that her injuries were too serious for them to perform a Caesarian section, so they recommended that Dianne have a normal delivery, even though the accident had broken her pelvic bone. The horror and loss of that night was too much for me to comprehend.

Dianne finished her story by sharing why she was attending college and why she was enrolled in my math class. During those many months of recovery, she had had plenty of time to consider what she should do next with her life. "My husband, John, was a beloved teacher," she said. "When I would visit his gravesite, I found that his students had also stopped there and left little bunches of flowers to remember him. After much thought, I decided to earn my degree in education and take John's place in the classroom." Dianne did fulfill that dream, and has spent the past twenty-five years enriching children's lives.

Rachel, another student from that class, had returned to college in her early thirties to finish her education. A dedicated worker with considerable talent, Rachel admitted that she didn't handle failure well. Yet, here she was attending a math class when her previous experiences had convinced her that she was not good at math. The first semester of the T series proved to be a test of her tenacity. On numerous occasions, I remember her saying, "I can't do this!"

Week by week, I taught the required skills, molding my presentation to the needs of the class. Through questions and answers in class discussion, we sorted out their math confusion. Once my students grasped a concept, we moved on to the next one. Rachel explained how she pictured these math concepts as building blocks of basic math knowledge. Learning math for her became a new language based on numbers.

Struggling through her homework assignments, asking questions in class, and studying the notes and examples, Rachel began to grasp the math understanding that had eluded her in the past. By the end of the first course in the T series, Rachel realized that she was not as dumb in math as she had feared. A large part of this success was that Rachel set high standards for herself and was driven to do her best.

At some point in our year together, Rachel realized that education in general and math in particular were well within her reach. By the end of the year, she found that math no longer scared her. Rachel had grown to love the challenge of numbers.

I wanted my students to understand that no matter the age, anyone could feel like a frightened child when it came to learning new concepts. And when these students eventually became teachers, they would possess the knowledge and skills to make learning easier for their students. I wanted each class member to get to hear their students exclaim, "Is that all there is to it!"

When Rachel was stumped by the subtraction of integers, she asked if I had a method to make it easier. I taught her the Keep, Change, Change rule. This rule helped guide students in knowing how to work with negative numbers and subtraction. When a problem, for example, 4−(-7), stumps students, math teachers use the Keep, Change, Change process to explain: Keep the 4;

Change the minus to plus; and Change the negative 7 to positive 7. Simplifying, the problem is now 4+ (+7) which equals 11. Besides using this rule to solve problems with negative numbers, Rachel also applied it to the way she approached math. Her take on it went something like this: Keep your basic knowledge; change your attitude of what you can and can't do; and then, change others with your skills. Now those are some words of wisdom.

Much to her surprise, Rachel was one of the few students in the T series who earned an A+. After graduation, she took her knowledge, her drive, and her ambition to the elementary classroom and became an inspiring teacher; one I would have been honored to have as a colleague. She taught her students in her own classroom with the same commitment and tenacity she had shown as a student, giving them her very best. I also learned from Rachel and the many other college students in my classes.

Statistics had been a challenging subject for me when I earned my master's degree, but teaching statistics proved to be even more challenging. Students often regard statistics as one of the most demanding college classes. I knew I would need to break down the complex statistical concepts into manageable, comprehensible components.

My students seemed to feel the most pressure while doing their homework assignments. I had heard plenty of their complaints and frustrations. Demonstrating how to work problems in stat class can require many steps and plenty of places where errors can happen. Locating where they had made mistakes, large or small, aggravated my students. I myself felt some of that same burden as I prepared lectures. My aim was to help them understand how the pieces fit together. I also knew that if my students and I didn't have occasional headaches, then we weren't working hard enough.

Since the statistics class met only one evening per week from September to middle December, the schedule didn't allow much time for me to get to know my students. Most, however, were like

Terry, a hardworking, motivated student who was taking the statistics class to further his education; his goal was to earn a business degree and create a better future for himself and his family. Understanding Terry's additional aspirations might have helped me to know how seriously he took his education.

Four weeks into the semester, my students took their first exam. I could see that Terry was upset when he found that he had gotten a D. After class that evening, Terry approached me and asked, "Could I go over this test with you?" I nodded yes and he continued, "I'd like to wait until it's almost time for our next test. Could we meet one week before the second exam? I'd like you to bring my test so I can have another look at my work." We set up an appointment time.

Three weeks later, we met, and Terry looked over his first exam. His reaction surprised me. "I can't believe some of the questions I missed," he remarked. "Now that I've learned more about statistics, I can see that I really hadn't studied enough when I took this test. I guess I'd better work harder before next week's exam. Thanks for meeting with me."

I thought Terry might look over the test and complain that I had asked too much of my students. Instead, he examined the questions and saw how his understanding of statistics had increased over time. No complaining from him.

Following that first test, Terry began to ask more questions in class and appeared to concentrate more on his assignments, substantially improving his homework average. Because of his hard work and dedication, Terry's exam scores also improved. And by the end of the semester, Terry had raised his grade to a B+, an admirable job considering the difficulty of the subject matter and his shaky beginning. Many of his classmates would have happily traded grades with him.

A year and a half later, I met Terry again at a spring recognition assembly where graduating seniors were being honored.

I asked what honor he was receiving that evening. "I'm here because of my grades," he said.

"How nice," I said. "Can you tell me about your grades?"

"Yes. I have all As except for one B+."

The magnitude of his comment hit me immediately. "Terry, I'm so sorry that the grade you received in my class kept you from having straight As."

"Don't be," he said. "That B+ means more to me than any of the As. You showed me what I was capable of. Before the statistics class, I thought I was using my ability, but your class stretched my thinking and I found more capacity than I knew I had. I want to thank you."

Over the years, I taught about two hundred college students, and they were clear when it came to explaining what they expected from their college education. They wanted teachers who would:

- Be encouraging and fair while clarifying the concepts.

- Relate the subject matter to real-world experiences.

- Create an appreciation of the subject through a deeper understanding of it.

- Explain and enrich perplexing concepts from the text.

- Exhibit concern for each individual in the class.

- Relate to the students' challenges.

- And, if possible, share laughter along with the trials.

Working with motivated college students enriched my teaching and my life.

God is not unjust; he will not forget your work and the love you have shown him as you have helped his people and continue to help them.

—Hebrew 6:10, NIV

Tried and True (For Me, Anyway)

Trust in the Lord with all your heart and lean not on your own understanding; in all your ways submit to him, and he will make your paths straight.

—Proverbs 3:5–6, NIV

My time in the classroom resembled a patchwork quilt: a mix of many different types of fabric cut into various sizes and shapes all stitched together in an eye-popping explosion of color. The top side of this quilt revealed a one-of-a-kind design while the underside exposed dangling threads, sloppy stitching, and frayed seams—the work accomplished over a lifetime. The following instructions reveal how parts of the quilt were created.

Borrow good ideas: My colleagues were a wonderful source of creative ideas. For instance, the junior high English staff was already using the "Celebrating Me" assignment when I joined the department. Even though this activity was not my idea, it was one of my favorite projects. Most of the students enjoyed this lengthy assignment, which showed in their interest and their achievement. But as I've often found, my students express their experiences best.

> I loved makeing (sic) it and my dad read and looked at mine. My mom said it made my dad cry.
>
> I had a lot of cute pictures I wanted to include, but didn't have room for them. That's why I included two extra pictures at the end.
>
> I wanted to be able to use more pictures because it seemed occward (sic) only being able to do 15.
>
> This project was very fun for me to do. I loved putting the pages together. Me and my mother enjoy scrapbooking so this was fun for me.

Making this project was awesome. I really had fun looking at all of the pictures and how funny they were. This was my favorite project ever—it was awesome. [I never heard this quiet student use the term *awesome* before or after this project.]

Collaborate: Some fun projects originated in grade level meetings when we teachers searched for ideas to enliven long-dead social studies topics such as ancient Egypt and Greek mythology. Here's an excerpt from a story printed in a local newspaper on one of our projects.

Students scurry around the gymnasium barefoot [and] wrapped in sheets. Many of them wear fake beards and carry homemade shields, swords or scrolls.

They are dressed as statues from ancient Greece and are "on display" in the gym. Other students tour the display.

Welcome to sixth-grade world history where the teachers treat history as if it were a giant playground.

So far this year, the Intermediate sixth-graders have made pyramids out of sugar cubes, created a museum out of the nurse's office overflowing with Egyptian artifacts, and re-enacted moments from Greece's past while dressed as historical, mythical or legendary characters. As always, their work is shared with the entire school.[1]

Reach out: I never knew where I would happen upon a clever idea that would inspire me. For instance, one January day, I read an article describing how a teacher felt she needed to lift her students' spirits. I liked her idea and thought about how I could incorporate this idea into my lesson to encourage my students. With Valentine's Day just around the corner, I listed each student's name on a paper, made a copy of this list for the class members, instructed them to write the characteristic they liked most or admired about their sixth-grade classmates, and then bring the papers to me the following Monday. I also asked that they not share their comments since I had a plan to use them.

After I collected their notes, I used a beautiful sheet of paper for each student and began by writing the class member's name in large letters. Then I combed through all of the student papers and copied each comment others had written to describe the classmate. This activity required a few hours to accomplish, so I was glad I had given myself plenty of time. The intervening time between filling out the papers and middle February when I planned to share them might help create a surprise for my students. As the students opened their cards that Valentine's Day, I enjoyed watching the reactions as each one read the collection of comments.

Here is an excerpt from an e-mail I received years later when one of these sixth graders was a sophomore in college.

> I was thinking of you today. In my Intro to Ed class, my professor read a story about a teacher who taught ninth-grade math. I think that you shared this story with me. It was the end of the week and her students were restless; she had them get out paper and write down a nice thing about everyone in their class. She then wrote all the things on a paper for each student. The story goes on and when one of her students is killed in Vietnam, she finds out what a difference those papers made.
>
> I remember in sixth grade when we did that and you gave us papers with all the nice stuff that our classmates had said about us. I still have the paper, and after class I got it out and read it. It just makes you feel good. Thanks.

Be inspiring: New ideas will pop up in the least expected places. One of my art lessons came to me when I was picking up a newly framed picture at the local graphic arts supply store. I noticed the many brochures of the latest art prints available through the gallery. I asked the owner if he would mind if I shared these beautiful pictures with my art class. "Take what you need. It's good to introduce the next generation to fine art," he said.

My students were fascinated by the variety of pictures I shared—paintings of nature, animals of all sorts, and whimsical fantasy. Their interest inspired me to create an art project by cutting these brochures apart. Students then used the small four-by-six-inch pictures to inspire their drawings. The eighteen-by-twenty-four-inch construction paper canvases produced some of their best work from our entire year together.

Years later when one of these students was studying to become a teacher, I received an e-mail request concerning this art lesson.

> My creative arts methods professor is interested in the lesson I described from your sixth-grade class where we used real artists to inspire our drawings. If you read this in a source, could you share it with me so I can pass it on? If it was an original idea, do you mind if I use it?

I was happy, even honored, to share this idea.

Create trust: My elementary students particularly enjoyed sharing a secret code. This simple but effective example illustrates one way my students and I built trust. On the occasions when the principal made an observation visit to my third-grade class, I would usually receive prior notice. One time when I knew my class would be getting a visit, I prepared my students with these directions.

> Let's impress the principal with your answers on his visit this month. Every time I ask a question, I want to see every hand in the air ready to answer. If you know the correct response, raise your right hand. If you are confused or don't know the answer, raise your left hand. I will call on students who have raised their right hands. I promise I will not call on anyone whose left hand is raised. If I ask a question and only see left hands in the air, I'll make a comment about how everyone already seems to know that answer so we'll just move on.

I don't remember any question that was unanswered with only left hands raised, but we were prepared just in case. My class seemed to appreciate our secret code. We had a wonderful, relaxed visit from the principal that even my students seemed to enjoy. And no one let on that we had made a trust promise.

Listen: A student's father appeared at my classroom door one afternoon thirty minutes after school had been dismissed. He asked for an explanation concerning the grades on his daughter's report card. I could sense that he was agitated, but he remained calm while he said, "I thought my daughter might have straight As on her grade card with the way she has been studying. I was just wondering how she got all Bs."

"Could I see her grade card?" I asked. He reached into his pocket and pulled out the carbonless copy paper form we used at that time for report cards. The particular benefit to this method of sending information home was that I had the imprint of the original, which I could retrieve from my file to compare with his copy.

"Maybe when I show you my daughter's grade card, you will understand why I am so upset," he added. "I can hardly read these grades. Are these Bs on her card?"

"Let me get my copy so we can compare them," I said.

His daughter did not have straight As or even straight Bs for that matter. Although she had been telling her dad one story, she knew that a different version was playing out at school. Also, I suspect she had thought that her dad would just accept the report card she gave him and would not bother to come to school. I was glad he had; it gave me a chance to straighten out the confusion.

I could tell that her dad was quite surprised when he compared the doctored form he held with the original one from my files. My copy of his daughter's report showed straight Cs. The sloppy writing came about when she tried to turn those Cs into Bs.

I also suspect that the true surprise most likely happened when her dad arrived home that day. However, I was grateful that he had been patient and had given me a chance to explain; not all parents wanted to know the facts.

Make it real: Some of my junior high students didn't understand the importance of the habits they practiced daily. Nor did they see how these behaviors could affect their futures. As William Shakespeare wrote in his play, *The Tempest*, if the past is prologue, then the students' daily behaviors shaped and predicted their destinies.

On occasion, I tried to translate the daily job requirements in junior high to the real world of job performance. "What would a boss do with an employee who showed up late, unprepared, and unwilling to work?" I asked my class. "Do you think any boss can afford to keep paying an employee who does careless work or no work at all?"

Some of my students unwittingly mirrored such discussions when they came to class day after day without their assignments, sporting bad attitudes, and treating classmates and staff disrespectfully. I knew I couldn't fire these lazy workers, but I could try to help them see their current work habits through a future boss's eyes rather than just through a teacher's perspective. "How would it work if teachers could fire chronic nonworkers?" This question not only got their attention, but usually caused a student to protest, "You can't do that!"

"Maybe not," I said, "but someday a future employer will do just that when you exhibit enough failure on the job. Consistently turning in D or F work to the boss who hired you and pays you will not secure your position for very long."

Take a chance: You have to trust your instincts. One year I had a group of sixth graders who entered my room each day engrossed in conversation. They were a wonderful bunch of kids, but I wasted precious class time pleading with them to quiet down. One day after class, I considered how to redirect their energy. I decided that I would take my own entertainment to class, and while the students entertained themselves with conversation, I would read.

That next day, I brought the newspaper and my library book with me. When my class arrived, I was seated at my desk—an unusual occurrence because I usually stood at the door and greeted them. This day, though, I remained at my desk, paid no attention to them, and acted as if I were absorbed in reading the newspaper. The bell rang to signal the beginning of class and the students took their seats. I, however, did not look up but continued reading the newspaper. The students seemed delighted to continue their conversations while I read. I finished the newspaper and then opened my reading book, never looking at my students. Their happy talk continued. About fifteen minutes into class time though, they became nervous. Their chatting slowed down as some students began to study me, trying to figure out why I wasn't shushing them.

These conditions were not conducive for enjoying a leisure book, but I was trying to give my students a new perspective. So I continued to focus on the page in front of me while I listened to the comments my students made to each other. "Do you think she knows we're here?" "I can't believe she hasn't started class." "Do you think we should approach her and ask for our assignment?" "What do you think is wrong?"

While I concentrated on my reading material, I sensed a shift in my students' attitudes. They quieted down and began whispering their comments. Before long, I heard one student say to her neighbor, "I think she is treating us like we treat her. We come in here and ignore her. Every day she has to ask us over and over to quiet down." Bingo.

I closed my book and laid it down. Then I slowly turned to my class and said, "Shelby just explained why I have spent the first twenty minutes of class reading. You come to class each day and fail to recognize the beginning of class when the bell rings, forcing me to ask you to settle in and calm down. Every day I waste time asking for you to quiet down so we can begin class, and I've decided not to do that anymore. If you want to talk at the beginning of class, then I will consider any time you use then as the study time I would normally give you at the end of class. Twenty minutes are gone from today's class, so we will work up until the bell rings. Let us open our books now to discuss chapter three. Who would like to share something new you have learned about life in ancient Greece?"

That evening, I attended a concert where I bumped into a college professor from ten years earlier. My Old Testament teacher, an educator with over twenty-five years' experience, had been an inspiration for me during my college days. After exchanging pleasantries, he asked how my teaching was going. I related the incident from my social studies class earlier that day. He looked surprised and asked, "What would have happened if you had lost them there and then?"

"I already had lost them," I answered. "I had to try something different since what I had been doing wasn't working."

That group of students calmed down, entered class in a more respectful manner after my lesson, and we accomplished our in-class assignments all while saving time for study at the end of class.

Be the difference: Consider how most classrooms resemble one another—desks, chairs, textbooks. Then consider the major difference—the teacher. I was the biggest difference when it came to my room. I was the one in front who set the tone, modeled the expected standards, and invested my individual talents to make my classroom a special place. The final success rested on my shoulders.

Give thanks: A former student—now a teaching colleague—and I bumped into one another one morning before school while checking our mailboxes. We took a few minutes to catch up on the latest news before she gathered her papers and prepared to leave. As she headed for the mailroom door, she turned back to me and said, "Well, I'm off to my room to enter my students' latest grades into my computer. And I bet you have no idea what my password is. One of the suggestions when I had to create my password was to use my favorite teacher's name. So after I enter 'Jeanne,' I'll get to work."

That piece of news certainly brightened my day. I have been blessed to be a blessing.

Instill confidence: I was fortunate enough to teach a variety of subjects throughout my career. But the two classes I taught the most, English and math, required very different teaching strategies. Students who were strong in math often struggled in English and vice versa. My high school math colleagues commented about how difficult the English classes had been in comparison to their math classes. More than once, a fellow math teacher brought me a memo to proofread before running the copies she was sending home.

I taught both of these subjects to the same students; I noticed how some students had opposite reactions to the subjects of English and math. Perhaps their reactions reflected their strengths and weaknesses, likes or dislikes, or even their earlier successes or failures in these subjects. I don't recall ever hearing anyone use the term *English anxiety*, although there is the term *writer's block*, but I certainly heard *math anxiety* more times than I (a math teacher) cared to count—from both students and parents. What's worse is that this apprehension seemed to be a genuine stumbling block for many students.

I often taught seventh-grade math followed by eighth-grade English. Many students seemed almost surprised to find that I was proficient at English once they had tagged me as a math teacher, thinking that math was all I knew. One student started his eighth-grade year by commenting on how strange it felt to be sitting in his seventh-grade math room, hearing his seventh-grade math teacher discuss sentence structure and grammar. More students may have felt the same confusion but just didn't say anything out loud. I do remember how much this particular eighth grader enjoyed some of our creative English lessons—the videos, the variety of topics, and the unusual guest speakers.

However, I was taken by complete surprise near the end of the school year when this eighth grader boldly announced to the teacher across the hall, "Do you know what Mrs. Nordstrom's problem is?" Later that day, when my math colleague related this story to me, I thought, "Oh no, what now!" But I needn't have been too worried because she told me how this student finished his thought. "She can teach everything!"

Of course there were subjects I would not have tackled, but this student's naïve confidence was inspiring.

Teachers who devote their entire career to the classroom will deal with a wide variety of problems throughout their years. Even mundane issues provide an opportunity to help students. For instance, my students even requested help in dealing with the body odor of classmates.

> I don't know if this issue has been brought to your attion (sic) but I'm tired of a classmate of mine *not* taking a bath. You know who it is and I would like you to do something about it for me. Thank you. Your student, Richie Meyer.

> Please talk to our class (4th block) about body odor. This is not a joke. Please either move me from where I sit or talk to our class. I'm sorry if this seems mean but one person that I sit by has a bodily odor and it really bothers me. I'm sorry again, I know you have enough to deal with and do in one day. But if you would *please* talk about it with our class or *please* move me! I would rather you move me because I don't think the talk would help because I think he wouldn't pay any attention to it. And I would hate for you to waste your time.

> — ♥ Megan

Take the lead: Good leaders really, really care about those they lead. Your job as teacher is important; don't shortchange or confuse your students by trying to be their peer. A good leader makes wise decisions on another's behalf. I've seen a few educators try to make peer relationships with students as if being their friend was more important than being their teacher. Trying to be their friend, or paying too much attention to what your students think about you, can cloud your judgment. Children can be manipulators by nature. Your job is to do what is best for them.

If you are not the leader in the classroom, discipline will become a bigger issue than it already is. When the strongest, most directed voice in the classroom, ideally that of the teacher, loses focus and control, the classroom can become a jungle. If the position of leadership is up for grabs, then count on the strongest student trying to take over and rule as a tyrant with only his own interests to guide him. In my experience, the fairest decisions came from the adult who cared about the well-being of all the students in the room.

Whether they liked it or not, my students knew that the leadership position was always filled by me. This assertiveness did not please would-be tyrants. But I had been hired for that position, trained for the task at hand, and was the most impartial, evenhanded person in the room. Being the leader did not prevent me from being kind, friendly, gracious, considerate, and respectful. It actually made it easier to express those qualities. It's important that the leader establish a classroom environment that protects students, maintains academic standards, encourages participation, and models both firmness and fairness.

Build on your best: I wanted to be professional and enthusiastic every day. These two ideas were concrete objectives for my daily decisions. Notes and comments from students reminded me and also directed me to focus energy and effort on attaining my goals for them. Sometimes students were inspired to leave notes on my desk at the end of the year after their grades were turned in telling me how they had changed in my class. The following note is representative.

> Although I was a little obnoxious (well maybe a lot). You are still the best teacher I have ever had. What I learned from you wasn't just stuff out of books or the lessons you taught in the front of class. I have learned that I am not going to get by in life with just slacking and not doing my work. I learned that life isn't like a box of chocolates, but it's more like school isn't like a box of chocolates. There are things thrown at you and obsticles (sic) that you have to achieve.
>
> You have taught me a lot and I want to let you know that I really appriceate (sic) it and I think that it will help me at another time in my life. Thank you! Debbie

At other times students included a special thank-you in a card. Here is a Mother's Day card I received from a former student.

> Hugs to you on Mother's Day…and every day of the year. Thanks for being someone I could confide in and for all of your inspiration. You have been like a second mom to me.
>
> – ♥Samantha

Even Valentine cards could move me with a heartfelt message.

> For my teacher-You're a teacher who's smart, helpful, and kind. I'm one lucky kid because you are mine! Happy Valentine's Day. Love, Amy

Then there were the letters that arrived in the mail many years after a student had moved on in life.

> I'm writing this letter to tell you how much I appreciate everything you have done for me. When I didn't believe in myself, you were always the one to believe in me. I can't possibly thank you enough for what you have done. I am so much more confident in myself because you showed me that I can do anything. You weren't just a teacher. When

my grades were down you helped me get them back up to where you knew I could get them to be. You showed that you cared about both my grades and me.

Ever since I had your class my life has changed so much. I now believe that I *can* do things. My grades have always been good since I had you as my teacher. I'm also more positive about things in my life. You not only taught me things for school you also taught me things for my life, and I thank you so much!! Lawrence

Eventually I even received e-mails.

How are you? This is Jeremy Thomas! I apologize that I have not spoken with you in a very long time, life is just hectic! I have married a truly wonderful woman. I am working in the area. Who would have ever thought that I would find a career that required people interaction skills? Furthermore, that I would love it. Life is going great especially since spring has finally sprung!

How are you these days? Still teaching I have gathered. I wasn't sure if you were close to retiring or not. I wish to thank you for all the advice you have shared over the years, and would like you to know how truly happy I have become! Your grateful student, Jeremy

Sometimes a message arrived in the end-of-year paragraph from the final exam where students were to demonstrate the paragraph, grammar, and vocabulary skills they had acquired during their time in English.

Today I was asked, as well as my classmates, what I have learned in English. So I thought about it, and I've learned quite a bit. From simple things like nouns to verbs, to 100 words, and sentence formats. This was what my first few thoughts were and then I thought some more.

Teaching English wasn't Mrs. Nordstrum's (sic) goal, but rather to teach her students things they truley (sic) would need to know. So when things seemed hard and frustrating, Mrs. Nordstrum (sic) was the voice of reason. But she could also be quite the humorous person if the time was right and that's what I have learned in English.

Bruce

Under promise, over deliver: What a pleasant surprise it was to see a student or coworker go the extra distance. I witnessed many empty promises accompanied by hollow excuses, especially when students tried to justify their failing work or missing assignments. It seemed to me that the level of inflated self-esteem—a societal problem in general and a student problem specifically—increased during my tenure in the classroom.

For many students, this sense of self-confidence did not need to be based on concrete facts or performance. An inflated self-worth seemed a lot like empty calories from junk food, tasty but not a good basis on which to build strong bodies. Colleagues commented that they felt the need to praise students too frequently for too little effort. The concept of everyone receiving a trophy, no matter what, has infiltrated the classroom. I found this notion counterproductive in trying to instill pride of personal achievement in students.

Model a cheerful, contagious attitude: To the best of your ability, be positive. Some days it may just not be possible, but whenever it is up to you and your choices, look on the bright side. Knowledge and good preparation are essential ingredients, but students also want to know that you truly care about them. I had my days when I didn't feel cheerful, but my students still needed that positive side of me.

One dark winter morning, one of my students reminded me how important my smile was. "You smile every day," he said. "You are the one teacher we count on to be cheerful. It's difficult for me to imagine you not smiling."

Most days I was happy to be teaching. On those days when I wasn't my best, I decided to fake it until I felt it. Did it always work? Absolutely not. But then again, many days it did work, and on those days, I benefited right alongside my students. A touch of Mary Poppins just might help some days.

Cultivate friendships: Throughout my career, I worked with wonderful colleagues who were kind and compassionate, not only to the students, but also to their coworkers. Halfway through my career, for example, I had a serious surgery in the middle of the school year. My coworkers visited, brought meals, and sent cards until I was well enough to return to work. Their kindness raised my spirits and helped speed up my recovery.

Many of us have found that retirement is the place where we get to make up for the limited time we shared friendship during our careers. Through the years of working together, many of us forged bonds that have held into retirement. There were times of disagreement between colleagues who worked together, but when we gathered in retirement, those old memories were left in the past. A group of ten to fifteen retired teachers gather monthly at a local restaurant to enjoy lively conversation and laughter. We are not a quiet group, but rather a joyous one. And the joy seems to linger as the retirees finish lunch, schedule the next month's location, and finally head their separate ways. We are continuing to cultivate friendship.

Keep growing: Teaching has good days, some great days, many average days, and a few that defy categorizing. Use what you get each day to build a broader base for the new experiences and students you will meet throughout your career.

Cherish gifts: Some remuneration in my career came in unsolicited creative writing, making my classroom experiences all the sweeter and more rewarding. Examples include a selection of the poems that students wrote for me.

A True Poem

[The poem mentions my former name]

Ms. Favreau's room fell apart today.

It happened all this way.

Ms. Favreau got sick,

The clock din't (sic) tick,

The pencill (sic) sharpener broke.

Everybody spoke,

What a terrible day for Ms. Favreau.

The End

Once upon a time, there was a foolish girl and a wise
    teacher.

The girl would never listen to what the teacher had to say,

But the teacher still tryed (sic) to help the girl every single
    day.

Then, one day the teacher said, "You need to stop and lis-
    ten up,

Your (sic) in the real world now and you need to start
    growing up!"

The girl then realized that she had been acting like a fool.

Because she wasn't following the teacher's rule.

Then the girl seen (sic) the error of her ways,

And her actions started improving over the days.

This poem is for Mrs. Nordstrom, a great teacher.

A smile so kind and eyes that glow,

Reminds me of someone I know.

I see her most every day,

She helps me out in every way.

When my thoughts begin to wonder (sic),

She leads me out of this terrible blunder.

A special thanks I send your way,

To you, Mrs. Nordstrom, I give an A.

"And surely I am with you always, to the very end of the age."

—*Matthew 28:20b,* NIV

View from the Custodial Cart

*Even youths grow tired and weary, and young men stumble
and fall; but those who hope in the Lord will renew their
strength. They will soar on wings like eagles; they will run
and not grow weary, they will walk and not be faint.*

—Isaiah 40:31, NIV

A t some point in the school year, students usually asked me
about jobs I had held before I became a teacher. One of the
jobs I told them about was the summer I worked as a maid cleaning college dormitories. The challenge of that job sent me back to
my college classes in the fall with renewed vigor, pushing me to
work hard preparing for my future. Those twelve weeks of summer labor also taught me to respect and appreciate even more the
effort required to maintain a school facility.

It was humbling work, and I wasn't paid much. But I did
receive the gift of empathy for the custodians who eventually
cleaned my classrooms.

Ever curious and full of questions, my students wanted details
about the specific responsibilities of that job. I explained that
cleaning dorm rooms was okay, but the working conditions were
less than desirable—hot, humid days in stuffy dormitories without air-conditioning accompanied by lots of sweaty, physical
labor. One of the best parts of that job was that I worked with
some very nice ladies.

The worst chore that summer, I thought, was scrubbing the
boys' dormitory restrooms. In the arsenal of cleaning supplies, we
had a special solution to sterilize bathrooms. The odor that met
us at the doorway to the boys' washroom made it clear that we
needed that sterilizing cleanser. This solution turned a dark green
whenever it contacted urine. When we applied the disinfectant
to the walls surrounding the toilets, the telltale green extended

seven feet up the wall. The maids wondered out loud if the boys had had contests to see who could reach the highest mark on the wall. I personally wondered if a stepladder had been involved since I needed a ladder to reach high enough to wash off the odd green color.

Although this job introduced me to only a few of the responsibilities that school custodians performed on a daily basis, it did grow my appreciation for the many chores required to maintain a clean, comfortable school environment.

Partway through my career, I heard excerpts from a graduation speech where the speaker emphasized the importance of custodians. In addressing the senior class, he described how important custodial coworkers are to the overall team. He urged the graduates to respect and honor the custodial and maintenance staff at their future places of employment for the vital contributions these faithful servants add to the company's image. He closed his speech by reminding the graduates that it was important to know the custodians' names and treat them with respect. It was important advice: most of the custodians I knew throughout my career were called friends.

Janitorial tasks are often performed out of sight, long after the school day is over. But even when the custodians cleaned during school hours, they went about their jobs quietly. And because most of the custodians were inconspicuous while cleaning, some people never noticed how hard they worked.

At one elementary school where I taught, the custodian who swept my room during my planning time was a grandfatherly type. He was always quiet when he entered my room so as not to disturb my work. I appreciated his methodical approach—checking the lights each day to see that no bulb had burned out, emptying the pencil sharpener before dumping the trash can, and straightening desks and chairs as he made his way around my room with his large dust mop. I looked forward to hearing stories about his family when something important happened in his life.

Through his soft-spoken nature, his work ethic, and his kindness, this custodian exemplified a true servant.

On days when the pressure of my job heated to the boiling point, the cleaning ladies brought their lighthearted laughter and tales of their antics with them as they cleaned my room, cheering me up in the process. They could relate to others' burdens because of the challenging and occasionally unpleasant tasks that came their way. Sometimes when one of them was sweeping my room at the end of the day, she would ask, "Did you hear our latest story?" Not yet, I'd answer. She then would plunge in, telling of their most recent adventure.

One day after the students had left, one of the cleaning ladies told me about working the school dance the previous Friday evening. It was very late by the time she locked up the building and headed to her car—alone. The timer on the south parking lot was set wrong, so the lights had gone out much earlier. The custodian found the path to her car really dark and scary as she crossed the parking lot after midnight. It was so dark that she didn't see the body lying on the pavement near her car and tripped over it. Now even more terrified, the custodian grabbed her cell phone and dialed 9–1–1. Next, the custodian called the principal and explained what she had found in the parking lot after the dance and relayed that an ambulance was on its way.

When the squad car arrived, the police determined that the person lying on the pavement required medical attention. The ambulance arrived within minutes, loaded the student, and headed to the hospital. After the ambulance left, the custodian called it a night and headed home. In the meantime, the principal had hurried to the hospital where he waited for the ambulance. It didn't take long for the doctors in the ER to diagnose intoxication, or in the students' terminology, passed out drunk. The next day, another custodian found the empty liquor bottle the drunken student had hidden the previous night in the parking lot.

Although some of the custodians' stories were serious, others were lighthearted or just plain entertaining. For example, each year the high school biology classes studied anatomy. One custodian shared the practical joke she played on her coworker at the end of a science unit where the biology classes had used dissected pigs for their anatomy unit. When the time came to dispose of the dissected specimens, one custodian set up a prank for her coworker by suspending one of the cast-off specimens in the dumpster in hopes her colleague would be startled when she unsuspectingly lifted the dumpster cover.

Later, when her friend headed out to empty the trash, the custodian watched from a nearby classroom window as her friend lifted the dumpster cover. However, her friend was not easily frightened and did not react when she saw the suspended pig. But a real surprise awaited both of them when a squirrel that had been scavenging in the dumpster shot out through the opened lid. The custodian inside the classroom squealed and jumped nearly as much as her friend did outside. The squirrel produced a scare for the two of them.

Whenever the students and staff heard the "all-call" page throughout the building summoning the custodial staff, speculation mounted on the details of the latest student prank. The custodians were usually the first to respond to the all-call of student tricks because the custodians had to clean up the mess. Here are follow-up memos circulated among the staff explaining some of these "call the custodians" episodes.

> Bobby admitted to super gluing the locks in three different doors. He will pay for the damages and serve three days out-of-school suspension.
>
> Found out what our boys are doing in the restroom is called toilet lasagna. [Without being too graphic, this group prank was a layering of human waste and toilet paper.] It is sick, and even sicker that someone thought it up, put it on the internet, and others have decided it

is something to copy. The janitors have [also] collected at least twenty folded triangles in the junior/senior high school. Students are flipping these with rubber bands.

Dip [tobacco] was found in the toilet of the second floor boys' bathroom. Please keep an eye out for dip because it is a mess to clean up.

The third-floor bathroom had paper put over the toilet-flush sensor and then multiple people used the toilet. Quite a mess for the custodians. The restroom had been checked at 2:00 after the halls had quieted down from the class change. If you can recall letting any boys out of class after that time, please contact the office and let us know. Because of this situation we will need to monitor those who leave class. Please don't let boys leave your rooms before the bell.

Our custodial staff normally accommodated all janitorial requests, but I recall an inappropriate demand from an administrator that was clearly outside legal bounds, not to mention beyond the limits of good judgment. Schools in my state were required to hold monthly fire drills during the school year. I experienced more than 350 of these evacuations throughout my career, but one fire drill in particular still stands out.

The administrator decided that the school needed to practice a closed exit drill, where an exit is blocked and egress must be rerouted. What should have been a simple exercise that day didn't work out as he had planned. To block an exit, this principal only needed to stand in front of the door, cross his arms, and announce: "This is a fire. You cannot exit here. Find another way out."

Instead, the principal directed the custodian to light a fire using a waste can filled with papers. The custodian resisted, saying, "I can't do that!" But the administrator instructed her to take the waste can filled with paper from the office, use a match, and light it by the nearest exit. Again the custodian protested, "I can't do that!" The principal then raised his voice and told her one more time to light the paper in the trash can. The custodian argued against it the third time by saying it was not legal. But then she reconsidered: the principal was her boss, and if she refused to perform a direct order, he could fire her for insubordination.

Very reluctantly and against her better judgment, the custodian got the trash can and lit the papers. After the papers caught fire, the principal pulled the fire alarm. For the staff and students in that end of the building, it appeared to be an actual fire. Smoke filled the halls and the children began coughing. All of our students safely evacuated the building that morning, but clearing the smoke took much more time than was allotted for a routine fire drill.

Astonishingly, the custodian, who bravely voiced her objections three times, did not lose her job for complying with her superior's direct order. Even more surprising was that the principal didn't lose his position either, even though lighting a fire in a school building is a felony. It appeared that he only received a reprimand from the superintendent. Later in the day, teachers in classrooms near the principal's office overheard the superintendent's scolding. The superintendent, who rarely showed his face in our building, traveled the eight-mile distance to personally deliver the reprimand. It would have been impossible for anyone in that wing of the building to avoid overhearing the dressing down that the superintendent, known for being soft-spoken and composed, shouted at the principal. *Wham!* His fist hit the desk. "You can't do that!" the superintendent yelled, followed by another loud whack on the desk. "I can't believe I am having to tell you this! Do you have any idea of the position you have put us in?" *Wham!*

Somehow, the superintendent managed to save the principal's job, and those of us who witnessed the whole episode will never think about "fire in the hole" in quite the same way again. More than one teacher wondered how this principal had kept his job. This wasn't the first time he had conducted himself improperly.

One teacher summed it up by saying, "How is that they hired him to lead *us*!"

Our custodians were never quite sure where or when the next big cleanup would happen, but somehow they were always up to the task, no matter how messy or disgusting. One messy situation that stands out occurred on a Monday, when the maintenance crew shut off the water in the elementary wing in order to make repairs. While the water was turned off, a fourth grader turned on the water faucet in the classroom sink. However, when no water flowed from the spigot, the student must have walked away with the drain plug securely in place. And by the end of the day, when the teacher locked her classroom door and headed home, there was still no indication of a problem.

Much later that day, after the repair work was completed, the maintenance workers turned the water on to that wing of the building. No more thought was given to this situation until some community members were taking their evening walk on the school grounds and discovered water pouring out of the eaves between the first and second floors, and it was not raining. The custodians were still cleaning in the high school wing when these community members found them and reported the problem they had discovered during their walk.

The custodians hurried to the second floor of the elementary wing and found four to five inches of water on the classroom floor. The water had overflowed the small sink, filled the storage drawers under the sink where many supplies were kept, and flooded the classroom. While one of the custodians shut off the water, the other one rushed to get the floor scrubbing machine, which could vacuum up the water. Besides working hard to clean up the mess, the custodians also called the classroom teacher so she could come and help save as much as possible from the water damage. This is the e-mail that teacher shared with the staff the next morning.

As most of you know, through a series of unfortunate events my room was flooded Monday evening. I recommend to all of you elementary teachers that you hide the stopper to your sink. A student left the plug in the classroom sink after turning on the faucet. I had gone home without discovering this prank. I have posters, maps, and various other educational things scattered around my room and throughout the upstairs hallway drying. I will be able to rescue most of it.

I deeply appreciate the hard work of our custodians and the fact that they were so considerate to call me at home so I could come in and start the recovery process right away. What a shock that would have been the next morning.

Thank you to all of the staff who pitched in Tuesday morning.

One of the most creative staff members I ever worked with happened to be a custodian. She dreamed up a wide range of costumes to celebrate school spirit during the fourteen years when she and I worked in the same school. Any time the students and staff dressed up for a celebration, we counted on Margie and her custodial crew for the best designs.

Margie recruited her fellow custodians each Christmas to brighten our holidays, using her artistic touch. Each December, she created a new Christmas card with her coworkers. Like the rest of the staff, I looked forward to that special envelope I'd find in my mailbox containing the latest fun holiday picture.

Three years of Christmas joy from our creative custodians.

Season's
Greetings

One Easter Monday when I opened my e-mail, I found a message titled "Did the Easter bunny visit you?" The picture attached to the e-mail showed the three custodians with bunny whiskers and bunny noses painted on their faces. They wore furry ears with pink satin centers, white fleece tops, and carried Easter baskets loaded with jelly beans. Their attire and cheerful attitudes brought many smiles that day as they went about their cleaning tasks.

The elementary principal made good use of the custodians' talents when he enlisted them as "ushers" for an end-of-the-year celebration. In honor of the last day of school, the elementary students enjoyed a movie in the auditorium. This assembly was also the time when honored students received prizes in recognition of their outstanding work from the previous nine months. The custodians transformed themselves into ushers by wearing white shirts with blue bowties that sported the school logo. To complete the look, they added blue vests that said Cinema I. Each usher carried a flashlight to direct students to their seats in the semidarkened auditorium. These ladies also passed out popcorn to the moviegoers. And before the assembly was over, they assisted in distributing the prizes to the students.

I reminded my students that while no one notices an empty trash can, people are certain to notice immediately when a restroom is dirty, a classroom is unkempt, a trash can is overflowing, a water fountain is broken, or a lightbulb is burned out.

So, for Margie and all the other unsung heroes who kept school buildings looking good and running smoothly, I say, "Thank you!" Custodians will never truly know how important their contributions are to the success of educating our future generations.

Be joyful in hope, patient in affliction, faithful in prayer. Share with the Lord's people who are in need. Practice hospitality.

—Romans 12:12–13, NIV

Time to Go

*The Lord will keep you from all harm – he will watch over
your life; the Lord will watch over your coming and going
both now and forevermore.*

—Psalm 121:7–8, NIV

There comes a time when you think you have seen enough. Enough changes, enough challenges, and enough craziness. Even enough abbreviations and acronyms that schools use on a regular basis and that seem to multiply with each year. This alphabet soup can quickly become a confusing shorthand for outsiders. IEP, IAT, SCA, WEP, OEASA/SAIL, NCATE, ESC, TAG, MAP, RAS, OGT, OAA, ACP, and AYP were just a few of those used at my school. The enhanced "vocabulary" was not limited to acronyms and abbreviations; a proliferation of buzz words also blossomed during my tenure, such as differentiated instruction, accreditation forum, best practices, output measures, cross-disciplinary techniques, institutional mission, smart goals, distance learning, benchmark, value-added, proactive, results-driven, and core competencies. Some people might have thought this jargon made us sound smarter when we talked, but I didn't see where these changes and added goals had fundamentally improved the quality of teaching and learning in the classroom. In fact, they might have had just the opposite affect: the focus on naming concepts drew attention away from the educational objectives. And even on occasion, former teaching strategies were recycled and presented as new techniques.

Although I liked learning, enjoyed it in fact, I discovered near the end of my career that my enthusiasm to attend yet another workshop was waning. During forty-one years in the classroom, I had attended more training meetings than I cared to count, and the ideas and information presented at the more recent in-service workshops began to sound and feel more and more like an exercise in recycling. In February of my final year when I received a memo about an upcoming summer math workshop, I drew a large smiley face on my copy and wrote "No, thank you" then slipped it into my stack of notes with a giddy sense of complete abandon.

Workshops and jargon weren't the only aspects of education that I would be content to leave behind. I found that the profusion of additional rules and regulations increasingly were impacting the classroom, and more often in ways that detracted from the amount of time available for learning. The Individual Educational Plan (IEP), a practice based on sound theory, first appeared on the educational horizon in 1975.[1] However, even the best ideas don't necessarily translate well in the reality of the everyday classroom. What is right in theory can sometimes turn out to be wrong in practice, especially in the hands of a calculating student.

Over the years I had worked with plenty of IEPs, and I had observed many students who benefited from this learning aid. But there were also those students who misused this educational tool by manipulating the system that had been designed to help them. Instead of working it to their educational advantage, they used it to take personal advantage.

One administrator, who had reached the breaking point with a particular student, summed up my feelings on the matter in this memo:

> I recently met with the regional education office and did not realize how much the government was destroying education. All students on IEP must continue to have interventions or modifications made until they are passing. Basically we cannot fail a student identified with learning difficulties.

This administrator's frustration was due to the fact that a few IEP students refused to complete their homework assignments. Such "failures" mandated a change be made somewhere, either in a student's IEP or the amount of assigned work and level of mastery. Unable to determine, much less prove, if students were truly giving their *best* efforts, teachers were reduced to dismal choices: either reduce the student's work requirements, even though it was readily apparent that the student was capable of more, or rewrite the IEP with lowered expectations, which didn't seem to serve the student's best interest long-term. Undoubtedly, some students must have felt rewarded for playing the system.

In recent years, society, and consequently my students, showed less respect for hard work, rules, other students, and school authority figures. I knew the schoolhouse was not a sanctuary, protected from the events of the world around it. Rather, it was—and is—a reflection of events and the changing morals and values outside the schoolhouse.

I taught junior high school in three different states over many years, and I saw plenty during that time. But two separate occurrences illustrated the potential for serious problems to be a part of the classroom, even on the junior high level. For example, one student who came to my class had shot and killed a family member prior to transferring to our school. The other instance, in a different year, involved a convicted child molester. Both of these students spent time in my classroom, causing me to take a closer look at the safety side of education. When these juvenile offenders first showed up in my classroom, I thought they would be there for the long haul, and I was concerned for the security of my other students. While I didn't know it at the time, both would move on before the school year ended.

A less frightening episode involved an innocent elementary-aged boy who was removed from his home by the authorities for his own protection. This happened just one day before he arrived in my fifth-grade class. I was never clear about the circumstances involving his family. The court officer in charge of this minor had been given short notice for placing this child and had done the best he could by housing this ten-year-old in jail overnight.

(Child placement has changed much since that time.) But I did not even learn this detail about his initial housing until the end of the year. All worked out well with this student, but with some background information, perhaps I could have helped more with this child's heavy burden.

Some students, such as this ten-year-old, have all sorts of reasons to act out, and yet choose to behave. Then there are students who don't seem to have experienced such extraordinary trauma but still focus on being unruly and rebellious at every opportunity.

I've heard first- and second-grade teachers say that they are not surprised by the unruly behavior of some middle school students; after all, these same individuals were the ones who were causing similar classroom disruptions as six- and seven-year-olds. Apparently, it was only the intensity, boldness, and inventiveness that had changed with time. Some students were so notorious that their troublemaking reputations preceded them. Their problems at school were so outrageous and public that everyone around them was aware of their misbehavior. For these children, their misbehavior usually accelerated to the level that they either could not or would not be able to escape its hold without outside help beyond what the school can provide. All too often it seems that the die is cast early for a handful of troubled students, and schools have limited influence, resources, or ability to redirect or intervene.

Jimmy was one of these students. He had been unruly since his primary schools days, and year after year after year, Jimmy's problem of acting out continued to accelerate. By the time he was in fifth grade, this pre-teen would drive to school. Yes, drive to school. Teachers would watch him pull up in the morning driving the family car, slide out, and then enter the building while his mom would take the wheel and drive away. Jimmy pretty much entered the classroom with the same bad-boy, take-charge attitude. He seemed to search out ways to be belligerent. And even though he was smart enough to do well in his studies, he wasn't at all interested in learning or growing in academic skills.

I was just one of Jimmy's many teachers who worked to redirect his disruptive behavior. But by the final nine weeks of his seventh-grade year, it was obvious that despite the concerted efforts we junior high teachers were making, we were failing to reach Jimmy.

His former teachers shared stories of some of the battles they fought trying to help him. The story details regarding Jimmy's lack of achievement and classroom misconduct had not changed much though the years. I was sorry for Jimmy's classmates who had suffered his disruptions day after day, week after week, and year after year.

The day Jimmy's school placement changed started out like most of the other days he had in my class. He arrived in his usual manner—lacking his homework, his supplies, and any respect for classmates, me, or school in general. The one difference for me that day was a conversation repeated to me by one of Jimmy's classmates. "Things seem extra bad with Jimmy today," this student whispered to me in the hall before Jimmy arrived. "During lunch, he was bragging that he would get himself kicked out of your math class. He said he would cause so much trouble that you wouldn't have any choice but to send him to the office."

As I entered my classroom, I promised myself that I would be calm, soft-spoken, low-key, and very patient. Jimmy didn't wait long to start the attack. While we were discussing the homework assignment, Jimmy made obnoxious noises. After we had covered the homework, I presented the lesson for the day. But Jimmy continued to stir up trouble. My goal had been to remain calm, refusing to engage in a contest of wills with him. However, each approach I tried failed. At first I isolated Jimmy from his classmates. Next I provided him with supplies because he had come to class without his, and finally I offered to tutor him individually since he was still protesting that he did not understand.

My calm approach was met at every turn with open defiance. I couldn't get Jimmy to write his name on his paper or look at the written explanations from the class lesson covering the math problems. Finally, I seated him by himself away from other distractions in hopes that a different location would help. Nothing I tried seemed to work.

Jimmy finally reached his breaking point and announced in a loud voice that he wasn't going to do any work. I made him take a seat even farther away from the other students who were trying to do their assignments. But this second seat placement did not help. Frustrated that I would not send him to the office, Jimmy finally got up and just walked out of my room. I followed a few steps behind him as he left. When I saw Jimmy was serious about leaving, I decided that he needed an escort to the office. I told my students I would return shortly and walked with him to the office.

The principal who had dealt with Jimmy on a regular, nearly daily, basis was not surprised to see Jimmy outside his office door. I do not know what transpired in the conference that followed because I returned to my classroom. But the principal must have had insurmountable evidence that public school was no longer working for this student. Throughout the years, so many staff members had worked hard to keep Jimmy in our school. With his history of office visits and classroom disruptions, Jimmy forced our school to find another placement for him.

Jimmy was right about one thing that day; he did get himself kicked out, and he never did return to my class. He also never returned to our school. I was thankful that I had not engaged in Jimmy's contest of wills. He accomplished his goal of getting kicked out all on his own.

Study hall, a near daily event in my career, offered interaction of a different kind with students. This assigned class had its own pros and cons; little had changed since my school days. Some students welcomed the opportunity to get help with a homework assignment. Others appreciated the extra work time so they wouldn't have to do as much at home later. However, a few students viewed study hall as a chance to write notes, sleep, stir up trouble, or goof off. Study hall helped some students while others were just biding their time until the bell rang.

Students who could have benefited from extra time and help were often the discipline problems who interfered with the learning environment. One student who was assigned to my study hall was also in my eighth-grade English class. I knew Shelly could use extra study time because she was carrying a 5 percent grade average in English, mostly because she refused to do her assignments or turn in the work. Shelly made it clear that she didn't intend to use study hall for its intended purpose. Texting or sleeping suited her better. I did my best to encourage Shelly by providing make-up assignments, but I was unable to get her to work. My basic goal shifted to ensuring that she didn't disrupt the whole class. However, that day, I fell far short of my goal.

Shelly had a short fuse; she had done her best to make sure that those around her understood this. In the few months that she had attended our school, she had bullied neighbors, teachers, and even administrators. An eighth-grade boy in study hall decided he was more than eager to light Shelly's short fuse. Whatever had started in math class a couple of hours earlier, now found its way into study hall when this boy entered the classroom taunting Shelly about the incident. I tried to defuse the situation but it was already approaching the boiling point when they walked into the room. The explosion that ensued after the bell rang involved cussing—an event that surprisingly had never before happened in my room. Realizing that this flare-up could quickly escalate, I enlisted the aid of two male teachers to escort Shelly to the office before this battle turned physical.

Here is the memo I sent to the principal to explain why Shelly was on her way to his office accompanied by two teachers.

Study hall doesn't seem to be a good time for Shelly. One student today started to tell of a problem in another teacher's room. (I was unaware of the problem, but I asked Robbie to stop.) However, Robbie decided to keep telling the story. I interrupted him and again asked him to stop, explaining that the other teacher had handled the problem. Before I could get Robbie back to his seat, Shelly exploded. I asked her to consider what she was saying before she said it. But, Shelly interrupted me and yelled, "I don't —— care!"

Mr. Green and Mr. Parker came and delivered her to your office.

Gosh, this job is fun.

That day I had to ask myself, had I stayed too long?

During my time in the classroom, much had changed in regard to behavioral standards for students. This was accompanied by a decline in the perceived value and importance of a good education. For example, I witnessed a downturn in student achievement, even with the grading standards relaxed by ten points. One might have thought more students would earn passing scores with this relaxation of standards, but that's not what my students' grades revealed. At the start of my career, the grading standard was:

A = 96–100

B = 88–95

C = 75–87

D = 70–74

F = 69 and below

These also were the same interval percentages in place when I was a student. But by the time I retired, the grading standard had been lowered to

A = 90–100

B = 80–89

C = 70–79

D = 60–69

F = 59 and below

Even with this system that allowed ten extra points before a grade was considered failing, I still witnessed a drastic increase in the number of failing students compared with my earlier teaching years.

These changes weren't restricted to just the students in my school. A fellow staff member shared the following reflections from a teacher in another district, and these sentiments clearly expressed my own frustrations.

> I spent twenty-three years as a statistician before deciding to teach high school math. Four years later, I'm back to being a statistician. During those four years I rarely had a good day, and I like kids.
>
> Instead of focusing on fancy, complicated approaches to teaching, we need to concentrate on the root problems of bad behavior, study skills, and fundamental understanding. Many of my math students were just not prepared for class, were fundamentally weak, disrespectful, disruptive, and didn't pay attention during explanations.

I wondered if he had been eavesdropping on my classes.

At the end of most of my years as a junior high math teacher, I liked to share *Stand and Deliver*, an inspiring movie about a master teacher's effects on students who were willing to make an extra effort and work diligently to achieve high goals. My math classes enjoyed seeing a teacher who was apparently more demanding than I was while they watched other students who struggled with some of the same challenges that they themselves had in math.

While I was preparing my students with background information on the movie, one of them asked an unusual question. "Does anyone get pregnant in this movie?"

No, I told the seventh-grade math student.

"Oh, darn," came the reply. This student did not represent the attitude of most of my students, but she did reveal how mores and standards had been changing over time. It was a good guess that this student would not benefit much from the uplifting message of this movie.

At a certain point, I felt weary from dealing with unrelenting behaviors from unrepentant students; it seemed to me that I had contacted enough disengaged parents concerning their children's disruptive or troubling behaviors and choices at school. I had to report on students who repeatedly lied about finishing their homework or who copied someone else's work. But worst of all were the students whose open defiance ruined the learning atmosphere for fellow classmates. And it seemed that my reporting poor student behavior to some parents elicited a bigger negative reaction toward me than toward their offspring; many parents appeared to make no apparent efforts to correct their child's conduct. This lack of consequences for what once was unacceptable behavior marked a big change from the values and expectations handed down to the next generation when I began my career. Long gone were the days when a simple phone call meant that I would be working closely with the parents to affect a positive change in a child.

In my final month of teaching, I once again had to contact a parent because of a student's missing work. The message this mom left on my school phone emphasized all the things I was to do. I wondered how different the situation might have been if the parents had shown this much resolve when dealing with their son.

> *You* need to give us a call. Timmy has two missing assignments in his locker. *You* didn't ask him for them so he

didn't turn them in… *You* need to get a hold of us because
we are really concerned. (Emphasis all from the parents.)

If it was my responsibility to hunt down late papers from a
student's locker, then what else, I wondered, did this parent think
I needed to be doing so that her thirteen-year-old would succeed.

Yes, the signs were clear to me. I knew I was ready to move
on; I had experienced enough changes. It seemed like the perfect
time had arrived for me to step aside. I still had permission from
my students to teach yet another year, but I also was feeling the
tug to try new things. I decided not to overstay my invitation. It
was time to open up the opportunity for another teacher to use
her skills and instruct the next generation in my place.

Whatever you do, work at it with all your heart, as working
for the Lord, not for human masters.

—*Colossians 3:23,* NIV

Permission to Retire

*This is the day which the Lord hath made; we will rejoice
and be glad in it.*

—*Psalm 118:24*, KJV

A s the end of my teaching career drew near, I eagerly began
to seek out words of wisdom from other teachers who had
already retired. For instance, on a hot, humid Sunday in July, I
found myself standing next to Becky, a friend and an elementary
teacher who had retired a year earlier. As we waited to greet the
minister following the early church service, I asked her, "How
is retirement?"

"I'm really loving my new freedom," said Becky, who had
enjoyed a successful career and had also transitioned well into a
fulfilling retirement lifestyle.

"How did you know that the time was right for you to retire?"
I asked.

"I had three rules in mind to determine when I was ready to
retire," she said. "One: I still had to enjoy teaching. Two: I still
had to be making a worthwhile contribution in the classroom. I
didn't want an administrator coming to me and telling me it was
time to go. And three: I had to have a good class. I don't think
I could have stood it for bad memories to follow me around. I
wanted to leave with happy feelings of success."

After a particularly trying day a few months later, I reflected
on Becky's words of wisdom as I drove home. Becky's third point
resonated in my head as I thought about the monumental discipline problems I had struggled with that day; I had dealt with
several students who were unprepared, and what's worse, they
didn't care. After the students had boarded the buses that afternoon and before I headed home, I had to attend a staff-parent
conference for a failing student. As I checked the student's math

grades, I noticed that he had received a zero that day on a simple math vocabulary assignment where the class had been assigned to make four flashcards. The definitions for these words were included in both the chapter and the glossary. So when it was my turn to speak in the conference, I asked the dad, "Did you realize your son failed to turn in this short assignment?"

"Yes," he answered, "he told me he didn't feel like doing it." The dad's comment cleared up a lot in my mind. And it became obvious that if I wanted to retire on a high note, then I wouldn't be retiring that year—there were too many challenges from way too many students and just not enough individual successes.

A few years later when I again contemplated retirement, thinking that I might be in my final year of teaching, Becky's second point came to mind. Would I need a principal to ask for my resignation in order to realize that I had passed my prime? I had taught many years without the perspective of a formal evaluation from a principal. But then one November morning, the principal showed up unexpectedly in my classroom: he was there to make an official observation of my teaching.

On that particular day of the principal's walk-through visit, I was reviewing a book my eighth-grade language arts classes had just finished reading. His official observation lasted from 10:30 a.m. to 10:40 a.m. The principal made notes as he watched me teach my final lesson on *The Miracle Worker* by the playwright William Gibson. Later that day, I found his evaluation in my mailbox. His assessment ranked my teaching as excellent in four areas: rapport with students, motivation, pertinence, and knowledge of subject. But what I found most revealing was that my principal hadn't listed any area of deficiency on my evaluation. I wrote this note to myself on the walk-through feedback form the principal had left in my mailbox: "It's reassuring for me to know that after all this time, I'll be able to finish strong."

A year before that November evaluation, a dear friend and gifted kindergarten teacher, Kris, who was sixty years old, woke up on Thanksgiving morning and knew intuitively that it was time for her to retire—as long as her financial adviser also agreed. She and I both knew of an effective and beloved educator who had waited until age eighty to retire, and I had suspected Kris would imitate this example because her dedication to her students ran deep. But that morning, the idea to retire was so strong that Kris couldn't ignore it. So at the first available opportunity, she scheduled an appointment with her financial planner. Kris carefully reviewed her economic situation, found herself financially prepared to retire, and then submitted her letter of resignation after thirty-eight years in the classroom. For the remainder of the school year, she concentrated her after-school hours and weekends on cleaning and sorting her classroom cabinets and files and began to plan her transition.

Stories from retired teachers provided additional insights or, at least, offered humor to my decision-making process. Sally, a former remedial reading instructor, described how she decided to retire. While she was teaching a small reading group one day, an outrageous thought crossed her mind suddenly out of the blue: I don't like doing this, she thought as she studied the students sitting around her little table. Caught off guard by this thought, Sally mentally reviewed recent experiences from her classroom. Although she had always enjoyed working with students, recently some of the magic that had once made it so rewarding for her had begun to dissipate. Had her time in the classroom come to an end, she wondered. If she no longer cherished helping students improve their reading skills, then perhaps it was time for her to move on. Throughout the day, Sally contemplated the idea of retiring. Had she reached the point that she had offered all she had to give, she asked herself. By the time the last students had left that afternoon, it was clear to Sally that she was indeed ready to retire.

That afternoon after school, Sally phoned the superintendent, explained that she was ready to retire, and scheduled an appointment to handle the paperwork. But another remarkable part of her day occurred at dinner that evening when her husband, a farmer, asked Sally how her day had gone.

"I surprised myself when I looked around my classroom today and decided that I no longer wanted to spend my time with children teaching them reading," she said. "So, I contacted the superintendent and started the paperwork to retire."

"You what?" her husband asked. "Without talking it over with me?"

"I didn't see you sitting in that classroom," Sally answered. And with that, the subject was closed.

Hearing this story for the first time, I just had to know one thing. "How did it work out for you?" I asked Sally.

"Fine!" she said. "The time was right. I left feeling like I had helped students. And eventually my husband understood."

During the first few months of a school year, many administrators will try to get a read on the teaching plans among the staff for the next year; who is staying and who might be quietly planning to move, quit, or retire. I've had principals approach me and say, "I'm not trying to pry, but as the superintendent and I were working on the staffing for next year, we wondered if you were considering retirement. I'm not trying to push you into a decision right now, I'm just interested in your plans." One year, the superintendent stopped by my room to tell me that another teacher was interested in my junior high position if I was planning to retire. I was still a few years from thinking about retirement then, and I told him that I was still enjoying my job and that this other teacher would need to wait a bit longer.

Shirley, a friend and kindergarten teacher from a neighboring school district, said her superintendent approached her one day in September and asked about her intent to continue teaching. Shirley had taught more than enough years to qualify for retirement. But she assured her superintendent that she was feeling fine and was not considering retirement.

Yet the following March, Shirley's years in the classroom caught up with her, and she decided that she was now teaching her last year. When she called the superintendent to notify him of her decision to retire at the end of the school year, he informed her that the deadline had already passed for her to submit her retirement paperwork. "Really?" Shirley asked. "If that is true, how is it that you just started your retirement process this month? Whatever paperwork you used, I'd like you to prepare a set for me. I am ready to retire, and it will be best for the students and the school if another teacher takes over in my classroom next year." He helped her start the process that day.

A chemistry teacher in a nearby district offered me this advice during his final year:

> When I arrived in my classroom thirty-five years ago, I had student textbooks and the accompanying teacher's manuals. Now that I am in my final year, I am clearing out my files one unit at a time. Each time I complete a chapter, I destroy those files. My year is half over and my files are half cleared. I will be ready to leave the room the way I found it all those years ago.

Then, there was my friend Vivian. She wondered aloud how the school she had worked for let her work for so long. Here's the humorous tale she shared with me at her retirement party.

> I started in one building. They transferred me to a second building and then to a third school. I was about halfway through my public school journey when they started closing buildings in my wake. First they moved me back to a previous location, but the administration closed and sold that building. So then I was sent back to the second building for a third time in just five years before they also closed that building and then demolished it.
>
> I've been back in the original school building for five years now and I'm surprised they even let me come here seeing how my work history foreshadows building clos-

ings. It's just best that I retire before something untoward happens to this building with me here.

As for me, the fact that I had dedicated so many years to the classroom would have been a surprise to my fifth-grade teacher. Even though he was one of my top three favorite teachers of all time, I rarely spoke a word in his room. He was a kind and gentle, yet firm, teacher who had started his teaching career in his mid-forties. And I was lucky enough to be in his first class. I knew I was shy, but one day at recess when my friends and I were clustered around him, I was surprised when he gently kidded me saying, "I thought Jeanne didn't have a voice because she never talks." No one, especially this favorite teacher, would have guessed that I would choose a career based on being in front of people and talking every day.

Most of my years in the classroom were gratifying. I had taught loads of wonderful, even delightful, students and had been allowed to instill in two generations of them a love of learning along with the rudiments of algebra or English or science. And I felt blessed that the committed learners far outnumbered the taxing ones and those who were downright defiant and recalcitrant. But now, the time had come when I began yearning for a change of pace and began to think that perhaps I had seen enough from the teacher's side of the desk. Even though students were still giving me permission to teach for yet another year, I was starting to warm to the idea of giving myself permission to retire and beginning to make alternate plans for my future.

Before I had even submitted my formal resignation to the school board, however, a fellow staff member surprised students and teachers alike at a February pep assembly when she named the four teachers slated to retire that year. I was probably the most stunned person that day when I heard my name called because I had not yet made my decision official, much less public, and I had yet to inform my students. This announcement, however, lifted a burden for me about when and how I would inform my classes.

A former student and now a junior, Jason found me outside the auditorium after the assembly and gave me a hug. With a catch in his voice, he asked, "Is it really true? Are you really going to retire? We don't want you to go."

"I think it's my time, Jason. I've taught many years and there comes a point in everyone's life when it's time to move on. Did you ever have a teacher you thought should have retired a few years earlier?" I asked.

"Yes," he nodded.

"Well, I don't want to be one of those teachers that students say 'Are you still here?'"

"I see your point, but I guess it just makes me sad to see some of my favorite teachers retiring," he said.

I appreciated Jason's vote of confidence, but God was urging me in new directions.

With more relief than melancholy, I submitted my letter of resignation the next month on the second Monday in March. It was a typical school day like any of the other more than 7,500 days I had spent in the classroom. That day in language arts classes, the students and I began the March Madness Poetry contest, shared twenty minutes of silent reading time, scored the English assignment, and studied some of the vocabulary from our 100 words list.

It seemed fitting that I would finish my career in such an ordinary manner. How fortunate for me that all of these ordinary days had added up to a lifetime of service. But one theme echoed across the years: every victory in my classroom, no matter how large or small, came through God's grace.

But grow in the grace and knowledge of our Lord and Savior Jesus Christ. To him be glory both now and forever! Amen.

—*2 Peter 3:18 (*NIV*)*

Epilogue

May the words of my mouth and the meditation of my heart
be pleasing in your sight, O Lord, my Rock and my Redeemer.

—*Psalm 19:14,* KJV

According to dictionary.com, a statue is "a three-dimensional work of art, as a representational or abstract form, carved in stone or wood, molded in a plastic material, cast in bronze or the like."

I'd like you to meet my statue. A red apple is depicted on a holographic disk that is perched atop an Ionic Greek column. The award weighs 5.43 ounces and stands six inches tall. The holographic background of vibrant blue to rich green makes the apple stand in sharp relief. My name and the name of the student who honored me are inscribed on the base.

Just one year after I retired, I received an invitation to attend the National Honor Society (NHS) luncheon to celebrate the graduating seniors. I had thought my retirement the previous spring marked the end of official school duties for me, at least as a teacher.

On my final day of work, I packed the last items from my desk, loaded the last box into my car, and headed for the next phase of my life with little fanfare. A dear friend and teaching colleague, who lived in the same town as I did, escorted me twelve miles to the edge of our hometown before she waved, honked, turned off the main road, and headed for her home. This simple, heartwarming gesture touched me and provided a fitting conclusion to my teaching days.

But here I was a year later returning to school after the longest period of absence from a school building since starting kindergarten at age four. However, the turf was still familiar and I felt at home.

I hummed a favorite hymn as I drove to school that beautiful May afternoon:

> To God be the glory great things he hath done!
>
> So loved he the world that he gave us his Son,
>
> who yielded his life an atonement for sin,
>
> and opened the lifegate that all may go in.[1]

After stopping at the office to check in as an official visitor, a first for me, I headed to the meeting of the National Honor Society. I could hear conversation and laughter spilling into the hall as I got near.

Todd Hayworth, one of the younger teachers on staff, was visiting with a group of teachers just inside the room, and I joined their conversation. As we caught up with each other's lives, I realized that Todd was unaware of the reason he had been invited to this lunch.

I had been the NHS academic adviser four years earlier, so I understood the significance of this meeting. This gathering, scheduled during the final week of school, was an opportunity to honor the senior NHS members as well as recognize the students' most influential teachers. Todd thought he had been invited for lunch, which was true, but that was not the most important reason he had been included in this group.

I looked around the room and saw many of my former eighth graders from four years earlier who were now graduating seniors. And if they hadn't been aware of the National Honor Society before eighth grade, they certainly learned about it from me that year because my duties as the society's adviser required me to be away from the classroom on two different occasions that year. Even though I was still in the building both times, my classes were taught by a substitute teacher. On one of those days, I supervised the NHS initiation ceremony, and on the other, I directed the Buy-a-Friend auction to raise money for the society's activities. My involvement with NHS also provided me with an opportunity to share the ideals—preparing student leaders for a life of service, learning, and success—of the National Honor Society with my eighth graders before they started their high school careers. I also viewed it as a way to teach them about a future opportunity, a goal they could aspire to achieve in high school years.

Because of our history together, joining these former eighth graders for lunch felt right. The familiar, friendly faces I saw that day had changed only a little through those intervening four years. The conversations I heard were happy, filled with eager anticipation of the upcoming graduation, summer plans, and the directions their lives would take in the fall.

The luncheon was scheduled for 12:45 during the usual high school lunchtime, late enough that everyone was eager to eat. The students and current staff members who had completed three-fourths of their school day seemed especially ready for lunch. The aroma of pizza from the favorite local snack shop filled the room.

The room fell silent when the superintendent began to pray, thanking God for the opportunity to gather and honor our graduating seniors. Following grace, we all lined up to fill our plates, then settled into an enjoyable mix of pizza and more conversation.

As everyone finished their pizza, the senior chosen to present the first award rose quietly, went to a counter at the back of the room, picked up a small statue hidden there, and stepped to the front of the group. Clearing her throat, she described how one special teacher had influenced her life. She then asked her kindergarten teacher to step forward and presented her with the inscribed statue.

One by one, each NHS senior acknowledged an exceptional teacher with a tribute and a statue, a cherished token of appreciation. The speeches illustrated how these teachers had made a difference in these students' lives.

Here the seniors were speaking in front of their teachers and school administrators. As I watched my former students pay tribute to their special teachers, I was transported back to eighth-grade language arts when these students practiced speaking in front of their classmates. I could almost hear their earlier complaints about any assignment which required public speaking: "I hate talking in front of others." "Do I have to get up in front of everybody?" "Couldn't I just sit at my seat and read what I have written?"

If the seniors were nervous about these speeches, their presentations didn't reveal it. Speaker after speaker described dedicated teachers who had shared knowledge, persistence, warmth, encouragement, devotion, and affection with their students. Through hard work and determination, these teachers had altered the lives of these seniors, affecting them in ways the teachers might not have imagined.

With the first student presentation, the purpose of the luncheon became clear to Todd Hayworth. When it was her turn, the senior who was honoring Mr. Hayworth cited examples of how he had enriched her education through the many experiments and classroom activities he had used to teach his students. Todd seemed genuinely surprised by the recognition, but also quite pleased and appreciative.

The seniors had kept mum about which teacher had been chosen by which student until they revealed their chosen recipient's identity in their individual presentations. The subject matter, such as music performance or chemistry lab, sometimes indicated immediately who the recipient would be. But many of the descriptions highlighted qualities and attributes shared by most teachers in attendance, increasing the suspense of wondering who the student had selected.

One of the seniors began his speech by revealing how he had felt lost in junior high, which included only seventh and eighth grades in our district. When he was in seventh grade, he said he had found a teacher who "wouldn't let go," and because of her persistence during those two years, he had found his way. As he spoke, I realized he was describing me. Besides tenacity, I had had time on my side when Neal was my student. Through a quirk in scheduling, Neal had been assigned to both my math class and my language arts class in eighth grade. So he and I got to spend a lot of classroom time together. I was both gratified and humbled to know that I had been an influential factor in his life.

Turning to me, Neal finished his tribute, "Mrs. Nordstrom has not only given me a good education, she cared for me. I learned there was no such thing as quitting. That when you feel like giving up, you don't because it makes you stronger." What a blessing Neal was to me, both then and at this moment.

As Neal handed me the statue with our names inscribed upon it, a Bible verse echoed in my mind, a favorite verse that is my guiding light and serves as an ever-present reminder of both who I am and whose I am.

> *His master replied, "Well done, good and faithful servant! You have been faithful with a few things; I will put you in charge of many things. Come and share your master's happiness!"*
>
> —*Matthew 25:21*, NIV

Notes

Ready or Not

1. *Economics of Education Review*, vol. 6, no. 4, p. 381, 1987 by Richard Murnane, Judith D. Singer, and John B. Willet, "Changes in Teacher Salaries During the 1970s: The Role of School District Demographics." Accessed June 24, 2014; http://www.seacademic.harvard.edu

2. http://nces.ed.gov/programs/digest/d13/tables/dt13_211.50.asp

Author, Author

1. E. B. White. 2004. Accessed June 24, 2014; http://encyclopediaofworldbiography.com

2. www.scholastic.com/teachers/contributions/e-b-white Accessed June 24, 2014

3. www.theparisreview.org/interview/4155/the-art-of-the-essay-no-1-e-b-white. Accessed June 24, 2014

4. William Caldwell. Enjoying Maine. (Augusta, Maine: Guy Gannett Publishing Co. and Bill Caldwell, 1977), 237.

5. E. B. White. 2004. Accessed June 24, 2014; http://encyclopediaofworldbiography.com

6. http://www.infoplease.com/ipea/A0203050.html. Listed as number one through the end of 2000. Accessed June 25, 2014

7. Caldwell, Enjoying, 234–236.

8. http://www.en.m.wikipedia.org/wiki/Stuart_Little.

9. Caldwell, Enjoying, 237.

You Only Cheat Yourself

1. "Cheating: An Academic Epidemic. Emily Flynn Vencat. Teen Newsweek, vol. 7, issue 24. April 24, 2006. 36; http://www.teennewsweek.com

Low Tide

1. "We Need Young People to Become Teachers." Randy Turner. January 1.2014. http://www.huffingtonpost.com

2. "Half of Teachers Quit in 5 Years." Lisa Lambert. Reuters. May 9, 2006. http://www.washingtonpost.com/wp-dyn/content/article/2006/05/08/AR2006050801344.html

You Reap What You Sow

1. "Invented by Mistake." Nannette Richford. April 16, 2007. Accessed June 18, 2014. http://voices.yahoo.com/invented-mistake-toll-house-cookies-mistake-286348.html?cat=23.

2. "Minnie Pearl." Accessed June 19, 2014. http://en.wikipedia.org/wiki/Minnie_Pearl

3. Ibid.

4. "Aspire to Inspire before You Expire." Eugene Bell Jr. November 26, 2012. Accessed June 18, 2014. http://www.giveyourselfthegreenlight.com

Tried and True (For Me, Anyway)

1. Keena D. Lykins. "Students Condemned to Repeat Past." Palladium-Item. Richmond, Ind., December 30, 1991.

Time to Go

1. http://www.specialed-news.com Accessed June 14, 2014.

Epilogue

1. Fanny Crosby. "To God Be the Glory." 1875. Accessed May 26, 2014. http://www.hymnsite.com/lyrics/umh098.sht.

Photo by James P. Chagares,
M. Photog., MEI, Cr, CPP, F-ASP